Table of Contents

Preface. ix

1. Zero Trust Fundamentals. 1
What Is a Zero Trust Network?   1
   Introducing the Zero Trust Control Plane   3
Evolution of the Perimeter Model   4
   Managing the Global IP Address Space   4
   Birth of Private IP Address Space   6
   Private Networks Connect to Public Networks   6
   Birth of NAT   7
   The Contemporary Perimeter Model   8
Evolution of the Threat Landscape   9
Perimeter Shortcomings   12
Where the Trust Lies   15
Automation as an Enabler   15
Perimeter Versus Zero Trust   16
Applied in the Cloud   18
Summary   19

2. Managing Trust. 21
Threat Models   23
   Common Threat Models   23
   Zero Trust's Threat Model   24
Strong Authentication   25
Authenticating Trust   28
   What Is a Certificate Authority?   28
   Importance of PKI in Zero Trust   29
   Private Versus Public PKI   29

    Public PKI Strictly Better Than None   30
  Least Privilege   30
  Variable Trust   33
  Control Plane Versus Data Plane   36
  Summary   38

3. Network Agents. 41
  What Is an Agent?   42
    Agent Volatility   42
    What's in an Agent?   43
  How Is an Agent Used?   43
    Not for Authentication   44
  How to Expose an Agent?   45
  No Standard Exists   46
    Rigidity and Fluidity, at the Same Time   46
    Standardization Desirable   47
    In the Meantime?   48
  Summary   48

4. Making Authorization Decisions. 51
  Authorization Architecture   51
  Enforcement   53
  Policy Engine   54
    Policy Storage   55
    What Makes Good Policy?   56
    Who Defines Policy?   58
  Trust Engine   58
    What Entities Are Scored?   59
    Exposing Scores Considered Risky   60
  Data Stores   60
  Summary   62

5. Trusting Devices. 65
  Bootstrapping Trust   65
    Generating and Securing Identity   66
    Identity Security in Static and Dynamic Systems   67
  Authenticating Devices with the Control Plane   70
    X.509   70
    TPMs   73
    Hardware-Based Zero Trust Supplicant?   77
  Inventory Management   78
    Knowing What to Expect   79

Zero Trust Networks
Building Secure Systems in Untrusted Networks

Evan Gilman and Doug Barth

Beijing · Boston · Farnham · Sebastopol · Tokyo

Zero Trust Networks

by Evan Gilman and Doug Barth

Copyright © 2017 Evan Gilman, Doug Barth. All rights reserved.

Printed in the United States of America.

Published by O'Reilly Media, Inc., 1005 Gravenstein Highway North, Sebastopol, CA 95472.

O'Reilly books may be purchased for educational, business, or sales promotional use. Online editions are also available for most titles (*http://oreilly.com/safari*). For more information, contact our corporate/institutional sales department: 800-998-9938 or *corporate@oreilly.com*.

Editors: Courtney Allen and Virginia Wilson	**Indexer:** Wendy Catalano
Production Editor: Kristen Brown	**Interior Designer:** David Futato
Copyeditor: Amanda Kersey	**Cover Designer:** Karen Montgomery
Proofreader: Jasmine Kwityn	**Illustrator:** Rebecca Demarest

July 2017:   First Edition

Revision History for the First Edition
2017-06-15:   First Release

See *http://oreilly.com/catalog/errata.csp?isbn=9781491962190* for release details.

978-1-491-96219-0

[LSI]

Secure Introduction   80
Renewing Device Trust   81
  Local Measurement   83
  Remote Measurement   83
Software Configuration Management   85
  CM-Based Inventory   85
  Secure Source of Truth   87
Using Device Data for User Authorization   88
Trust Signals   89
  Time Since Image   89
  Historical Access   89
  Location   89
  Network Communication Patterns   90
Summary   90

6. Trusting Users. 93
Identity Authority   93
Bootstrapping Identity in a Private System   95
  Government-Issued Identification   95
  Nothing Beats Meatspace   96
  Expectations and Stars   97
Storing Identity   97
  User Directories   97
  Directory Maintenance   98
When to Authenticate Identity   99
  Authenticating for Trust   99
  Trust as the Authentication Driver   99
  The Use of Multiple Channels   100
  Caching Identity and Trust   101
How to Authenticate Identity   101
  Something You Know: Passwords   102
  Something You Have: TOTP   103
  Something You Have: Certificates   104
  Something You Have: Security Tokens   104
  Something You Are: Biometrics   105
  Out-of-Band Authentication   106
  Single Sign On   106
  Moving Toward a Local Auth Solution   107
Authenticating and Authorizing a Group   108
  Shamir's Secret Sharing   108
  Red October   109
See Something, Say Something   110

Trust Signals   110
Summary   111

7. Trusting Applications. **113**
Understanding the Application Pipeline   114
Trusting Source   115
   Securing the Repository   116
   Authentic Code and the Audit Trail   116
   Code Reviews   118
Trusting Builds   118
   The Risk   118
   Trusted Input, Trusted Output   120
   Reproducible Builds   120
   Decoupling Release and Artifact Versions   121
Trusting Distribution   122
   Promoting an Artifact   122
   Distribution Security   123
   Integrity and Authenticity   123
   Trusting a Distribution Network   125
Humans in the Loop   126
Trusting an Instance   127
   Upgrade-Only Policy   127
   Authorized Instances   128
Runtime Security   130
   Secure Coding Practices   130
   Isolation   131
   Active Monitoring   132
Summary   134

8. Trusting the Traffic. **137**
Encryption Versus Authentication   137
   Authenticity Without Encryption?   138
Bootstrapping Trust: The First Packet   139
   fwknop   140
A Brief Introduction to Network Models   142
   Network Layers, Visually   142
   OSI Network Model   143
   TCP/IP Network Model   145
Where Should Zero Trust Be in the Network Model?   145
   Client and Server Split   147
The Protocols   150
   IKE/IPsec   150

Mutually Authenticated TLS	155
Filtering	163
Host Filtering	164
Bookended Filtering	167
Intermediary Filtering	169
Summary	171
9. Realizing a Zero Trust Network.	**173**
Choosing Scope	173
What's Actually Required?	174
Building a System Diagram	178
Understanding Your Flows	180
Controller-Less Architecture	182
"Cheating" with Configuration Management	182
Application Authentication and Authorization	183
Authenticating Load Balancers and Proxies	184
Relationship-Oriented Policy	185
Policy Distribution	185
Defining and Installing Policy	186
Zero Trust Proxies	187
Client-Side Versus Server-Side Migrations	189
Case Studies	190
Case Study: Google BeyondCorp	190
The Major Components of BeyondCorp	192
Leveraging and Extending the GFE	194
Challenges with Multiplatform Authentication	196
Migrating to BeyondCorp	197
Lessons Learned	199
Conclusion	201
Case Study: PagerDuty's Cloud Agnostic Network	202
Configuration Management as an Automation Platform	202
Dynamically Calculated Local Firewalls	203
Distributed Traffic Encryption	204
Decentralized User Management	205
Rollout	206
Value of a Provider-Agnostic System	207
Summary	207
10. The Adversarial View.	**209**
Identity Theft	210
Distributed Denial of Service	210
Endpoint Enumeration	211

Untrusted Computing Platform   212
Social Engineering   212
Physical Coercion   213
Invalidation   214
Control Plane Security   215
Summary   216

Index. **217**

Preface

Thank you for choosing to read *Zero Trust Networks*! Building trusted systems in hostile networks has been a passion of ours for many years. In building and designing such systems, we have found frustration in the pace of progress toward solving some of the more fundamental security problems plaguing our industry. We'd very much like to see the industry move more aggressively toward building the types of systems which strive to solve these problems.

To that end, we are proposing that the world take a new stance toward building and maintaining secure computer networks. Rather than being something which is layered on top, considered only after some value has been built, security must be fundamentally infused with the operation of the system itself. It must be ever-present, enabling operation rather than restricting it. As such, this book sets forth a collection of design patterns and considerations which, when heeded, can produce systems that are resilient to the vast majority of modern-day attack vectors.

This collection, when taken as a whole, is known as the zero trust model. In this model, nothing is taken for granted, and every single access request—whether it be made by a client in a coffee shop or a server in the datacenter—is rigorously checked and proven to be authorized. Adopting this model practically eliminates lateral movement, VPN headaches, and centralized firewall management overhead. It is a very different model indeed; one that we believe represents the future of network and infrastructure security design.

Security is a complicated and ever-changing field of engineering. Working on it requires a deep understanding of many layers of a system and how bugs or weaknesses in those layers can allow an attacker to subvert access controls and protections. While this makes defending a system challenging, it's also a lot of fun to learn about! We hope you'll enjoy learning about it as much as we have!

Who Should Read This Book

Have you found the overhead of centralized firewalls to be restrictive? Perhaps you've even found their operation to be ineffective? Have you struggled with VPN headaches, TLS configuration across a myriad of applications and languages, or compliance and auditing hardships? These problems represent just a small subset of those addressed by the zero trust model. If you find yourself thinking that there just has to be a better way, then you're in luck—this book is for you.

Network engineers, security engineers, CTOs, and everyone in between can benefit from zero trust learnings. Even without a specialized skillset, many of the principles included within can be clearly understood, helping leaders make decisions that get them closer to realizing the zero trust model, improving their overall security posture incrementally.

Additionally, readers with experience using configuration management systems will see the opportunity of using those same ideas to build a more secure and operable networked system—one in which resources are secure by default. They will be interested in how automation systems can enable a new network design that is able to apply fine-grained security controls more easily.

Finally, this book also explores mature zero trust design, enabling those who have already incorporated the basic philosophies to further the robustness of their security systems.

Why We Wrote This Book

We started speaking about our approach to system and network design at industry conferences in 2014. At the time, we were using configuration management systems to rigorously define the system state, applying changes programmatically as a reaction to topological changes. As a result of leveraging automation tools for this purpose, we naturally found ourselves programmatically calculating the network enforcement details instead of managing such configuration by hand. We found that using automation to capture the system design in this way was enabling us to deploy and manage security features, including access control and encryption, much more easily than in systems past. Even better, doing so allowed us to place much less trust in the network than other systems might normally do, which is a key security consideration when operating in and across public clouds.

Around that same time, Google's first BeyondCorp paper was published, describing how they were rethinking system and network design to remove trust from the network. We saw a lot of philosophical similarities in how Google was approaching their network security, and how we approached similar problems in our own systems. It was clear that reducing trust in the network was not only our own design preference/

---

opinion, but the general direction the industry was headed. With the realizations gained from comparing the BeyondCorp paper to our own efforts, we started sharing broader understandings of this architecture and philosophy at various conferences.

Attendees were engaged and interested in what we were doing, but the question we frequently heard was "Where can I learn more about how to do this in my own system?" Unfortunately, the answer was typically "Well, there's not a whole lot…come see me afterward." The lack of publicly available information and guidance became a glaring gap—one we wanted to correct. This book aims to fill that gap.

While writing this book, we spoke to individuals from dozens of companies to understand their perspective on network security designs. We found that many of those companies were themselves reducing the trust of their internal networks. While each organization took a slightly different approach in their own system, it was clear that they all were working under the same threat model and were as a result building solutions that shared many properties.

Our goal with this book isn't to present one or two particular solutions to building these types of systems, but rather to define a system model that places no trust in its communication network. Therefore, this book won't be focused on using specific software or implementations, but rather it will explore the concepts and philosophies that are used to build a zero trust network. We hope you will find it useful to have a clear mental model for how to construct this type of system when building your own system, or even better, reusable solutions for the problems described herein.

Zero Trust Networks Today

The zero trust model was originally conceived by Forrester's John Kindervag in 2010. He worked for many years to set forth architectural models and guidance for building zero trust networks and has advised many large companies on how to evolve their security posture in order to attain zero trust guarantees. John was, and still is, an important figure in the field. His work in the area greatly informed our understanding of the state of the union, and we thank him for popularizing zero trust during its formative years.

Today's zero trust networks are largely built using off-the-shelf software components with custom software and glue to integrate the components in novel ways. As such, when reading this text, please be aware that deploying this type of system isn't as easy as installing and configuring some ready-made hardware or software…yet.

It could be said that the lack of easily deployable components that work well together is an opportunity. A suite of open source tools could help drive adoption of zero trust networks.

Navigating This Book

This book is organized as follows:

- Chapters 1 and 2 discuss the fundamental concepts at play in a zero trust network.
- Chapters 3 and 4 explore the new concepts typically seen in mature zero trust networks: network agents and trust engines.
- Chapters 5–8 detail how trust is established among the actors in a network. Most of this content is focused on existing technology that could be useful even in a traditional network security model.
- Chapter 9 brings all this content together to discuss how you could begin building your own zero trust network and includes two case studies.
- Chapter 10 looks at the zero trust model from an adversarial view. It explores potential weaknesses, discussing which are well mitigated, and which are not.

Conventions Used in This Book

The following typographical conventions are used in this book:

Italic
> Indicates new terms, URLs, email addresses, filenames, and file extensions.

`Constant width`
> Used for program listings, as well as within paragraphs to refer to program elements such as variable or function names, databases, data types, environment variables, statements, and keywords.

`Constant width bold`
> Shows commands or other text that should be typed literally by the user.

`Constant width italic`
> Shows text that should be replaced with user-supplied values or by values determined by context.

 This element signifies a tip or suggestion.

This element signifies a general note.

 This element indicates a warning or caution.

O'Reilly Safari

 Safari (formerly Safari Books Online) is a membership-based training and reference platform for enterprise, government, educators, and individuals.

Members have access to thousands of books, training videos, Learning Paths, interactive tutorials, and curated playlists from over 250 publishers, including O'Reilly Media, Harvard Business Review, Prentice Hall Professional, Addison-Wesley Professional, Microsoft Press, Sams, Que, Peachpit Press, Adobe, Focal Press, Cisco Press, John Wiley & Sons, Syngress, Morgan Kaufmann, IBM Redbooks, Packt, Adobe Press, FT Press, Apress, Manning, New Riders, McGraw-Hill, Jones & Bartlett, and Course Technology, among others.

For more information, please visit *http://oreilly.com/safari*.

How to Contact Us

Please address comments and questions concerning this book to the publisher:

O'Reilly Media, Inc.
1005 Gravenstein Highway North
Sebastopol, CA 95472
800-998-9938 (in the United States or Canada)
707-829-0515 (international or local)
707-829-0104 (fax)

We have a web page for this book, where we list errata, examples, and any additional information. You can access this page at *http://bit.ly/zeroTrustNetworks*.

To comment or ask technical questions about this book, send email to *bookquestions@oreilly.com*.

For more information about our books, courses, conferences, and news, see our website at *http://www.oreilly.com*.

Find us on Facebook: *http://facebook.com/oreilly*

Follow us on Twitter: *http://twitter.com/oreillymedia*

Watch us on YouTube: *http://www.youtube.com/oreillymedia*

Acknowledgments

We would like to thank our editor, Courtney Allen, for her help and guidance during the writing process. Thanks also to Virginia Wilson, Nan Barber, and Maureen Spencer for their help during the review.

We had the opportunity to meet with many people during the writing of this content, and we appreciate their willingness to speak with us and provide intros to other folks working in this space. Thanks to Rory Ward, Junaid Islam, Stephen Woodrow, John Kindervag, Arup Chakrabarti, Julia Evans, Ed Bellis, Andrew Dunham, Bryan Berg, Richo Healey, Cedric Staub, Jesse Endahl, Andrew Miklas, Peter Smith, Dimitri Stiliadis, Jason Chan, and David Cheney.

A special thanks to Betsy Beyer for writing the Google BeyondCorp case study included in the book. We really appreciate your willingness to work on getting that content included. Thanks!

Thanks to our technical reviewers, Ryan Huber, Kevin Babcock, and Pat Cable. We found your comments invaluable and appreciate the time you took to read through the initial drafts.

Doug would like to thank his wife, Erin, and daughters, Persephone and Daphne, for being so very understanding of the time it took to write this book.

Evan thanks his partner, Kristen, for all of her support through the writing of this book. He would also like to thank Kareem Ali and Kenrick Thomas—without them, none of this would have been possible.

CHAPTER 1

Zero Trust Fundamentals

In a time where network surveillance is ubiquitous, we find ourselves having a hard time knowing who to trust. Can we trust that our internet traffic will be safe from eavesdropping? Certainly not! What about that provider you leased your fiber from? Or that contracted technician who was in your datacenter yesterday working on the cabling?

Whistleblowers like Edward Snowden and Mark Klein have revealed the tenacity of government-backed spy rings. The world was shocked at the revelation that they had managed to get inside the datacenters of large organizations. But why? Isn't it exactly what you would do in their position? Especially if you knew that traffic there would not be encrypted?

The assumption that systems and traffic within a datacenter can be trusted is flawed. Modern networks and usage patterns no longer echo those that made perimeter defense make sense many years ago. As a result, moving freely within a "secure" infrastructure is frequently trivial once a single host or link there has been compromised.

Zero trust aims to solve the inherent problems in placing our trust in the network. Instead, it is possible to secure network communication and access so effectively that physical security of the transport layer can be reasonably disregarded. It goes without saying that this is a lofty goal. The good news is that we've got pretty good crypto these days, and given the right automation systems, this vision is actually attainable.

What Is a Zero Trust Network?

A zero trust network is built upon five fundamental assertions:

- The network is always assumed to be hostile.
- External and internal threats exist on the network at all times.

- Network locality is not sufficient for deciding trust in a network.
- Every device, user, and network flow is authenticated and authorized.
- Policies must be dynamic and calculated from as many sources of data as possible.

Traditional network security architecture breaks different networks (or pieces of a single network) into zones, contained by one or more firewalls. Each zone is granted some level of trust, which determines the network resources it is permitted to reach. This model provides very strong defense-in-depth. For example, resources deemed more risky, such as web servers that face the public internet, are placed in an exclusion zone (often termed a "DMZ"), where traffic can be tightly monitored and controlled. Such an approach gives rise to an architecture that is similar to some you might have seen before, such as the one shown in Figure 1-1.

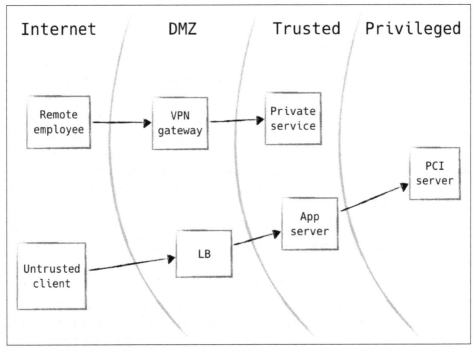

Figure 1-1. Traditional network security architecture

The zero trust model turns this diagram inside out. Placing stopgaps in the network is a solid step forward from the designs of yesteryear, but it is significantly lacking in the modern cyberattack landscape. There are many disadvantages:

- Lack of intra-zone traffic inspection
- Lack of flexibility in host placement (both physical and logical)
- Single points of failure

It should be noted that, should network locality requirements be removed, the need for VPNs is also removed. A VPN (or virtual private network) allows a user to authenticate in order to receive an IP address on a remote network. The traffic is then tunneled from the device to the remote network, where it is decapsulated and routed. It's the greatest backdoor that no one ever suspected.

If we instead declare that network location has no value, VPN is suddenly rendered obsolete, along with several other modern network constructs. Of course, this mandate necessitates pushing enforcement as far toward the network edge as possible, but at the same time relieves the core from such responsibility. Additionally, stateful firewalls exist in all major operating systems, and advances in switching and routing have opened an opportunity to install advanced capabilities at the edge. All of these gains come together to form one conclusion: the time is right for a paradigm shift.

By leveraging distributed policy enforcement and applying zero trust principles, we can produce a design similar to the one shown in Figure 1-2.

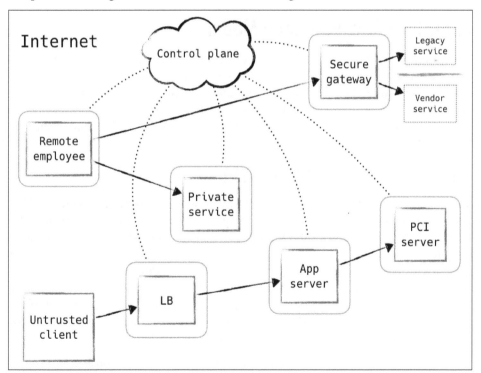

Figure 1-2. Zero trust architecture

Introducing the Zero Trust Control Plane

The supporting system is known as the *control plane*, while most everything else is referred to as the *data plane*, which the control plane coordinates and configures.

Requests for access to protected resources are first made through the control plane, where both the device and user must be authenticated and authorized. Fine-grained policy can be applied at this layer, perhaps based on role in the organization, time of day, or type of device. Access to more secure resources can additionally mandate stronger authentication.

Once the control plane has decided that the request will be allowed, it dynamically configures the data plane to accept traffic from that client (and that client only). In addition, it can coordinate the details of an encrypted tunnel between the requestor and the resource. This can include temporary one-time-use credentials, keys, and ephemeral port numbers.

While some compromises can be made on the strength of these measures, the basic idea is that an authoritative source, or trusted third party, is granted the ability to authenticate, authorize, and coordinate access in real time, based on a variety of inputs.

Evolution of the Perimeter Model

The traditional architecture described in this book is often referred to as the *perimeter model*, after the castle-wall approach used in physical security. This approach protects sensitive items by building lines of defenses that an intruder must penetrate before gaining access. Unfortunately, this approach is fundamentally flawed in the context of computer networks and no longer suffices. In order to fully understand the failure, it is useful to recall how the current model was arrived at.

Managing the Global IP Address Space

The journey that led to the perimeter model began with address assignment. Networks were being connected at an ever-increasing rate during the days of the early internet. If it wasn't being connected to the internet (remember the internet wasn't ubiquitous at the time), it was being connected to another business unit, another company, or perhaps a research network. Of course, IP addresses must be unique in any given IP network, and if the network operators were unlucky enough to have overlapping ranges, they would have a lot of work to do in changing them all. If the network you are connecting to happens to be the internet, then your addresses must be *globally* unique. So clearly some coordination is required here.

The Internet Assigned Numbers Authority (IANA), formally established in 1998, is the body that today provides that coordination. Prior to the establishment of the IANA, this responsibility was handled by Jon Postel, who created the internet map shown in Figure 1-3. He was the authoritative source for IP address ownership records, and if you wanted to guarantee that your IP addresses were globally unique, you would register with him. At this time, everybody was encouraged to register for

IP address space, even if the network being registered was not going to be connected to the internet. The assumption was that even if a network was not connected now, it would probably be connected to another network at some point.

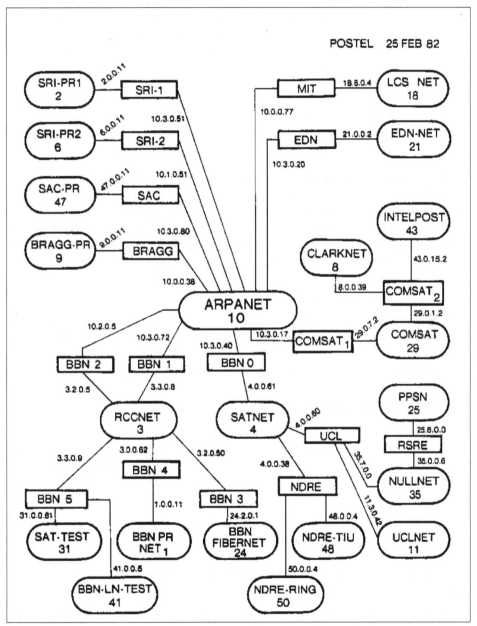

Figure 1-3. A map of the early internet created by Jon Postel, dated February 1982

Birth of Private IP Address Space

As IP adoption grew through the late 1980s and early 1990s, frivolous use of address space became a serious concern. Numerous cases of truly isolated networks with large IP address space requirements began to emerge. Networks connecting ATMs and arrival/departure displays at large airports were touted as prime examples. These networks were considered truly isolated for various reasons. Some devices might be isolated to meet security or privacy requirements (e.g., networks meant for ATMs). Some might be isolated because the scope of their function was so limited that having broader network access was seen as exceedingly unlikely (e.g., airport arrival and departure displays). RFC 1597 (*https://tools.ietf.org/html/rfc1597*), Address Allocation for Private Internets, was introduced to address this wasted public address space issue.

In March of 1994, RFC 1597 announced that three IP network ranges had been reserved with IANA for general use in private networks: 10.0.0.0/8, 172.16.0.0/12, and 192.168.0.0/16. This had the effect of slowing address depletion by ensuring that the address space of large private networks never grew beyond those allocations. It also enabled network operators to use non-globally unique addresses where and when they saw fit. It had another interesting effect, which lingers with us today: networks using private addresses were more secure, because they were fundamentally incapable of joining other networks, particularly the internet.

At the time, very few organizations (relatively speaking) had an internet connection or presence, and as such, internal networks were frequently numbered with the reserved ranges. Additionally, security measures were weak to nonexistent because these networks were typically confined by the walls of a single organization.

Private Networks Connect to Public Networks

The number of interesting things on the internet grew fairly quickly, and soon most organizations wanted at least *some* sort of presence. Email was one of the earliest examples of this. People wanted to be able to send and receive email, but that meant they needed a publicly accessible mail server, which of course meant that they needed to connect to the internet somehow.

With established private networks, it was often the case that this mail server would be the *only* server with an internet connection. It would have one network interface facing the internet, and one facing the internal network. With that, systems and people on the internal private network got the ability to send and receive internet email via their connected mail server.

It was quickly realized that these servers had opened up a physical internet path into their otherwise secure and private network. If one was compromised, an attacker might be able to work their way into the private network, since hosts there can communicate with it. This realization prompted strict scrutiny of these hosts and their network connections. Network operators placed firewalls on both sides of them to restrict communication and thwart potential attackers attempting to access internal systems from the internet, as shown in Figure 1-4. With this step, the perimeter model was born. The internal network became the "secure" network, and the tightly controlled pocket that the external hosts laid in became the *DMZ*, or the *demilitarized zone*.

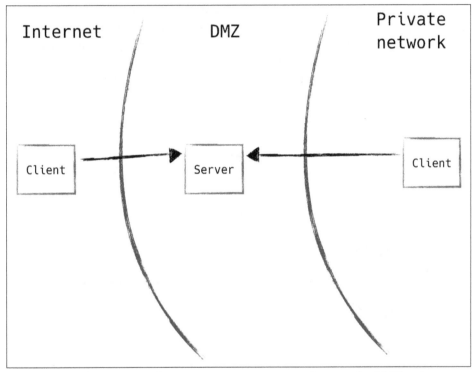

Figure 1-4. Both internet and private resources can access hosts in the DMZ; private resources, however, cannot reach beyond the DMZ, and thus do not gain direct internet access

Birth of NAT

The number of internet resources desired to be accessed from internal networks was growing rapidly, and it quickly became easier to grant general internet access to internal resources than it was to maintain intermediary hosts for every application desired. *NAT*, or *network address translation*, solved that problem nicely.

RFC 1631 (*https://tools.ietf.org/html/rfc1631*), *The IP Network Address Translator*, defines a standard for a network device that is capable of performing IP address translation at organizational boundaries. By maintaining a table that maps public IPs and ports to private ones, it enabled devices on private networks to access arbitrary internet resources. This lightweight mapping is application-agnostic, which meant that network operators no longer needed to support internet connectivity for particular applications; they needed only to support internet connectivity in general.

These NAT devices had an interesting property: because the IP mapping was many-to-one, it was not possible for incoming connections from the internet to access internal private IPs without specifically configuring the NAT to handle this special case. In this way, the devices exhibited the same properties as a stateful firewall. Actual firewalls began integrating NAT features almost instantaneously, and the two became a single function, largely indistinguishable. Supporting both network compatibility and tight security controls meant that eventually you could find one of these devices at practically every organizational boundary, as shown in Figure 1-5.

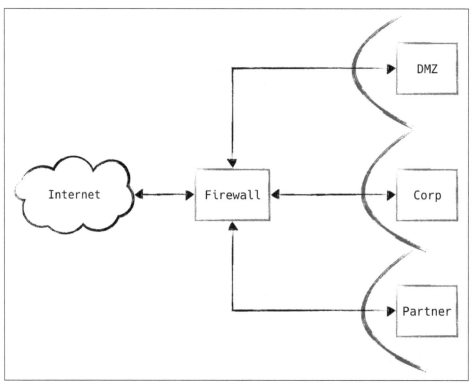

Figure 1-5. Typical (and simplified) perimeter firewall design

The Contemporary Perimeter Model

With a firewall/NAT device between the internal network and the internet, the security zones are clearly forming. There is the internal "secure" zone, the DMZ (demilitarized zone), and the untrusted zone (aka the internet). If at some point in the future, this organization needed to interconnect with another, a device would be placed on that boundary in a similar manner. The neighboring organization is likely to become a new security zone, with particular rules about what kind of traffic can go from one to the other, just like the DMZ or the secure zone.

Looking back, the progression can be seen. We went from offline/private networks with just one or two hosts with internet access to highly interconnected networks with security devices around the perimeter. It is not hard to understand: network operators can't afford to sacrifice the perfect security of their offline network because they had to open doors up for various business purposes. Tight security controls at each door minimized the risk.

Evolution of the Threat Landscape

Even before the public internet, communicating with a remote computer system was highly desirable. This was commonly done over the public telephone system. Users and computer systems could dial in and, by encoding data into audible tones, gain connectivity to the remote machine. These dial-in interfaces were the most common attack vector of the day, since gaining physical access was much more difficult.

Once organizations had internet-connected hosts, attacks shifted from occurring over the telephone network to being launched over the internet. This triggered a change in most attack dynamics. Incoming calls to dial-in interfaces tied up a phone line, and were a notable occurrence when compared to a TCP connection coming from the internet. It was much easier to have a covert presence on an IP network than it was on a system that needed to be dialed into. Exploitation and brute force attempts could be carried out over long periods of time without raising too much suspicion...though an additional and more impactful capability rose from this shift: malicious code could then listen for internet traffic.

By the late 1990s, the world's first (software) Trojan horses had begun to make their rounds. Typically, a user would be tricked into installing the malware, which would then open a port and wait for incoming connections. The attacker could then connect to the open port and remotely control the target machine.

It wasn't long after that people realized it would be a good idea to protect those internet-facing hosts. Hardware firewalls were the best way to do it (most operating systems had no concept of a host-based firewall at the time). They provided policy enforcement, ensuring that only whitelisted "safe" traffic was allowed in from the internet. If an administrator inadvertently installed something that exposed an open port (like a Trojan horse), the firewall would physically block connections to that port until explicitly configured to allow it. Likewise, traffic to the internet-facing servers from inside the network could be controlled, ensuring that internal users could speak to them, but not vice versa. This helped prevent movement into the internal network by a potentially compromised DMZ host.

DMZ hosts were of course a prime target (due to their connectivity), though such tight controls on both inbound and outbound traffic made it hard to reach an internal network through a DMZ. An attacker would first have to compromise the firewalled server, then abuse the application in such a way that it could be used for covert communication (they need to get data *out* of that network, after all). Dial-in interfaces remained the lowest hanging fruit if one was determined to gain access to an internal network.

This is where things took an interesting turn. NAT was introduced to grant internet access to clients on internal networks. Due in some part to NAT mechanics and in some part to real security concerns, there was still tight control on inbound traffic, though internal resources wishing to consume external resources might freely do so. There's an important distinction to be made when considering a network with NAT'd internet access against a network without it: the former has relaxed (if any) outbound network policy.

This significantly transformed the network security model. Hosts on the "trusted" internal networks could then communicate directly with untrusted internet hosts, and the untrusted host was suddenly in a position to abuse the client attempting to speak with it. Even worse, malicious code could then send messages to internet hosts from within the internal network. Today, we know this as *phoning home*.

Phoning home is a critical component of most modern attacks. It allows data to be exfiltrated from otherwise-protected networks; but more importantly, since TCP is bidirectional, it allows data to be *injected* as well.

A typical attack involves several steps, as shown in Figure 1-6. First, the attacker will compromise a single computer on the internal network by exploiting the user's browser when they visit a particular page, by sending them an email with an attachment that exploits some local software, for example. The exploit carries a very small payload, just enough code to make a connection out to a remote internet host and execute the code it receives in the response. This payload is sometimes referred to as a *dialer*.

The dialer downloads and installs the real malware, which more often than not will attempt to make an additional connection to a remote internet host controlled by the attacker. The attacker will use this connection to send commands to the malware, exfiltrate sensitive data, or even to obtain an interactive session. This "patient zero" can act as a stepping stone, giving the attacker a host on the internal network from which to launch additional attacks.

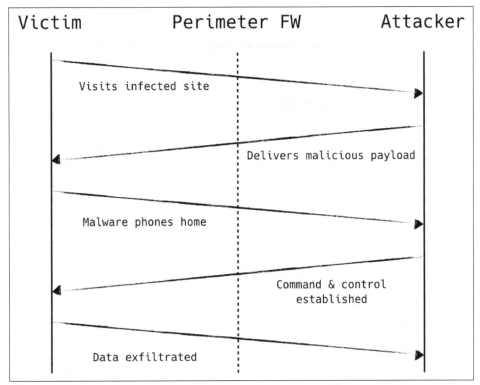

Victim	Perimeter FW	Attacker

Visits infected site

Delivers malicious payload

Malware phones home

Command & control
established

Data exfiltrated

Figure 1-6. Client initiates all attack-related connections, easily traversing perimeter firewalls with relaxed outbound security

Outbound Security

Outbound network security is a very effective mitigation measure against dialer-based attacks, as the phone home can be detected and/or blocked. Oftentimes, however, the phone home is disguised as regular web traffic, possibly even to networks that are seemingly benign or "normal." Outbound security tight enough to stop these attacks will oftentimes cripple web usability for users. This is a more realistic prospect for back-office systems.

The ability to launch attacks from hosts within an internal network is a very powerful one. These hosts almost certainly have permission to talk to other hosts in the same security zone (lateral movement) and might even have access to talk to hosts in zones more secure than their own. To this effect, by first compromising a low-security zone on the internal network, an attacker can move through the network, eventually gaining access to the high-security zones.

Taking a step back for a moment, it can be seen that this pattern very effectively undermines the perimeter security model. The critical flaw enabling attack progression is subtle, yet clear: security policies are defined by network zones, enforced only at zone boundaries, using nothing more than the source and destination details.

Perimeter Shortcomings

Even though the perimeter security model still stands as the most prevalent model by far, it is increasingly obvious that the way we rely on it is flawed. Complex (and successful) attacks against networks with perfectly good perimeter security occur every day. An attacker drops a remote access tool (or RAT) into your network through one of a myriad of methods, gains remote access, and begins moving laterally. Perimeter firewalls have become the functional equivalent of building a wall around a city to keep out the spies.

The problem comes when architecting security zones into the network itself. Imagine the following scenario: you run a small ecommerce company. You have some employees, some internal systems (payroll, inventory, etc.), and some servers to power your website. It is natural to begin classifying the kind of access these groups might need: employees need access to internal systems, web servers need access to database servers, database servers don't need internet access but employees do, and so on. Traditional network security would codify these groups as zones and then define which zone can access what, as shown in Figure 1-7. Of course, you need to actually enforce these policies; and since they are defined on a zone-by-zone basis, it makes sense to enforce them wherever one zone can route traffic into another.

As you might imagine, there are always exceptions to these generalized rules... they are, in fact, colloquially known as *firewall exceptions*. These exceptions are typically as tightly scoped as possible. For instance, your web developer might want SSH access to the production web servers, or your HR representative might need access to the HR software's database in order to perform audits. In these cases, an acceptable approach is to configure a firewall exception permitting traffic from that individual's IP address to the particular server(s) in question.

Now let's imagine that your archnemesis has hired a team of hackers. They want to have a peek at your inventory and sales numbers. The hackers send emails to all the employee email addresses they can find on the internet, masquerading as a discount code for a restaurant near the office. Sure enough, one of them clicks the link, allowing the attackers to install malware. The malware phones home and provides the attackers with a session on the now-compromised employee's machine. Luckily, it's only an intern, and the level of access they gain is limited.

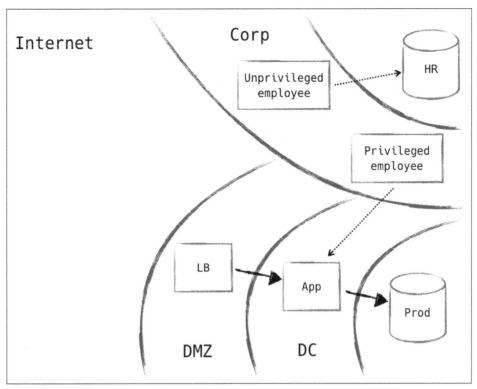

Figure 1-7. Corporate network interacting with the production network

They begin searching the network and find that the company is using file sharing software on its network. Out of all the employee computers on the network, *none* of them have the latest version and are vulnerable to an attack that was recently publicized. One by one, the hackers begin searching for a computer with elevated access (this process of course can be more targeted if the attacker has advanced knowledge). Eventually they come across your web developer's machine. A keylogger they install there recovers the credentials to log into the web server. They SSH to the server using the credentials they gathered; and using the sudo rights of the web developer, they read the database password from disk and connect to the database. They dump the contents of the database, download it, and delete all the log files. If you're lucky, you might actually discover that this breach occurred. They accomplished their mission, as shown in Figure 1-8.

Wait, what? As you can see, many failures at many levels led to this breach, and while you might think that this is a particularly contrived case, successful attacks just like this one are staggeringly common. The most surprising part however goes unnoticed all too often: what happened to all that network security? Firewalls were meticulously placed, policies and exceptions were tightly scoped and very limited, everything was done right from a network security perspective. So what gives?

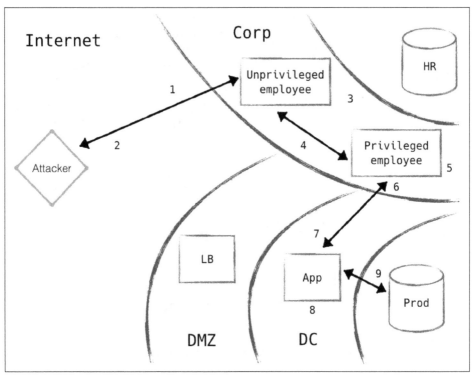

Figure 1-8. Attacker movement into corporate network, and subsequently production into network

Example Attack Progression

1. Employees targeted via phishing email
2. Corporate machine compromised, shell shoveled
3. Lateral movement through corporate network
4. Privileged workstation located
5. Local privilege escalation on workstation—keylogger installed
6. Developer password stolen
7. Compromised prod app host from privileged workstation
8. Developer password used to elevate privileges on prod app host
9. Database credentials stolen from app
10. Database contents exfiltrated via compromised app host

When carefully examined, it is overwhelmingly obvious that this network security model is not enough. Bypassing perimeter security is trivial with malware that phones home, and firewalls between zones consider nothing more than source and destination when making enforcement decisions. While perimeters can still provide some value in network security, their role as the primary mechanism by which a network's security stance is defined needs to be reconsidered.

The first step of course is to search for existing solutions. Sure, the perimeter model is the accepted approach to securing a network, but that doesn't mean we haven't learned better elsewhere. What is the worst possible scenario network security-wise? It turns out that there is actually a level of absoluteness to this question, and the crux of it lies in trust.

Where the Trust Lies

When considering options beyond the perimeter model, one must have a firm understanding of what is trusted and what isn't. The level of trust defines a lower limit on the robustness of the security protocols required. Unfortunately, it is rare for robustness to exceed what is required, so it is wise to trust as little as possible. Once trust is built into a system, it can be very hard to remove.

A zero trust network is just as it sounds. It is a network that is completely untrusted. Lucky for us, we interact with such a network very frequently: the internet.

The internet has taught us some valuable security lessons. Certainly an operator will secure an internet-facing server much differently than it secures its locally accessible counterpart. Why is that? And if the pains associated with such rigor were cured (or even just lessened), would the security sacrifice still be worth it?

The zero trust model dictates that all hosts be treated as if they're internet-facing. The networks they reside in must be considered compromised and hostile. Only with this consideration can you begin to build secure communication. With most operators having built or maintained internet-facing systems in the past, we have at least some idea of how to secure IP in a way that is difficult to intercept or tamper with (and, of course, how to secure those hosts). Automation enables us to extend this level of security to all of the systems in our infrastructure.

Automation as an Enabler

Zero trust networks do not require new protocols or libraries. They do, however, use existing technologies in novel ways. Automation systems are what allow a zero trust network to be built and operated.

Interactions between the control plane and the data plane are the most critical points requiring automation. If policy enforcement cannot be dynamically updated, zero trust will be unattainable; therefore it is critical that this process be automatic and rapid.

There are many ways that this automation can be realized. Purpose-built systems are most ideal, though more mundane systems like traditional configuration management can fit here as well. Widespread adoption of configuration management represents an important stepping stone for a zero trust network, as these systems often maintain device inventories and are capable of automating network enforcement configuration in the data plane.

Due to the fact that modern configuration management systems can both maintain a device inventory and automate the data plane configuration, they are well positioned to be a first step toward a mature zero trust network.

Perimeter Versus Zero Trust

The perimeter and zero trust models are fundamentally different from each other. The perimeter model attempts to build a wall between trusted and untrusted resources (i.e., local network and the internet). On the other hand, the zero trust model basically throws the towel in, and accepts the reality that the "bad guys" are everywhere. Rather than build walls to protect the soft bodies inside, it turns the entire population into a militia.

The current approaches to perimeter networks assign some level of trust to the protected networks. This notion violates the zero trust model and leads to some bad behavior. Operators tend to let their guard down a bit when the network is "trusted" (they *are* human). Rarely are hosts that share a trust zone protected from themselves. Sharing a trust zone, after all, seems to imply that they are equally trusted. Over time, we have come to learn that this assumption is false, and it is not only necessary to protect your hosts from the outside, but it is also necessary to protect them from *each other*.

Since the zero trust model assumes the network is fully compromised, you must also assume that an attacker can communicate using any arbitrary IP address. Thus, protecting resources by using IP addresses or physical location as an identifier is not enough. All hosts, even those which share "trust zones," must provide proper identification. Attackers are not limited to active attacks though. They can still perform passive attacks in which they sniff your traffic for sensitive information. In this case, even host identification is not enough—strong encryption is also required.

There are three key components in a zero trust network: *user/application authentication*, *device authentication*, and *trust*. The first component has some duality in it due to the fact that not all actions are taken by users. So in the case of automated action (inside the datacenter, for instance), we look at qualities of the application in the same way that we would normally look at qualities of the user.

Authenticating and authorizing the device is just as important as doing so for the user/application. This is a feature rarely seen in services and resources protected by perimeter networks. It is often deployed using VPN or NAC technology, especially in more mature networks, but finding it between endpoints (as opposed to network intermediaries) is uncommon.

NAC as a Perimeter Technology

NAC, or *Network Access Control*, represents a set of technologies designed to strongly authenticate devices in order to gain access to a sensitive network. These technologies, which include protocols like 802.1X and the Trusted Network Connect (TNC) family, focus on admittance to a network rather than admittance to a service and as such are independent to the zero trust model. An approach more consistent with the zero trust model would involve similar checks as close to the service being accessed as possible (something which TNC can address—more on this in Chapter 5). While NAC can still be employed in a zero trust network, it does not fulfill the zero trust device authentication requirement due to its distance from the remote endpoint.

Finally, a "trust score" is computed, and the application, device, and score are bonded to form an agent. Policy is then applied against the agent in order to authorize the request. The richness of information contained within the agent allows very flexible yet fine-grained access control, which can adapt to varying conditions by including the score component in your policies.

If the request is authorized, the control plane signals the data plane to accept the incoming request. This action can configure encryption details as well. Encryption can be applied at the device level, application level, or both. At least one is required for confidentiality.

With these authentication/authorization components, and the aide of the control plane in coordinating encrypted channels, we can assert that every single flow on the network is authenticated and expected. Hosts and network devices drop traffic that has not had all of these components applied to it, ensuring sensitive data can never leak out. Additionally, by logging each of the control plane events and actions, network traffic can be easily audited on a flow-by-flow or request-by-request basis.

Perimeter networks can be found which have similar capability, though these capabilities are enforced at the perimeter only. VPN famously attempts to provide these qualities in order to secure access to an internal network, but the security ends as soon as your traffic reaches a VPN concentrator. It is apparent that operators know what internet-strength security is supposed to look like; they just fail to implement those strong measures throughout.

If one can imagine a network that applies these measures homogeneously, some brief thought experiment can shed a lot of light on this new paradigm. Identity can be proven cryptographically, meaning it no longer matters what IP address any given connection is originating from (technically, you can still associate risk with it—more on that later). With automation removing the technical barriers, VPN is essentially obsoleted. "Private" networks no longer mean anything special: the hosts there are just as hardened as the ones on the internet. Thinking critically about NAT and private address space, perhaps zero trust makes it more obvious that the security arguments for it are null and void.

Ultimately, the perimeter model flaw is lack of universal protection and enforcement. Secure cells with soft bodies inside. What we're really looking for is hard bodies, bodies that know how to check IDs and speak in a way they can't be overheard. Having hard bodies doesn't necessarily preclude you from also maintaining the security cells. In very sensitive installations, this would still be encouraged. It does, however, raise the security bar high enough that it wouldn't be unreasonable to lessen or remove those cells. Combined with the fact that the majority of the zero trust function can be done with transparency to the end user, the model almost seems to violate the security/convenience trade-off: stronger security, more convenience. Perhaps the convenience problem (or lack thereof) has been pushed onto the operators.

Applied in the Cloud

There are many challenges in deploying infrastructure into the cloud, one of the larger being security. Zero trust is a perfect fit for cloud deployments for an obvious reason: you can't trust the network in a public cloud! The ability to authenticate and secure communication without relying on IP addresses or the security of the network connecting them means that compute resources can be nearly commoditized.

Since zero trust advocates that every packet be encrypted, even within the same datacenter, operators need not worry about which packets traverse the internet and which don't. This advantage is often understated. Cognitive load associated with when, where, and how to encrypt traffic can be quite large, particularly for developers who may not fully understand the underlying system. By eliminating special cases, we can also eliminate the human error associated with them.

Some might argue that intra-datacenter encryption is overkill, even with the reduction in cognitive load. History has proven otherwise. At large cloud providers like AWS, a single "region" consists of many datacenters, with fiber links between them. To the end user, this subtlety is often obfuscated. The NSA was targeting precisely links like these in 2013, and internet-backbone links even earlier in rooms like the one shown in Figure 1-9.

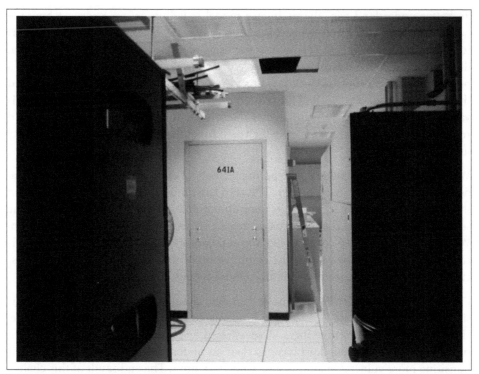

Figure 1-9. Room 641A—NSA interception facility inside an AT&T datacenter in San Francisco

There are additionally risks in the network implementation of the provider itself. It is not impossible to think that a vulnerability might exist in which neighbors can see your traffic. A more likely case is network operators inspecting traffic while trouble-shooting. Perhaps the operator is honest, but how about the person who stole his/her laptop a few hours later with your captures on the disk? The unfortunate reality is that we can no longer assume that our traffic is protected from snooping or modifica-tion while in the datacenter.

Summary

This chapter explored the high-level concepts that have led us toward the zero trust model. The zero trust model does away with the perimeter model, which attempts to ensure that bad actors stay out of the trusted internal network. Instead, the zero trust system recognizes that this approach is doomed to failure, and as a result, starts with the assumption that malicious actors are within the internal network and builds up security mechanisms to guard against this threat.

To better understand why the perimeter model is failing us, we reviewed how the perimeter model came into being. Back at the internet's beginning, the network was fully routable. As the system evolved, some users identified areas of the network that didn't have a credible reason to be routable on the internet, and thus the concept of a private network was born. Over time, this idea took hold, and organizations modeled their security around protecting the trusted private network. Unfortunately, these private networks aren't nearly as isolated as the original private networks were. The end result is a very porous perimeter, which is frequently breached in regular security incidents.

With the shared understanding of perimeter networks, we are able to contrast that design against the zero trust design. The zero trust model carefully manages trust in the system. These types of networks lean on automation to realistically manage the security control systems that allow us to create a more dynamic and hardened system. We introduced some key concepts like the authentication of users, devices, and applications, and the authorization of the combination of those components. We will discuss these concepts in greater detail throughout the rest of this book.

Finally, we talked about how the move to public cloud environments and the pervasiveness of internet connectivity have fundamentally changed the threat landscape. "Internal" networks are now increasingly shared and sufficiently abstracted away in such a way that end users don't have as clear an understanding of when their data is transiting more vulnerable long-distance network links. The end result of this change is that data security is more important than ever when constructing new systems.

The next chapter will discuss the high-level concepts that need to be understood in order to build systems that can safely manage trust.

CHAPTER 2

Managing Trust

Trust management is perhaps the most important component of a zero trust network. We are all familiar with trust to some degree—you probably trust members of your family, but not a stranger on the street, and certainly not a stranger who looks threatening or menacing. Why is that?

For starters, you actually *know* your family members. You know what they look like, where they live; perhaps you've even known them your whole life. There is no question of who they are, and you are more likely to trust them with important matters than others.

A stranger, on the other hand, is someone completely unknown. You might see their face, and be able to tell some basic things about them, but you don't know where they live, and you don't know their history. They might appear perfectly cromulent, but you likely wouldn't rely on one for important matters. Watch your stuff for you while you run to the bathroom? Sure. Make a quick run to the ATM for you? Definitely not.

At the end, you are simply taking in all the information you can tell about the situation, a person, and all you may know about them, and deciding how trustworthy they are. The ATM errand requires a very high level of trust, where watching your stuff needs much less, but not zero.

You may not even trust yourself completely, but you can definitely trust that actions taken by you were taken by you. In this way, trust in a zero trust network always originates with the operator. Trust in a zero trust network seems contradictory, though it is important to understand that when you have no *inherent* trust, you must source it from somewhere and manage it carefully.

There's a small wrinkle though: the operator won't always be available to authorize and grant trust! Plus, the operator just doesn't scale :). Luckily, we know how to solve that problem—we delegate trust as shown in Figure 2-1.

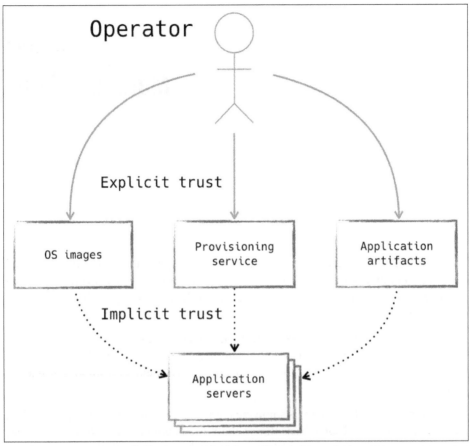

Figure 2-1. An operator declares trust in a particular system, which can in turn trust another, forming a trust chain

Trust delegation is important because it allows us to build automated systems that can grow to large scale and to operate in a secure and trusted way with minimal human intervention. The trusted operator must assign some level of trust to a system, enabling it to take actions on behalf of the operator. A simple example of this is autoscaling. You want your servers to provision themselves as needed, but how do you know a new server is one of yours and not some other random server? The operator must delegate the responsibility to a provisioning system, granting it the ability to assign trust to, and create, new hosts. In this way, we can say that we trust the new server is indeed our own, because the provisioning system has validated that it has taken the action to create it, and the provisioning system can prove that the operator has granted it the ability to do so. This flow of trust back to the operator is often referred to as a *trust chain*, and the operator can be referred to as a trust anchor.

Threat Models

Defining threat models is an important first step when designing a security architecture. A *threat model* enumerates the potential attackers, their capabilities and resources, and their intended targets. Threat models will normally define which attackers are in scope, rationally choosing to mitigate attacks from weaker adversaries before moving onto more difficult adversaries.

A well-defined threat model can be a useful tool to focus security mitigation efforts. When building security systems, like most engineering exercises, there is a tendency to focus on the fancier aspects of the engineering problem to the detriment of the more boring but still important parts. This tendency is especially worrisome in a security system, since the weakest link in the system is where attackers will quickly focus their attention. Therefore, the threat model serves as a mechanism for focusing our attention on a single threat and fully mitigating their attacks.

Threat models can also be useful when prioritizing security initiatives. Fighting state-level actors is pointless if a system's security measures are insufficient to defend against a simple brute force attack on a user's poor password. As such, it is important to start first with simpler personas when building a threat model.

Common Threat Models

There are many different techniques for threat modeling in the security field. Here are some of the more popular ones:

- STRIDE (*https://msdn.microsoft.com/en-us/library/ee823878(v=cs.20).aspx*)
- DREAD (*https://www.owasp.org/index.php/Threat_Risk_Modeling#DREAD*)
- PASTA (*http://bit.ly/2rQGNoa*)
- Trike (*http://octotrike.org/*)
- VAST (*http://threatmodeler.com/threat-modeling-methodology/*)

The varying threat modeling techniques provide different frameworks for exploring the threat space. Each of them is after the same goal: to enumerate threats to the system and further enumerate the mitigating systems and processes for those threats.

Different threat models approach the problem from different angles. Some modeling systems might focus on the assets that an attacker would be targeting. Others might look at each software component in isolation and enumerate all the attacks that could be applied to that system. Finally, some models might look at the system as a whole from the attacker's perspective: as an attacker, how might I approach penetrating this system. Each of these approaches has pros and cons. For a well-diversified mitigating strategy, a blend of the three approaches is ideal.

If we were to look at the attacker-based threat modeling methodology, we are able to categorize attackers into a list of increasing capabilities (ordered from least to most threatening):

1. *Opportunistic attackers*

   So-called script kiddies, who are unsophisticated attackers taking advantage of well-known vulnerabilities with no predetermined target.

2. *Targeted attackers*

   Attackers who craft specialized attacks against a particular target. Spear phishing and corporate espionage might fall under this bucket.

3. *Insider threats*

   A credentialed but everyday user of a system. Contractors and unprivileged employees generally fall into this bucket.

4. *Trusted insider*

   A highly trusted administrator of a system.

5. *State-level actor*

   Attackers backed by foreign or domestic governments and assumed to have vast resources and positioning capabilities to attack a target.

Categorizing threats like this is a useful exercise to focus discussion around a particular level to mitigate against. We will discuss which level zero trust targets in the next section.

Zero Trust's Threat Model

In RFC 3552, the Internet Threat Model (*https://tools.ietf.org/html/rfc3552#section-3*) is described. Zero trust networks generally follow the Internet Threat Model to plan their security stance. While reading the entire RFC is recommended, here is a relevant excerpt:

> The Internet environment has a fairly well understood threat model. In general, we assume that the end-systems engaging in a protocol exchange have not themselves been compromised. Protecting against an attack when one of the end-systems has been compromised is extraordinarily difficult. It is, however, possible to design protocols which minimize the extent of the damage done under these circumstances.

> By contrast, we assume that the attacker has nearly complete control of the communications channel over which the end-systems communicate. This means that the attacker can read any PDU (Protocol Data Unit) on the network and undetectably remove, change, or inject forged packets onto the wire. This includes being able to generate packets that appear to be from a trusted machine. Thus, even if the end-system with which you wish to communicate is itself secure, the Internet environment provides no assurance that packets which claim to be from that system in fact are.

Zero trust networks, as a result of their control over endpoints in the network, expand upon the Internet Threat Model to consider compromises at the endpoints. The response to these threats is generally to first harden the systems proactively against compromised peers, and then facilitate detection of those compromises. Detection is aided by scanning of devices and behavioral analysis of the activity from each device. Additionally, mitigation of endpoint compromise is achieved by frequent upgrades to software on devices, frequent and automated credential rotation, and in some cases frequent rotation of the devices themselves.

An attacker with unlimited resources is essentially impossible to defend against, and zero trust networks recognize that. The goal of a zero trust network isn't to defend against all adversaries, but rather the types of adversaries that are commonly seen in a hostile network.

From our earlier discussion of attacker capabilities, a zero trust network is generally attempting to mitigate attacks up to and including attacks originating from a "trusted insider" level of access. Most organizations do not experience attacks that exceed this level of sophistication. Developing mitigations against these attackers will defend against the vast majority of compromises and would be a dramatic improvement for the industry's security stance.

Zero trust networks generally do not try to mitigate all state-level actors, though they do attempt to mitigate those attempting to compromise their systems remotely. State-level actors are assumed to have vast amounts of money, so many attacks that would be infeasible for lesser organizations are available to them. Additionally, local governments have physical and legal access to many of the systems that organizations depend upon for securing their networks.

Defending against these localized threats is exceedingly expensive, requiring dedicated physical hardware, and most zero trust networks consider the more extreme forms of attacks (say a vulnerability being inserted into a hypervisor which copies memory pages out of a VM) out of scope in their threat models. We should be clear that while security best practices are still very much encouraged, the zero trust model only requires the safety of information used to authenticate and authorize actions, such as on-disk credentials. Further requirements on endpoints, say full disk encryption, can be applied via additional policy.

Strong Authentication

Knowing how much to trust someone is useless without being able to associate a real-life person with that identity you know to trust. Humans have many senses to determine if the person in front of them is who they think they are. Turns out, combinations of senses are hard to fool.

Computer systems, however, are not so lucky. It's more like talking to someone on the phone. You can listen to their voice, read their caller ID, ask them questions...but you can't see them. Thus we are left with a challenge: how can one be reasonably assured that the person (or system) on the other end of the line is in fact who they say they are?

Typically, operators examine the IP address of the remote system and ask for a password. Unfortunately, these methods alone are insufficient for a zero trust network, where attackers can communicate from any IP they please and insert themselves between yourself and trusted remote host. Therefore, it is very important to employ strong authentication on every flow in a zero trust network.

The most widely accepted method to accomplish this is a standard named X.509, which most engineers are familiar with. It defines a certificate standard that allows identity to be verified through a chain of trust. It's popularly deployed as the primary mechanism for authenticating TLS (formerly SSL) connections.

SSL is Anonymous

The most widely consumed TLS configuration validates that the client is speaking to a trusted resource, but not that the resource is speaking to a trusted client. This poses an obvious problem for zero trust networks.

TLS additionally supports mutual authentication, in which the resource also validates the client. This is an important step in securing private resources; otherwise, the client device will go unauthenticated. More on zero trust TLS configuration in "Mutually Authenticated TLS" on page 155.

Certificates utilize two cryptographic keys: a *public key* and a *private key*. The public key is distributed, and the private key is held as a secret. The public key can encrypt data that the private key can decrypt, and vice versa, as shown in Figure 2-2. This allows one to prove they are in the presence of the private key by correctly decrypting a piece of data that was encrypted by the well-known (and verifiable) public key. In this way, identity can be validated without ever exposing the secret.

Certificate-based authentication lets us be certain that the person on the other end of the line has the private key, and also lets us be certain that someone listening in can't steal the key and reuse it in the future. It does, however, still rely on a secret, something that can be stolen. Not necessarily by listening in, but perhaps by a malware infection or physical theft.

So while we can validate that credentials are legitimate, we might not trust that they have been kept a secret. For this reason, it is desirable to use multiple secrets, stored in different places, which in combination grant access. With this approach, a potential attacker must steal multiple components.

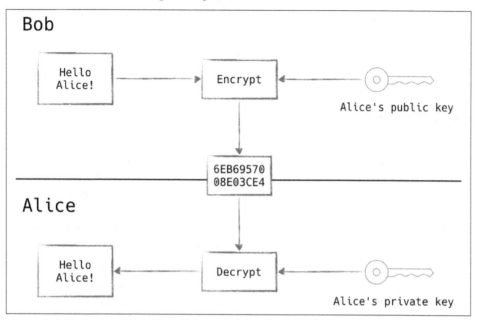

Figure 2-2. Bob can use Alice's well-known public key to encrypt a message that only Alice is able to decrypt

While having multiple components goes a long way in preventing unauthorized access, it is still conceivable that all these components can be stolen. Therefore, it is critical that all authentication credentials be time-boxed. Setting an expiration on credentials helps to minimize the blast radius of leaked or stolen keys and gives the operator an opportunity to reassert trust. The act of changing, or renewing, keys/passwords is known as *credential rotation*.

Credential rotation is essential for validating that no secrets have been stolen, and revoking them when required. Systems utilizing keys/passwords that are hard or impossible to rotate should be avoided at all cost, and when building new systems this fact should be taken into account early on in the design process. The rotation frequency of a particular credential is often inversely proportional to the cost of rotation.

Examples of Secrets Expensive to Rotate

- Certificates requiring external coordination
- Hand-configured service accounts
- Database passwords requiring downtime to reset
- A site-specific salt that cannot be changed without invalidating all stored hashes

Authenticating Trust

We spoke a little bit about certificates and public key cryptography. However, certificates alone don't solve the authentication issue. For instance, you can be assured that a remote entity is in possession of a private key by making an assertion using its public key. But how do you obtain the public key to begin with? Sure, public keys don't need to be secret, but you must still have a way to know that you have the *right* public key. *Public key infrastructure*, or PKI, defines a set of roles and responsibilities that are used to securely distribute and validate public keys in untrusted networks.

The goal of a PKI is to allow unprivileged participants to validate the authenticity of their peers through an existing trust relationship with a mutual third party. A PKI leverages what is known as a *registration authority* (RA) in order to bind an identity to a public key. This binding is embedded in the certificate, which is cryptographically signed by the trusted third party. The signed certificate can then be presented in order to "prove" identity, so long as the recipient trusts the same third party.

There are many types of PKI providers. The most popular two are *certificate authorities* (CAs) and *webs of trust* (WoTs). The former relies on a signature chain that is ultimately rooted in the mutually trusted party. The latter allows systems to assert validity of their peers, forming a web of endorsements rather than a chain. Trust is then asserted by traversing the web until a trusted certificate is found. While this approach is in relatively wide use with Pretty Good Privacy (PGP) encryption, this book will focus on PKIs that employ a CA, the popularity of which overshadows the WoT provider.

What Is a Certificate Authority?

Certificate authorities act as the trust anchor of a certificate chain. They sign and publish public keys and their bound identities, allowing unprivileged entities to assert the validity of the binding through the signature.

CA certificates are used to represent the identity of the CA itself, and it is the private key of the CA certificate that is used to sign client certificates. The CA certificate is well known, and is used by the authenticating entity to validate the signature of the presented client certificate. It is here that the trusted third-party relationship exists, issuing and asserting the validity of digital certificates on behalf of the clients.

The trusted third-party position is very privileged. The CA must be protected at all costs, since its subversion would be catastrophic. Digital certificate standards like X.509 allow for chaining of certificates, which enables the root CA to be kept offline. This is considered standard practice in CA-based PKI security. We'll talk more about X.509 security in Chapter 5.

Importance of PKI in Zero Trust

All zero trust networks rely on PKI to prove identity throughout the network. As such, it acts as the bedrock of identity authentication for the majority of operations. Entities that might be authenticated with a digital certificate include:

- Devices
- Users
- Applications

Binding Keys to Entites

PKI can bind an identity to a public key, but what about a private key to the entity it is meant to identify? After all, it is the private key which we are really authenticating. It is important to keep the private key as close to the entity it was meant to represent as possible. The method by which this is done varies by the type of entity. For instance, a user might store a private key on a smart card in their pocket, where a device might store a private key in an onboard security chip. We'll discuss which methods best fit which entities in Chapters 5, 6, and 7.

Given the sheer number of certificates that a zero trust network will issue, it is important to recognize the need for automation. If humans are required in order to process certificate signing requests, the procedure will be applied sparingly, weakening the overall system. That being said, certificates deemed highly sensitive will likely wish to retain a human-based approval process.

Private Versus Public PKI

PKI is perhaps most popularly deployed as a public trust system, backing X.509 certificates in use on the public internet. In this mode, the trusted third party is publicly trusted, allowing clients to authenticate resources that belong to other organizations. While public PKI is trusted by the internet at large, it is not recommended for use in a zero trust network.

Some might wonder why this is. After all, public PKI has some defensible strengths. Factors like existing utilities/tooling, peer-reviewed security practices, and the promise of a better time to market are all attractive. There are, however, several drawbacks to public PKI that work against it. The first is cost.

The public PKI system relies on publicly trusted authorities to validate digital certificates. These authorities are businesses of their own, and usually charge a fee for signing certificates. Since a zero trust network has many certificates, the signing costs associated with public authorities can be prohibitive, especially when considering rotation policies.

Another significant drawback to public PKI is the fact that it's hard to *fully* trust the public authorities. There are lots of publicly trusted CAs, operating in many countries. In a zero trust network leveraging public PKI, any one of these CAs can cut certificates that your network trusts. Do you trust the laws and the governments associated with all of those CAs too? Probably not. While there are some mitigation methods here, like certificate pinning or installing trust in a single public CA, it remains challenging to retain trust in a disjoint organization.

Finally, flexibility and programmability can suffer when leveraging public CAs. Public CAs are generally interested in retaining the public's trust, so they do employ good security measures. This might include policies about how certificates are formed, and what information can be placed where. This can adversely affect zero trust authentication in that it is often desirable to store site-specific metadata in the certificate, like a role or a user ID. Additionally, not all public CAs provide programmable interfaces, making automation a challenge.

Public PKI Strictly Better Than None

While the drawbacks associated with public PKI are significant, and the authors heavily discourage its use within a zero trust network, it remains superior to no PKI at all. A well-automated PKI is the first step, and work will be required in this area no matter which PKI approach you choose. The good news is that if you choose to leverage public PKI initially, there is a clear path to switch to private PKI once the risk becomes too great. It begs the question, however, if it is even worth the effort, since automation of those resources will still be required.

Least Privilege

The principle of least privilege is the idea that an entity should be granted only the privileges it needs to get its work done. By granting only the permissions that are always required, as opposed to sometimes desired, the potential for abuse or misuse by a user or application is greatly reduced.

In the case of an application, that usually means running it under a service account, in a container or jail, etc. In the case of a human, it commonly manifests itself as policies like "only engineers are allowed access to the source code." Devices must also be considered in this regard, though they often assume the same policies as the user or application they were originally assigned to.

Privacy as Least Privilege

The application of encryption in the name of privacy is an often-overlooked application of least privilege. Who *really* needs access to the packet payload?

Another effect of this principle is that if you *do* need elevated access, that you retain those access privileges for only as long as you need them. It is important to understand what actions require which privileges so that they may be granted only when appropriate. This goes one step beyond simple access control reviews.

This means that human users should spend most of their time executing actions using a nonprivileged user account. When elevated privileges are needed, the user needs to execute those actions under a separate account with higher privileges.

On a single machine, elevating one's privileges is usually accomplished by taking an action that requires the user to authenticate themselves. For example, on a Unix system, invoking a command using the sudo command will prompt the user to enter their password before running that command as a different role. In GUI environments, a dialog box might appear requiring the user's password before performing the risky operation. By requiring interaction with the user, the potential for malicious software to take action on behalf of the user is (potentially) mitigated.

In a zero trust network, users should similarly operate in a reduced privilege mode on the network most of the time, only elevating their permissions when needed to perform some sensitive operation. For example, an authenticated user might freely access the company's directory or interact with project planning software. Accessing a critical production system, however, should require additional confirmation that the user or the user's system is not compromised. For relatively low-risk actions, this privilege elevation could be as simple as reprompting for the user's password, requesting a second factor token, or sending a push notification to the user's phone. For high-risk access, one might choose to require active confirmation from a peer via an out-of-band request.

Human-Driven Authentication

For particularly sensitive operations, an operator may rely on the coordination of multiple humans, requiring a number of people to be actively engaged in order to authenticate a particular action. Forcing authentication actions into the real world is a good way to ensure a compromised system can't interfere with them. Be careful, however—these methods are expensive and will become ineffective if employed too frequently.

Like users, applications should also be configured to have the fewest privileges necessary to operate on the network. Sadly, applications deployed in a corporate setting are often given fairly wide access on the network. Either due to the difficulty of defining policies to rein in applications, or the assumption that compromised users are the more likely target, it's now become commonplace for the first step in setting up a machine to be disabling the application security frameworks that are meant to secure the infrastructure.

Beyond the traditional consideration of privilege for users and applications, zero trust networks also consider the privilege of the device on the network. It is the combination of user or application and the device being used that determines the privilege level granted. By joining the privilege of a user to the device being used to access a resource, zero trust networks are able to mitigate the effects of lost or compromised credentials. Chapter 3 will explore how this marriage of devices and users works in practice.

Privilege in a zero trust network is more dynamic than in traditional networks. Traditional networks eventually converge on policies that stay relatively static. If new use cases appear that require greater privilege, either the requestor must lobby for a change in policy; or, perhaps more frequently, they ask someone with greater privilege (a sysadmin, for example) to perform the operation for them. This static definition of policy presents two problems. First, in more permissive organizations, privilege will grow over time, lessening the benefit of least privilege. Second, in both permissive and restrictive organizations, admins are given greater access, which has resulted in malicious actors purposefully targeting sysadmins for phishing attacks.

A zero trust network, by contrast, will use many attributes of activity on the network to determine a riskiness factor for the access being requested currently. These attributes could be temporal (access outside of the normal window activity for that user is more suspicious), geographical (access from a different location than the user was last seen), or even behavioral (access to resources the user does not normally access). By considering all the details of an access attempt, the determination of whether the action is authorized or not can be more granular than a simple binary answer. For example, access to a database by a given user from their normal location during typical working hours would be granted, but access from a new location at

---

different working hours might require the user to authenticate using an additional factor.

The ability to actively adjust access based on the riskiness of activity on a network is one of the several features that make zero trust networks more secure. By dynamically adjusting policies and access, these networks are able to respond autonomously to known and unknown attacks by malicious actors.

Variable Trust

Managing trust is perhaps the most difficult aspect of running a secure network. Choosing which privileges people and devices are allowed on the network is time consuming, constantly changing, and directly affects the security posture the network presents. Given the importance of trust management, it's surprising how under-deployed network trust management systems are today.

Defining trust policies is typically left as a manual effort for security engineers. Cloud systems might have managed policies, but those policies provide only basic isolation (e.g., super user, admin, regular user) which advanced users typically outgrow. Perhaps in part due to the difficulty of defining and maintaining them, requests to change existing policies can be met with resistance. Determining the impact of a policy change can be difficult, so prudence pushes the administrators toward the status quo, which can frustrate end users and overwhelm system administrators with change requests.

Policy assignment is also typically a manual effort. Users are granted policies based on their responsibilities in the organization. This role-based policy system tends to produce large pools of trust in the administrators of the network, weakening the overall security posture of the network. These pools of trust have created a market for hackers to "hunt sys admins" (*http://bit.ly/2sYnfNQ*), seeking out and compromising system administrators. Perhaps the gold standard for a secure network is one without highly privileged system administrators.

These pools of trust underscore the fundamental issue with how trust is managed in traditional networks: policies are not nearly dynamic enough to respond to the threats being leveled against the network. Mature organizations will have some sort of auditing process in place for activity on their network, but audits can be done too infrequently, and are frankly so tedious that doing them well is difficult for humans. How much damage could a rogue sysadmin do on a network before an audit discovered their behavior and mitigated it? A more fruitful path might be to rethink the actor/trust relationship, recognizing that trust in a network is ever evolving and based on the previous and current actions of an actor within the network.

This model of trust, considering all the actions of an actor and determining their trustworthiness, is not novel. Credit agencies have been performing this service for many years. Instead of requiring organizations like retailers, financial institutions, or even an employer to independently define and determine one's trustworthiness, a credit agency can use actions in the real world to score and gauge the trustworthiness of an individual. The consuming organizations can then use their credit score to decide how much trust to grant that person. In the case of a mortgage application, an individual with a higher credit score will receive a better interest rate, which mitigates the risk to the lender. In the case of an employer, one's credit score might be used as a signal for a hiring decision. On a case-by-case basis, these factors can feel arbitrary and opaque, but they serve a useful purpose; providing a mechanism for defending a system against arbitrary threats by defining policy based not only on specifics, but also on an ever-changing and evolving score.

A zero trust network utilizes this insight to define trust within the network, as shown in Figure 2-3. Instead of defining binary policy decisions assigned to specific actors in the network, a zero trust network will continuously monitor the actions of an actor on the network to update their trust score. This score can then be used to define policy in the network based on the severity of breach of that trust (Figure 2-4). A user viewing their calendar from an untrusted network might require a relatively low trust score. However, if that same user attempted to change system settings, they would require a much higher score and would be denied or flagged for immediate review. Even in this simple example, one can see the benefit of a score: we can make fine-grained determinations on the checks and balances needed to ensure trust is maintained.

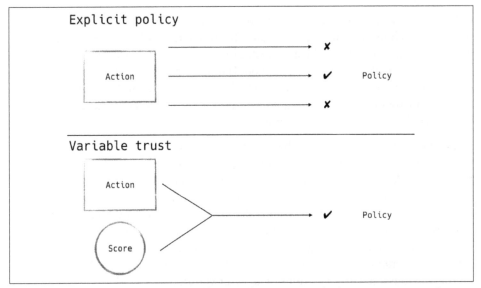

Figure 2-3. Using a trust score allows fewer policies to provide the same amount of access

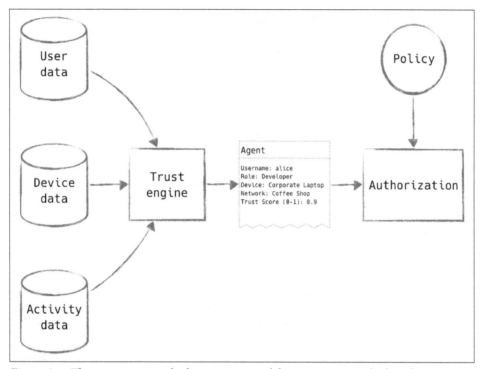

Figure 2-4. The trust engine calculates a score and forms an agent, which is then compared against policy in order to authorize a request. We'll talk more about agents in Chapter 3.

Monitoring Encrypted Traffic

Since practically all flows in a zero trust network are encrypted, traditional traffic inspection methods don't work as well as intended. Instead, we are limited to inspecting what we can see, which in most cases is the IP header and perhaps the next protocol header (like TCP in the case of TLS). If a load balancer or proxy is in the request path, however, there is an opportunity for deeper inspection and authorization, since the application data will be exposed for examination.

Clients begin sessions as untrusted. They must accumulate trust through various mechanisms, eventually accruing enough to gain access to the service they're requesting. Strong authentication proving that a device is company-owned, for instance, might accumulate a good bit of trust, but not enough to allow access to the billing system. Providing the correct RSA token might give you a good bit more trust, enough to access the billing system when combined with the trust inferred from successful device authentication.

Strong Policy as a Trust Booster

Things like score-based policies, which can affect the outcome of an authorization request based on a number of variables like historical activity, drastically improve a network's security stance when compared to static policy. Sessions that have been approved by these mechanisms can be trusted more than those that haven't. In turn, we can rely (a little bit) less on user-based authentication methods to accrue the trust necessary to access a resource, improving the overall user experience.

Switching to a trust score model for policies isn't without its downsides. The first hurdle is whether a single score is sufficient for securing all sensitive resources. In a system where a trust score can decrease based on user activity, a user's score can also increase based on a history of trustworthy activity. Could it be possible for a persistent attacker to slowly build their credibility in a system to gain more access?

Perhaps slowing an attacker's progress by requiring an extended period of "normal" behavior would be sufficient to mitigate that concern, given that an external audit would have more opportunity to discover the intruder. Another way to mitigate that concern is to expose multiple pieces of information to the control plane so that sensitive operations can require access from trusted locations and persons. Binding a trust score to device and application metadata allows for flexible policies that can declare absolute requirements yet still capture the unknown unknowns through the computed trust score.

Loosening the coupling between security policy and a user's organizational role can cause confusion and frustration for end users. How can the system communicate to users that they are denied access to some sensitive resource from a coffee shop, but not from their home network? Perhaps we present them with increasingly rigorous authentication requirements? Should new members be required to live with lower access for a time before their score indicates that they can be trusted with higher access? Maybe we can accrue additional trust by having the user visit a technical support office with the device in question. All of these are important points to consider. The route one takes will vary from deployment to deployment.

Control Plane Versus Data Plane

The distinction between the control plane versus the data plane is a concept that is commonly referenced in network systems. The basic idea is that a network device has two logical domains with a clear interface between those domains. The data plane is the relatively dumb layer that manages traffic on the network. Since that layer is handling high rates of traffic, its logic is kept simple and often pushed to specialized hardware. The control plane, conversely, could be considered the brains of the network device. It is the layer that system administrators apply configuration to, and as a result is more frequently changed as policy evolves.

Since the control plane is so malleable, it is unable to handle the high rate of traffic on the network. Therefore, the interface between the control plane and the data plane needs to be defined in such a way that nearly any policy behavior can be implemented at the data layer with infrequent requests being made to the control plane (relative to the rate of traffic).

A zero trust network also defines a clear separation between the control plane and data plane. The data plane in such a network is made up of the applications, firewalls, proxies, and routers that directly process all traffic on the network. These systems, being in the path of all connections, need to quickly make a determination of whether traffic should be allowed. When viewing the data plane as a whole, it has broad access and exposure throughout the system, so it is important that the services on the data plane cannot be used to gain privilege in the control plane and thereby move laterally within the network. We'll discuss control plane security in Chapter 4.

The control plane in a zero trust network is made up of components that receive and process requests from data plane devices that wish to access (or grant access to) network resources, as shown in Figure 2-5. These components will inspect data about the requesting system to make a determination on how risky the action is, and examine relevant policy to determine how much trust is required. Once a determination is made, the data plane systems are signaled or reconfigured to grant the requested access.

The mechanism by which the control plane affects change in the data plane is of critical importance. Since the data plane systems are often the entry point for attackers into a network, the interface between it and the control plane must be clear, helping to ensure that it cannot be subverted to move laterally within the network. Requests between the data plane and control plane systems must be encrypted and authenticated using a non-public PKI system to ensure that the receiving system is trustworthy. The control/data plane interface should resemble the user/kernel space interface, where interactions between those two systems are heavily isolated to prevent privilege escalation.

This concern with the interface between the control plane and the data plane belies another fundamental property of the control plane: the control plane is the trust grantor for the entire network. Due to its far-reaching control of the network's behavior, the control plane's trustworthiness is critical. This need to have an actor on the network with a highly privileged role presents a number of interesting design requirements.

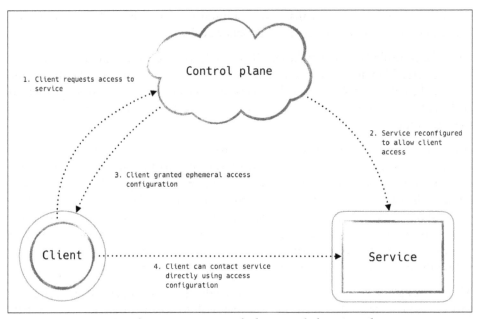

Figure 2-5. A zero trust client interacting with the control plane in order to access a resource

The first requirement is that the trust granted by the control plane to another actor in the data plane should have limited real-time value. Trust should be temporary, requiring regular check-ins between the truster and trustee to ensure that the continued trust is reasonable. When implementing this tenet, leased access tokens or short lifetime certificates are the most appropriate solution. These leased access tokens should be validated not just within the data plane (e.g., when the control plane grants a token to an agent to move through the data plane), but also between the interaction between the data plane and the control plane. By limiting the window during which the data plane and control plane can interact with a particular set of credentials, the possibility for physical attacks against the network is mitigated.

Summary

This chapter discussed the critical systems and concepts that are needed to manage trust in a zero trust network. Many of these ideas are common in traditional network security architectures, but it is important to lay the foundation of how trust is managed in a network without any.

Trust originates from humans and flows into other systems via trust mechanisms that a computer can operate against. This approach makes logical sense: a system can't be considered trusted unless the humans who use it feel confident that it is faithfully executing their wishes.

Security has frequently been viewed as a set of best practices, which are passed down from one generation of engineers to the next. Breaking out of this cycle is important, since each system is unique, and so we discussed the idea of threat models. Threat models attempt to define the security posture of a system by enumerating the threats against the system and then defining the mitigating systems and processes which anticipate those threats. While a zero trust network assumes a hostile environment, it is still fundamentally grounded in the threat model, which makes sense for the system. We enumerated several present-day threat-modeling techniques so that readers can dig deeper. We also discussed how the zero trust model is based on the internet threat model and expands its scope to the endpoints that are under the control of zero trust system administrators.

Having trust in a system requires the use of strong authentication throughout the system. We discussed the importance of this type of authentication in a zero trust network. We also briefly talked a bit about how strong authentication can be achieved in today's technology. We will discuss these concepts more in later chapters.

In order to effectively manage trust in a network, you must be able to positively identify trusted information, particularly in the case of authentication and identity. Public key infrastructure (or PKI) provides the best methods we have today for asserting validity and trust in a presented identity. We discussed why PKI is important in a zero trust network, the role of a certificate authority, and why private PKI is preferred over public PKI.

Least privilege is one of the key ideas in these types of networks. Instead of constructing a supposedly safe network over which applications can freely communicate, the zero trust model assumes that the network is untrustworthy, and as a result, components on the network should have minimal privileges when communicating. We explained what the concept of least privilege is and how it is similar and different than least privilege in standalone systems.

One of the most exciting ideas of zero trust networks is the idea of variable trust. Network policy has traditionally focused on which systems are allowed to communicate in what manner. This binary policy framework results in policy that is either too rigidly defined (creating human toil to continually adjust) or too loosely defined (resulting in security systems that assert very little). Additionally, policy that is defined based on concrete details of interactions will invariably be stuck in a cat-and-mouse game of adjusting policy based on past threats. The zero trust model leans on the idea of variable trust, a numeric value representing the level of trust in a component. Policy can then be written against this number, effectively capturing a number of conditions without complicating the policy with edge cases. By defining policy in less concrete details, and considering the trust score while making an authorization decision, the authorization systems are able to adjust to novel threats.

Zero trust networks make a clear distinction between the control plane systems and the data plane systems. We discussed at a high level how these two systems interact with each other to allow expected communication to flow through the network. In later chapters we will flesh out more of the control and data plane systems that manage communication in the network.

The next chapter digs into a fundamental entity in zero trust networks that is used to authorize actions on the network.

CHAPTER 3

Network Agents

Imagine you're in a security-conscious organization. Each employee is given a highly credentialed laptop to do their work. With today's work and personal life blending together, some also want to view their email and calendar on their phone. In this hypothetical organization, the security team applies fine-grained policy decisions based on which device the user is using to access a particular resource.

For example, perhaps it is permissible to commit code from the employee's company-issued laptop, but doing so from their phone would be quite a strange thing. Since source code access from a mobile device is decidedly riskier than from an enrolled laptop, the organization blocks such access.

The story described here is a fairly typical application of zero trust, in that multiple factors of authentication and authorization take place, concerning both the user and the device. In this example, however, it is clear that one factor has influenced the other—a user which might "normally" have source code access won't enjoy such access from their mobile device. Additionally, this organization does not want authenticated users to commit code from just any trusted device—they expect users to use their own device.

This marriage of user and device is a new concept that zero trust introduces, which we are calling a *network agent*. In a zero trust network, it is insufficient to treat the user and device separately, because policy often needs to consider the two together to accurately enforce desired behavior. By defining a network agent formally in the system, we are able to capture this relationship and use it to drive policy decisions.

This chapter will define what a network agent is and how it is used. In doing that, we will discuss the types of data that are included in an agent, some of which is potentially sensitive. Given the nature of that data, we will discuss when and how an agent should be exposed to data plane systems. A network agent, being a new concept, could benefit from standardization. We will explore the benefits of standardizing this agent.

What Is an Agent?

A *network agent* is the term given to the combination of data known about the actors in a network request, typically containing a user, application, and device. Traditionally, these entities have been authorized separately, but zero trust networks recognize that policy is best captured as a combination of all participants in a request. By authorizing the entire context of a request, the impact of credential theft is greatly mitigated.

It's best to think of a network agent as an ephemeral entity that is formed on demand to evaluate a policy. The data that is used to form an agent—user or device information—will typically be stored in persistent storage and queried to form an agent. When this data is queried, the union of the data at that point in time is what we call an *agent*.

Agent Volatility

Some fields in the agent are made available specifically to mitigate against active attacks, and are therefore expected to change rapidly relative to the infrequent changes that IT organizations normally expect. *Trust scores* are an example of this type of dynamic data. Trust score systems can evaluate each request in the network, using that activity feed to update the trust scores of users, applications, and devices. Therefore, in order for a trust score to mitigate a novel attack, it needs to be updated as close to real time as possible.

In addition to rapidly changing data, agents will frequently have sparse data. A device undergoing bootstrapping is an example scenario where the agent will have less data when compared to a mature device. During the bootstrapping process, little is known about the device, yet it must still interact with corporate infrastructure to perform tasks like device enrollment and software installation. In this case, the bootstrapping device is not yet assigned to a user and can run into problems if policy expects an assigned user to be present in the agent. This scenario should be expected and reflected in authorization policy.

Sparse data isn't just found in bootstrapping scenarios. Autonomous systems in a zero trust network will frequently have sparse data when compared to human-operated systems. These systems, for example, will likely not authenticate the user account the application runs under, relying instead on the security of the configuration management system that created that user.

What's in an Agent?

The granularity of data contained within an agent can vary based on needs and maturity. It can be as high level as a user's name or a device's manufacturer, or as low level as serial numbers and place of residence or issue. It should be noted that the more detailed data is more likely to have data cleanliness issues, which must be dealt with.

Agent Data Fields

The type of data stored in an agent can greatly vary in both presence and granularity. Here are some examples of data that one might find in an agent:

- Agent trust score
- User trust score
- User role or groups
- User place of residence
- User authentication method
- Device trust score
- Device manufacturer
- TPM manufacturer and version
- Current device location
- IP address

Another point of consideration is if the data contained in the agent is trusted or not. For instance, device data populated during the procurement process is more trusted than device data which is reported back from an agent running on it. This difference in trust arises from difficulties in ensuring the accuracy and integrity of the reported information in the event that the device is compromised.

How Is an Agent Used?

When making an authorization decision in a zero trust network, it is the agent that is in fact authorized. While it is tempting to authorize the device and user separately, this approach is not recommended. Since the agent is the entity which is authorized, it is also the thing against which policy is written.

As noted in the previous section, the agent carries many pieces of information. So while more "traditional" authorization information like IP address can still be used, leveraging the agent also unlocks the use of "nontraditional" authorization information like device type or city of residence. As such, zero trust network policy is written against the agent as a whole, as opposed to crafting disjoint user and device policy.

Using an agent to drive authorization policy encourages authors to consider the totality of the communication context. The marriage of user and device is very important in zero trust authorization decisions, and colocating the data in an agent makes it difficult to ignore one or the other. As with other portions of the zero trust architecture, lowering barrier to entry is key, and colocating the data to make device/user comparisons easier is no different.

An agent, being the primary actor in the network, plays an additional role in the calculation of trust scores. The trust engine can use recorded actions, in addition to data contained within the agent itself, to score agents for their trustworthiness. This trust score will then be exposed as an additional attribute on the agent against which most policy should be defined. We'll talk more about how the trust score is calculated in the next chapter.

Not for Authentication

It is important to understand the difference between authentication and authorization in the context of an agent. Agents serve solely as authorization components and do not play any part in authentication. In fact, authentication is a precursor to agent formation and is generally performed separately for user and device. For example, devices could be authenticated with X.509 certificates, while users might be authenticated through a traditional multifactor approach.

Following successful authentication, the canonical identifiers for users and devices can be used to form an agent and its details. A device-specific certificate might be used as the canonical identifier for the device and therefore be used to populate information like device type or device owner. Similarly, a username might serve as the lookup key to populate user information like their role in the company.

Typically authentication is session oriented, but in the case of authorization, it is best to be request oriented. As a result, caching the outcome of an authentication request is permissible, but caching an agent or the result of an authorization request is ill advised. This is because details in the agent, which are used to make authorization decisions, can change rapidly based on a number of factors, and it is desirable to make authorization decisions using the latest data. This is in contrast to authentication materials, which change much less often and don't directly affect authorization itself.

Finally, the act of generating an agent should be as lightweight as possible. If agent generation is expensive, it will discourage frequent authorization requests due to performance reasons. We will talk more about how performance affects authorization in the next chapter.

Revoke Authorization First, Credentials Second

Successful authentication is the act of proving one's identity to a remote system. That verified identity is then used to determine if the user actually has rights to access the resource in question (the authorization). In the event that access must be revoked, updating authorization is more effective than changing authentication credentials. This is doubly so when considering that authentication results are typically cached and assigned to session identifier. The act of validating an authenticated session is really an authorization decision.

How to Expose an Agent?

The data contained in a network agent is potentially sensitive. Personally identifiable user information (e.g., name, address, phone number) will usually be present on the agent to facilitate detailed authorization decisions. This data should be treated with care to protect the privacy of users.

The sensitive nature of the data extends beyond users, however. Device details can also be sensitive data when it falls into the hands of a determined attacker. An attacker with detailed knowledge of a user's device could use that data to craft a targeted remote attack, or even learn a pattern of that user's physical location to steal the device.

To adequately secure the sensitive agent details, the entirety of the agent lifecycle should be contained to trusted control plane systems, which themselves are heavily secured. These systems should be logically and physically separated from the data plane systems, have clear boundaries, and change infrequently.

Most policy decisions will be made in the control plane systems, since the agent data is needed to make those decisions. However, it will often be the case that the authorization engine in the control plane is not in the best position to enforce application-centric policy, despite its ability to enforce authorization on a request-by-request basis. This is especially so in user-facing systems. As a result, some agent details will need to be exposed to data plane systems.

Let's look at an example. An administrative application stores details on all the customers of a particular company. This system exposes that data to employees based on their role within the company. A search feature allows employees to search within the subset of data that they are allowed to access. The application needs to implement this logic, and it needs access to the role of the user in order to do so.

In order to allow applications to implement their own fine-grained authorization logic, agent details can be exposed to applications via a trusted communication channel. This could be as simple as injecting headers into network requests that flow through a reverse proxy. The proxy, being a zero trust control plane system, can view the agent to enforce its own authorization decisions and expose a subset of the data to the downstream application for further authorization.

Exposing agent details to the downstream application can also be useful to enable compatibility with pre-existing applications that have a rich authorization system. This compatibility goal highlights that agent details should be exposed to the application in a format that is is preferred by the application. For third-party applications, the format of the agent data will vary. For first-party applications, a common structure for the agent data will ease management of the system.

No Standard Exists

A zero trust network comprises many systems that concern themselves with the agent. In order to make room for reusability in these systems, standardization of the agent must occur. At the time of this writing, most zero trust networks consist of systems built in-house; and while those systems have developed their own agent standards, a public standard would unlock the control plane, allowing components to be mixed and matched.

Rigidity and Fluidity, at the Same Time

Knowing the format of an agent, and where to find particular pieces of data within it, is very important when considering how and by what it will be consumed. The "coordinates" of certain pieces of data must be fixed and well known in order to ensure consistency across control plane systems. A good analogy here is the schema of a relational database, which applications accessing the data must have knowledge of in order to extract the right pieces of information.

This data compatibility is extremely important when it comes to implementing and maintaining zero trust control plane systems. Zero trust networks, particularly more mature ones, are likely to construct an agent from multiple systems and data sources. Without a schema of sorts, not only will it be difficult to surface the data in a consistent manner, but it will also contribute negatively to the amount of effort required to introduce *new* control plane systems or agent data, something which is considered critical for a maturing zero trust network.

One thing to keep in mind, however, is that agent data is likely to be fairly sparse, thanks to the practically unavoidable data cleanliness issues encountered in source systems like device inventories. The result is a "best-effort" agent, where many fields may be unpopulated for one reason or another. Rather than seeking data cleanliness (a problem that only gets harder with scale), it is best to accept reality and craft policy that understands that not all data may be present. So while one may still require a particular piece of data to be present in the agent, it is a useful thought exercise to consider alternative pieces of data in its absence.

Standardization Desirable

One might wonder how it would be possible to standardize a data format that is so seemingly inextricably tied to the organization consuming it. After all, an agent is likely to contain information types that relate to business logic or other proprietary/local information. Is standardization even feasible in such a case?

Luckily, there are already some standards out there defining data formats that behave in such a way. One of the best examples is the *Simple Network Management Protocol* (SNMP), and its associated *management information base* (MIB).

SNMP is a protocol frequently used for network device management, allowing devices to expose data to operators and management systems in a standard yet flexible way. The MIB component describes the format of the data itself, which is a collection of *OIDs*, or *object identifiers*. Each OID describes (and is reserved for) a particular piece of data and is registered with ISO, a global standardization body. This lends itself well to widely accepted "coordinates" for certain pieces of data.

Let's look at an example, shown in Figure 3-1, of a simplified set of nodes in an OID tree.

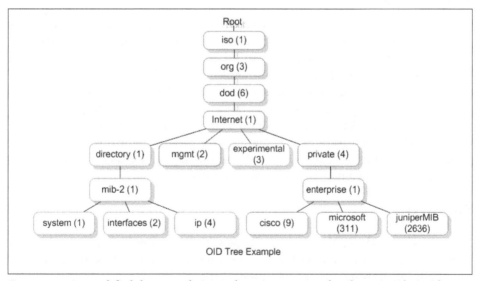

Figure 3-1. A simplified diagram showing the organization of nodes in an object identifier (OID) tree

In this example, the "ip" node and associated data would be addressed as *1.3.6.1.1.1.4*. A MIB arranges and gives color to a set of OIDs. For example, a Cisco MIB might provide definitions for all OIDs under the *1.3.6.1.4.1.9* portion of the tree, including human-readable descriptions.

Of course, this registered list can be extended, and oftentimes chunks of OID space are carved out for organizations or manufacturers. In this way, an OID can be compared to an IP address, where an IP address globally identifies a computer system and an OID globally identifies a piece of data.

Unfortunately, there is no good OID equivalent of private IP address space, which would be useful for ad hoc or site-specific data. The best available compromise is to register (*http://pen.iana.org/pen/PenApplication.page*) for a *Private Enterprise Number* with IANA, which will give you a dedicated OID prefix for private use. Luckily, such registration is free and with few questions asked. There have been some efforts to create a private range similar to that found in IP. However, such efforts have been unsuccessful.

Despite the lack of a truly free/private OID space for experimental or internal use, SNMP remains a useful analogy to make when considering the standardization of an agent. It describes the format and packaging of a set of data—data that is easily found and identified using their unique OIDs—and how that data can be transmitted and understood from one system to another.

In the Meantime?

At the time of this writing, zero trust networks are still quite new, and the field is under active development. As such, no standard describing an agent exists today, and it will be some time before one can be ratified. In the meantime, agents take the form of least resistance, given the needs of the implementor. Whether it be a JSON blob or a custom binary format, it is recommended to ensure that the data contained within it be flexible and easily extensible. Loose typing or no typing should be preferred over strong typing, as the latter will make introducing new data and systems more difficult. Pluggable design patterns may help in moving to a standardized agent in the future. However, this is far from required, and should not be pursued if they impede the adoption of agent authorization in your network.

Summary

This chapter introduced the concept of a network agent, a new entity in a zero trust network against which authorization decisions are made. Adding this concept is critical to realizing the benefits of a zero trust network.

We explored what goes into creating an agent. Agents contain rapidly changing data and frequently have data that is unavailable or inconsistent. Accepting that reality is important for success when introducing the agent concept.

Agents are used purely for making authorization decisions. Authentication is a separate concern, and the current authentication status is reflected in the properties of an agent. Control plane systems use the agent to authorize requests. These systems are the primary enforcers of authorization in a zero trust network, but sometimes they must expose agent details to applications that are better positioned to implement fine-grained authorization decisions. We explored how to expose this data to applications while maintaining privacy.

Zero trust network administration is still very new, and as a result, no standard yet exists for network agents. Defining a standard would allow for better reuse and interoperability of zero trust systems, aiding the adoption of this technology. We discussed a possible approach for standardizing the definition of an agent.

The next chapter will focus on the systems that are responsible for authorizing all requests in a zero trust network.

CHAPTER 4

Making Authorization Decisions

Authorization is arguably the most important process occurring within a zero trust network, and as such, making an authorization decision should not be taken lightly. Every flow and/or request will ultimately require a decision be made.

The databases and supporting systems we will discuss here are the key systems that come together to make and affect those decisions. Together, they are authoritative for access control and thus need to be rigorously isolated. Careful distinction should be made between these responsibilities, particularly when deciding whether to collapse them into a single system, which should generally be avoided if possible.

The zero trust model is still very new, and this area is undergoing rapid evolution. Some of the content included in this chapter is considered state of the art at the time of this writing. Known implementations still vary wildly in their approaches, and most are not publicly available. That being said, the major components and responsibilities are understood.

Taking reality into account, this chapter will focus on high-level architectural arrangement of the components required to make zero trust authorization decisions, as well as how they fit together and enforce said decisions.

Authorization Architecture

The zero trust authorization architecture comprises four main components, as shown in Figure 4-1:

- Enforcement
- Policy engine
- Trust engine
- Data stores

These four components are distinct in their responsibilities, and as a result, we treat them as separate systems. From a security standpoint, it is highly desirable that these components be isolated from each other. These systems represent the practical crown jewels of the zero trust security model, so special care should be taken in their maintenance and security posture. Carefully evaluate any proposals that suggest collapsing these responsibilities into a single system.

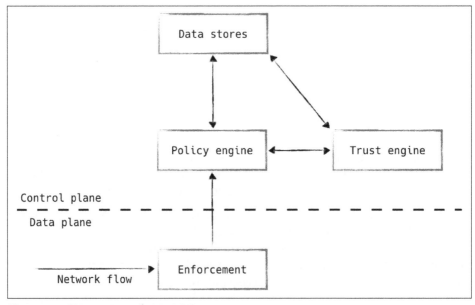

Figure 4-1. Zero trust authorization systems

The enforcement component will exist in large numbers throughout the system and should be as close to the workload as possible. It is the one that actually affects the outcome of the authorization decision. It is typically manifested as a load balancer, proxy, or even a firewall. This component interacts with the policy engine, which is the piece that we use to make the actual decision. The enforcement component ensures that clients are authenticated, and passes the context of each flow/request to the policy engine. The policy engine compares the request and its context to policy, and informs the enforcer whether the request will be permitted or not.

The trust engine is leveraged by the policy engine for risk analysis purposes. It leverages multiple data sources in order to compute a risk score, similar to a credit score. This score can be used to protect against unknown unknowns, and helps keep policy strong and robust without complicating it with edge cases and signatures. It is used by the policy engine as an additional component by which an authorization decision can be made. Google's BeyondCorp is widely recognized as having pioneered this technology.

Finally, we have the various data stores that represent the source of truth for the data being used to inform authorization. This data is used to paint a full contextual picture of a particular flow/request, using small authenticated bits of data as the primary lookup keys (i.e., a username or a device's serial number). These data stores, be they user data, device data, or otherwise, are heavily leveraged by both the policy engine and trust engine, and represent the backing against which all decisions are measured.

Enforcement

The enforcement component (depicted in Figure 4-2) is a natural place to start. It sits on the "front line" of the authorization flow and is responsible for carrying out decisions made by the rest of the authorization system.

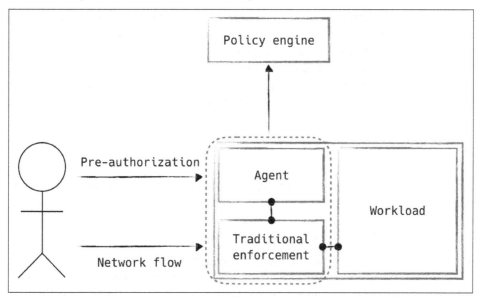

Figure 4-2. An agent receives a pre-authorization signal to grant access to a system using traditional enforcement mechanisms. These systems together form the enforcement component.

Enforcement can be broken down into two primary responsibilities. First, an interaction with the policy engine must occur. This is generally the authorization request itself (e.g., a load balancer has received a request and needs to know whether it is authorized or not). The second is the actual installation and ongoing enforcement of the decision. While these two responsibilities represent a single component in the zero trust authorization architecture, you can choose whether they are fulfilled together or separately.

The way you choose to handle this will likely depend on your use case. For instance, an identity-aware proxy can call the policy engine to actively authorize a request it has received, and in the same step use the response to either service or reject the request. This is an example of treating the concerns as unified. Alternatively, perhaps a pre-authorization daemon receives a request for access to a particular service, which then calls the policy engine for authorization. Upon successful authorization, the daemon can manipulate local firewall rules to allow the specific request. With this approach, we rely on "standard" enforcement mechanisms that are informed/programmed by the zero trust control plane. It should be noted, however, that this approach requires a client-side hook in order to notify the control plane of the authorization request. This may or may not be acceptable, depending on the level of control over your devices and applications.

Placement of the enforcement component is very important. Since it represents our control point within the data plane, we must ensure that enforcement components are placed as close to the endpoints as possible. Otherwise, trust can pool "behind" the enforcement component, undermining zero trust security. Luckily, the enforcement component can be modeled as a client of sorts and applied liberally throughout the system. This is in contrast to the rest of the authorization components, which are modeled as services.

Policy Engine

The policy engine is the component that has the power to make a decision. It compares the request coming from the enforcement component against policy in order to determine whether the request is authorized or not. Once determined, the result is returned to the enforcement piece for actual realization.

The arrangement of the enforcement layer and policy engine allows for dynamic, point-in-time decisions to be made, allowing revocation to occur rapidly. As such, it is important that these components be considered separately and independently. That is not to say, however, that they cannot be co-located.

Depending on a number of factors, a policy engine may be found hosted side by side with the enforcement mechanism. An example of this might be a load balancer that authorizes requests through *inter-process communication* (IPC) instead of a remote call. The most attractive benefit of this architecture is the lower latency to authorize the request. A low-latency authorization system enables fine-grained and comprehensive authorization of network activity; for example, individual HTTP requests could be authorized instead of the session-level authorization that commonly is deployed.

It should be noted that it is best to maintain process-level isolation between the policy engine and enforcement layer. The enforcement layer, being in the user's data path, is more exposed; therefore, integrating the policy engine in the same process could expose it to unwanted risk. Deploying the policy engine as its own process goes a long way to ensure that bugs in the enforcement layer don't result in a policy engine compromise.

What Ever Happened to RADIUS?

The relationship between the policy engine and the enforcement layer is a familiar one for most network engineers. In 1997, the IETF ratified a standard describing the *RADIUS* protocol, which provides authentication, authorization, and accounting for network services. RADIUS stands for *Remote Authentication Dial-In User Service*—the name alone shows its age. While the protocol itself is hopelessly insecure (it uses MD5 for authenticity assertions), it is specifically written for the task at hand. What would it look like to use RADIUS between the enforcement layer and the policy engine? RADIUS could be protected with other protocols discussed in this book, but that feels like a kludge. Perhaps there is an opportunity to create a RADIUS-like project, which takes into account the threat reality of today's systems.

Policy Storage

The rules referenced by the policy engine need to be stored. These policy rules are ultimately loaded into the policy engine, but it is strongly recommended that the rules are captured outside of the policy engine itself. Storing the policy rules in a version control system is ideal and provides several benefits:

- Changes to policy can be tracked over time.
- Rationale for changing policy is tracked in the version control system.
- The expected current policy state can be validated against the actual enforcement mechanisms.

Many of these benefits have historically been implemented using rigorous change management procedures. In that system, changes to the system's configuration are requested and approved before ultimately being applied. The resulting change management log can be used to determine why the system is in the current state.

Moving policy definitions into version control is the logical conclusion of change management procedures when the system can be configured programmatically. Instead of relying on human system administrators to load desired policy into the system, we can instead capture the policy as data that a program can read and apply. In many ways, loading policy is then similar to deployable software. As a result, system administrators can use standard software development procedures (namely code review and promotion pipelines) to manage the changes in policy.

What Makes Good Policy?

Policy in a zero trust network is in some ways similar to traditional network security, and in other ways substantially different.

 Zero Trust Policy Is Still Not Standardized

The reality today is that zero trust policy is still not standardized in the same way as a network-oriented policy. As a result, defining the standard policy language used in a zero trust network is a great opportunity.

Let's look at what's similar first. Good policy in a zero trust network is fine-grained. The level of granularity will vary based on the maturity of the network, but the desired goal is policy that is scoped to the individual resource being secured. This is not very different than a traditional network security model that aims to segment the network to decrease attack surface area.

The zero trust model starts to diverge from traditional network security in the control mechanisms that are used to define policy. Instead of defining policy in terms of network implementation details (IP addresses and ranges), policy is best defined in terms of logical components in the network. These components will generally consist of:

- Network services
- Device endpoint classes
- User roles

Defining policy from logical components that exist in the network allows the policy engine to calculate the enforcement decisions based on its knowledge of the current state of the network. To put this in concrete terms, a web service running on one server today might be on a different server tomorrow, or might even move between servers automatically as directed by a workload scheduler. The policy that we define needs to be divorced from these implementation details to adapt to this reality. An example of this style of policy from the Kubernetes project is shown in Figure 4-3.

```
metadata:
 name: test-network-policy
 namespace: default
spec:
 podSelector:
  matchLabels:
    role: db
 ingress:
  - from:
    - namespaceSelector:
      matchLabels:
        project: myproject
    - podSelector:
      matchLabels:
        role: frontend
```

Figure 4-3. A snippet from a Kubernetes network policy. These policies use workload labels, computing the underlying IP-based enforcement rules when and where necessary.

Policy in a zero trust network also leans on trust scores to anticipate unknown attack vectors. By defining policy with a trust score component, administrators are able to mitigate risk that otherwise can't be captured with a specific policy. Therefore, most policy should include a trust score component. We'll talk more about the score component in the next section.

No Standard Exists

Currently, mature zero trust networks implement their own policy language/format on a case-by-case basis, typically being developed fully in-house. Simpler zero trust networks may embed policy in an existing structure, such as in Figure 4-3. While the latter is generally acceptable, it is typically outgrown as the network evolves and adds features. The advantages of a standardized/interoperable policy language can be clearly seen. However, such work remains an open research question.

Policy should not rely on trust score alone. Specific characteristics of the request being authorized can also be part of the policy definition. An example of this might be certain user roles should only have access to a particular service.

Who Defines Policy?

Zero trust network policy should be fine-grained, which can place an extraordinary burden on system administrators to keep the policy up to date. To help spread the load of this configuration burden, most organizations decide to distribute policy definition across the teams so they can help maintain policy for the services they own.

Opening up policy definition to an entire organization can present certain risks, like well-meaning users who create overly broad policies, thereby increasing the attack surface area of the system they intended to constrain. Zero trust systems lean on two organizational workflows to counteract this exposure.

First, since policy is typically stored under version control, having another person review changes to the policy helps ensure that changes are well considered. Security teams can additionally review the changes and ask probing questions to ensure that the policy being defined is as tightly scoped as possible. Since the policy is defined using logical intent instead of physical components, the policy will change less rapidly than if it was defined in physical terms.

The second organizational measure used is to layer broad infrastructure policy on top of fine-grained policy. For example, an infrastructure group might rightly require that only a certain set of roles be allowed to accept traffic from the internet. The infrastructure team will therefore define policy that enforces that restriction, and no user-defined policy will be allowed to circumvent it. Enforcing this constraint could take several forms: an automated test of proposed policy, or perhaps a policy engine that will simply refuse overly broad policy assertions from untrusted sources. Such enforcement can also be useful for compliance and regulatory requirements.

Trust Engine

The *trust engine* is the system in a zero trust network that performs risk analysis against a particular request or action. This system's responsibility is to produce a numeric assessment of the riskiness of allowing a particular request/action, which the policy engine uses to make an ultimate authorization decision.

The trust engine will frequently pull from data contained in authoritative inventory systems to check attributes of an entity when computing its score. A device inventory, for example, could provide the trust engine with information like the last time a device was audited, or whether it has a particular hardware security feature.

Creating a numeric assessment of risk is a difficult task. A simple approach would be to define a set of ad hoc rules that score an entity's riskiness. For example, a device that is missing the latest software patches could have its score reduced. Similarly, a user who is continually failing to authenticate could have their trust score reduced.

While ad hoc trust scoring might be simple to get started with, a set of statically defined rules will be insufficient to meet the desired goal of defending against unexpected attacks. As a result, in addition to using static rules, mature trust engines use machine learning techniques to derive a scoring function.

Machine learning derives a scoring function by calculating observable facts from a subset of activity data known as *training data*. The training data is raw observations that have been associated with trusted or untrusted entities. From this data, features are extracted and used to derive a computer-generated scoring function. This scoring function, a model in machine learning terms, is then run against a set of data that is in the same format as the training data. The resulting scores are compared against human-defined risk assessments, and the model's quality can then be refined based on its ability to correctly predict risk of the data being analyzed. A model that has sufficient accuracy can then be said to be predictive of the riskiness of yet unseen requests in the network.

While machine learning is increasingly used to solve hard computational problems, it does not obviate the need for more explicit rules in the trust engine. Whether due to limitation of the derived scoring models or for desired customization of the scoring function, trust engines will typically use a mixture of ad hoc and machine learning scoring methods.

What Entities Are Scored?

Deciding which components of a zero trust network should be scored is an interesting consideration. Should scores be calculated for each individual entity (user, device, and application), for the network agent as a whole, or for both? Let's look at some scenarios.

Imagine a user's credentials are being brute forced by a malicious third party. Some systems will mitigate this threat by locking the user's account, which can present a denial-of-service attack against that particular user. If we were to score a user negatively based on that activity, a zero trust network would suffer the same problem. A better approach is to realize that we're authenticating the network agent, and so the attacker's network agent is counteracted, leaving the legitimate user's network agent unharmed. This scenario makes a case that the network agent is the entity that should be scored.

But just scoring the network agent can be insufficient against other attack vectors. Consider a device that has been associated with malicious activity. A user's network agent on that device may be showing no signs of malicious behavior, but the fact that the agent is being formed with a suspected device should clearly have an impact on the trust score for all requests originating from that device. This scenario strongly suggests that the device should be scored.

Finally, consider a malicious human user (the infamous internal threat) is using multiple kiosk devices to exfiltrate trade secrets. We'd like the trust engine to recognize this behavior as the user hops across devices and to reflect the decreasing level of trust in their trust score for all future authorization decisions. Here again, we see that scoring the network agent alone is insufficient for mitigating common threats.

Taken as a whole, it seems like the right solution is to score both the network agent itself and the underlying entities that make up the agent. These scores can be exposed to the policy engine, which can choose the correct component(s) to authorize based on the policy being written.

Presenting so many scores for consideration when writing policy, however, can make the task of crafting policy more difficult and error prone. In an ideal world, a single score would be sufficient, but that approach presents extra availability requirements on the trust engine. A system that tries to create a single score would likely need to move to an online model, where the trust engine is interactively queried during the policy decision making. The engine would be given some context about the request being authorized so it could choose the best scoring function for that particular request. This design is clearly more complex to build and operate. Additionally, for policy where a system administrator specifically wishes to target a particular component (say, only allow deploys from devices with a score above X), it seems rather roundabout.

Exposing Scores Considered Risky

While the scores assigned to entities in a zero trust network are not considered confidential, exposing the scores to end users of the system should be avoided. Seeing one's score could be a signal to would-be attackers that they are increasing or decreasing their trustworthiness in the system. This desire to withhold information should be balanced against the frustration of end users' ability to understand how their actions are affecting their own trust in the system. A good compromise from the fraud industry is to show users their scores infrequently, and to highlight contributing factors to their score determination.

Data Stores

The data stores used to make authorization decisions are very simply the sources of truth for the current and past state of the system. Information from these data stores flows through the control plane systems, providing a large portion of the basis on which authorization decisions are made, as demonstrated in Figure 4-4.

We previously spoke about the trust engine leveraging these data stores in order to produce a trust score, which in turn is considered by the policy engine. In this way, information from control plane data stores has flowed through the authorization system, finally reaching the policy engine where the decision was made. These data stores are used by the policy engine, both directly and indirectly, but they can be useful to other systems that need authoritative data about the state of the network.

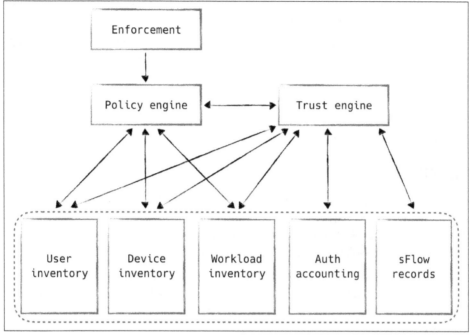

Figure 4-4. Authoritative data stores are used by the policy engine both directly and indirectly through the trust engine

Zero trust networks tend to have many data stores, organized by function. There are two primary types: *inventory* and *historical*. An inventory is a single consistent source of truth, recording the current state of the resource(s) it represents. An example is a user inventory that stores all user information, or a device inventory that records information about devices known to the company.

In an inventory, a primary key exists which uniquely represents the tracked entity. In the case of a user, the likely choice is the username; for a device, perhaps it's a serial number. When a zero trust agent undergoes authentication, it is authenticating its identity against this primary key in the inventory. Think about it like this: a user authenticates against a given username. The policy engine gets to know the username, and that the user was successfully authenticated. The username is then used as the primary key for lookup against the user inventory. Keeping this flow and purpose in mind will help you choose the right primary keys, depending on your particular implementation and authentication choices.

A historical data store is a little bit different. Historical data stores are kept primarily for risk analysis purposes. They are useful for examining recent/past behavior and patterns in order to assess risk as it relates to a particular request or action. Trust engine components are most likely to be consuming this data, as trust/risk determinations are the engine's primary responsibility.

One can imagine many types of historical data stores, and when it comes to risk analysis, the sky's the limit. Some common examples include user accounting records and sFlow data. Regardless of the data being stored, it must be queryable using the primary key from one of the inventory systems.

We will talk about various inventory and historical data stores as we introduce related concepts throughout this book.

Summary

This chapter focused on the systems that are responsible for making the ultimate decision of whether a particular request should be authorized in a zero trust network. This decision is a critical component of such a network, and therefore should be carefully designed and isolated to ensure it is trustworthy.

We broke this responsibility down into four key systems: enforcement, policy engine, trust engine, and data stores. These components are logical areas of responsibility. While they could be collapsed into fewer physical systems, the authors prefer an isolated design.

The enforcement system is responsible for ensuring that the policy engine's authorization decision takes effect. This system, being in the data path of user traffic, is best implemented in a manner where the policy decision is referenced and then enforced. Depending on the architecture chosen, the policy engine might be notified before a request occurs, or during the processing of that same request.

The policy engine is the key system that computes the authorization decision based on data available to it and the policy definitions that have been crafted by the system administrators. This system should be heavily isolated. The policy that is defined should ideally be stored separately from the engine and should use good software development practices to ensure that changes are understood, reviewed, and not lost as the policy moves from being proposed to being implemented. Furthermore, since zero trust networks expect to have much finer-grained policy, mature organizations choose to distribute the responsibility of defining that policy into the organization with security teams reviewing the proposed changes.

The trust engine is a new concept in security systems. This engine is responsible for calculating a trust score of components of the system using static and inferred algorithms derived from past behavior. The trust score is a numerical determination of the trustworthiness of a component and allows the policy writers to focus on the level of trust required to access some resource instead of the particular details of what actions might reduce that trust.

The final component of this part of the system is the authoritative data sources that capture current and historical data that can be used to make the authorization decision. These data stores should focus on being sources of truth. The policy engine, the trust engine, and perhaps third-party systems can leverage this data so the collection of this data will have a decent return on investment from capturing it.

The next chapter will dig into how devices gain and maintain trust.

CHAPTER 5

Trusting Devices

Trusting devices in a zero trust network is extremely critical; it's also an exceedingly difficult problem. Devices are the battlegrounds upon which security is won or lost. Most compromises involve a malicious actor gaining access to a trusted device; and once that access is obtained, the device cannot be trusted to attest to its own security.

This chapter will discuss the many systems and processes that need to be put in place to have sufficient trust of devices deployed in the network. We will focus on the role that each of these systems plays in the larger goal of truly trusting a device. Each technology is complicated in its own right. While we can't go into exhaustive detail on each protocol or system, we will endeavor to give enough details to help you understand the technology and avoid any potential pitfalls when using it.

We start with learning how devices gain trust in the first place.

Bootstrapping Trust

When a new device arrives, it is typically assigned an equal level of trust as that of the manufacturer and distributor. For most people, that is a fairly high level of trust (whether warranted or not). This inherited trust exists purely in meatspace though, and it is necessary to "inject" this trust into the device itself.

There are a number of ways to inject (and keep) this trust in hardware. Of course, the device ecosystem is massive, and the exact approach will differ on a case-by-case basis, but there are some basic principles that apply across the board. These principles reduce most differences to implementation details.

The first of those principles has been known for a long time: *golden images*. No matter how you receive your devices, you should always load a known-good image on them. Software can be hard to vet; rather than doing it many times hastily (or not at all), it makes good sense to do it once and certify an image for distribution.

Loading a "clean" image onto a device grants it a great deal of trust. You can be reasonably sure that the software running there is validated by you, and secure. For this reason, recording the last time a device was imaged is a great way to determine how much trust it gets on the network.

Secure Boot

There are of course ways to subvert devices in a manner that they retain the implant across reimaging and other low-level operations, as the implant in these cases are usually themselves fairly low level.

Secure Boot is one way to help fend against these kinds of attacks. It involves loading a public key into the device's firmware, which is used to validate driver and OS loader signatures to ensure that nothing has been slipped in between. While effective, support is limited to certain devices and operating systems. More on this later.

Being able to certify the software running on a device is only the first step. The device still needs to be able to identify itself to the resources that it is attempting to access. This is typically done by generating a unique device certificate that is signed by your private certificate authority. When communicating with network resources, the device presents its signed certificate. This certificate proves not only that it is a known device, but it also provides an identification method. Using details embedded in the certificate, the device can be matched with data from the device inventory, which can be used for further decision making.

Generating and Securing Identity

In providing a signed certificate by which a device may be identified, it is necessary to store the associated private key in a secure manner. This is not an easy task. Theft of the private key would enable an attacker to masquerade as a trusted device. This is the worst possible scenario for device authentication.

A simple yet insecure way to do this is to configure access rights to the key in such a way that only the most privileged user (root or administrator) can access it. This is the least desirable storage method, as an attacker who gains elevated access can exfiltrate the unprotected key.

Another way to do this is to encrypt the private key. This is better than relying on simple permissions, though it presents usability issues because a password (or other secret material) must be furnished in order to decrypt and use the key. This may not pose a problem for an end-user device, as the user can be prompted to enter the password, though this is usually not feasible for server deployments; human interaction is required for every software restart.

The best way by far to store device keys is through the use of secure cryptoprocessors. These devices, commonly referred to as a *hardware security module* (HSM) or a *trusted platform module* (TPM), provide a secure area in which cryptographic operations can be performed. They provide a limited API that can be used to generate asymmetric encryption keys, where the private key never leaves the security module. Since not even the operating system can directly access a private key stored by a security module, they are very difficult to steal.

Identity Security in Static and Dynamic Systems

In relatively static systems, it is common for an operator to be involved when new hosts are provisioned. This makes the injection story easy—the trusted human can directly cut the new keys on behalf of the hosts. Of course, as the infrastructure grows, this overhead will become problematic.

In automating the provisioning and signing process, there is an important decision to make: should a human be involved when signing new certificates? The answer to this largely depends on your sensitivity.

A signed device certificate carries quite a bit of power, and serves to identify anything with the private key as an authentic and trusted device. Just as we go through measures to protect their theft locally, we must also protect against their frivolous generation. If your installation is particularly sensitive, you might choose to involve a human every time a new certificate is signed.

Pwning the Signing Service

In 2011, a company named DigiNotar suffered a security breach. This breach was significant because DigiNotar was a publicly trusted certificate authority. The attackers managed to compromise the certificate signing infrastructure, and used this position to sign certificates of their choosing. It is estimated that over 300,000 users had their private data exposed by these fraudulent certificates. DigiNotar's certificates were immediately blacklisted by browsers around the world, and the company declared bankruptcy not long after. This breach underscores the importance of a secure signing infrastructure and process.

If provisioning is automated, but still human-driven, it makes a lot of sense to allow the human driving that action to also authorize the associated signing request. Having a human involved every time is the best way to prevent unauthorized requests from being approved. Humans are not perfect though. They are susceptible to fatigue and other shortcomings. For this reason, it is recommended that they be responsible for approving only requests that they themselves have initiated.

It is possible to accomplish provisioning and signature authorization in a single step through the use of a *temporal one-time password* (TOTP). The TOTP can be provided along with the provisioning request and passed through to the signing service for verification, as shown in Figure 5-1. This simple yet strong mechanism allows for human control over the signing of new certificates while imposing only minimal administrative overhead. Since a TOTP can only be used once, a TOTP verification failure is an important security event.

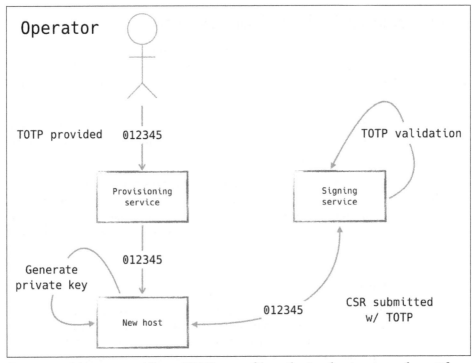

Figure 5-1. A human providing a TOTP can safely authorize the signature of a certificate.

It goes without saying that none of this applies if you want to *fully* automate the provisioning of new hosts. Frequently referred to as "auto-scaling," systems that can grow and shrink themselves are commonly found in large, highly automated installations. Allowing a system to scale itself decreases the amount of care and feeding required, significantly reducing administrative overhead and cost.

Signing a certificate is an operation that requires a great deal of trust; and just as with other zero trust components, this trust must be sourced from somewhere. There are three common choices:

- A human
- The resource manager
- The image or device

The human is an easy and secure choice for relatively static infrastructure or end user devices, but is an obvious nonstarter for automated infrastructure. In this case, you must choose the resource manager or the image...or both.

The resource manager is in a privileged position. It has the ability to both grow and shrink the infrastructure, and is likely able to influence its availability. It provides a good analog to a human in a more static system. It is in a position to assert, "Yes, I turned this new host on, and here is everything I know about it." It can use this position to either directly or indirectly authorize the signing of a new certificate.

Depending on your needs, it might be desirable to not grant this ability wholly to the resource manager. In this case, credentials can be baked into an image. This is generally not advised as a primary mechanism, as it places too much responsibility on the image store; and protecting and rotating images can be fraught with peril. In a similar way, HSMs or TPMs can be leveraged to provide a device certificate that is tied to the hardware. This is better than baking material into the image, though requiring a TPM-backed device to sign a new certificate is still not ideal, especially when considering cloud-based deployments.

One good way to mitigate these concerns is to require *both* the resource manager and a trusted image/device. Generic authentication material baked into the image (or a registered TPM key) can be used to secure communication with the signing service and can serve as a component in a multifaceted authorization. The following are examples of components for authorization consideration:

- Registered TPM key or image key
- Correct IP address
- Valid TOTP (generated by resource manager)
- Expected certificate properties (i.e., expected common name)

By validating all of these points, the certificate signing service can be relatively certain that the request is legitimate. The resource manager alone cannot request a certificate, and since it does not have access to the hosts it provisions, the most an attacker could do is impact availability. Similarly, a stolen image alone cannot request a certificate, as it requires the resource manager to validate that it has provisioned the host and expects the request.

By splitting these responsibilities and requiring multiple systems to assert validity, we can safely (well, as safely as is possible) remove humans from the loop.

Resource Managers and Containers

Sometimes it all comes down to terminology. In host-centric systems, resource managers create auto-scaling systems, making decisions about when and where capacity is needed. In containerized environments, the same decisions are made and executed by a resource scheduler. For the purposes of zero trust application, these components are practically identical, and the principles apply equally to host-centric and container-centric environments.

Authenticating Devices with the Control Plane

Now that we know how to store identity in a new device or host, we have to figure out how to validate that identity over the network. Luckily, there are a number of open standards and technologies available through which to accomplish this. Here, we'll discuss two of those technologies and why they are so important to device authentication: first we'll cover X.509 before moving on to look at TPMs.

These technologies enjoy widespread deployment and support, though this was not always the case. While we discuss real-world approaches to securing legacy devices in Chapter 8, we'll additionally explore here what the future might hold for zero trust support in legacy hardware.

X.509

X.509 is perhaps the most important standard we have when it comes to device identity and authentication. It defines the format for public key certificates, revocation lists, and methods through which to validate certification chains. The framework it puts forth aids in the formation of identity used for secure device authentication in nearly every protocol we'll discuss in this book.

One of the coolest things about X.509 is that the public/private key pairs it uses to prove identity can also be used to bootstrap encrypted communication. This is just one of many reasons that X.509 is so valuable for internet security.

Certificate chains and certification authorities

For a certificate to mean anything, it has to be trusted. A certificate can be created by anyone, so just having one with the right name on it does not mean much. A trusted party must endorse the validity of the certificate by digitally signing it. A certificate without a "real" signature is known as a self-signed certificate and is typically only used for testing purposes.

It is the responsibility of the registration authority (a role commonly filled by the certificate authority) to ensure that the details of the certificate are accurate before allowing it to be signed. In signing the certificate, a verifiable link is created from the signed certificate to the parent. If the signed certificate has the right properties, it can sign further certificates, resulting in a chain. The certificate authority lies at the root of this chain.

By trusting a certificate authority (CA), you are trusting the validity of all the certificates signed by it. This is quite a convenience, because it allows us to distribute only a small number of public keys in advance—the CA public keys, namely. All certificates furnished from there on can be linked back to the known trusted CA, and therefore also be trusted. We spoke more about the CA concept and PKI in general in Chapter 2.

Device identity and X.509

The primary capability of an X.509 certificate is to prove identity. It leverages two keys instead of one: a public key and a private key. The public key is distributed, and the private key is held by the owner of the certificate. The owner can prove they are in presence of the private key by encrypting a small piece of data, which can only be decrypted by the public key. This is known as *public key cryptography*, or *asymmetric cryptography*.

The X.509 certificate itself contains a wealth of configurable information. It has a set of standard fields, along with a relatively healthy ecosystem of extensions, which allow it to carry metadata that can be used for authorization purposes. Here is a small sample of typical information found within an X.509 certificate:

```
Certificate:
    Data:
        Version: 3 (0x2)
        Serial Number:
            ea:78:b1:33:90:2e:2b:a0
        Signature Algorithm: sha1WithRSAEncryption
        Issuer: C=US, ST=California, L=San Francisco,
                O=production, OU=web, CN=web01.example.com
        Validity
            Not Before: Oct 27 23:33:33 2016 GMT
            Not After : Oct 27 23:33:33 2017 GMT
        Subject: C=US, ST=California, L=San Francisco,
                O=production, OU=web, CN=web01.example.com
        Subject Public Key Info:
            Public Key Algorithm: rsaEncryption
            RSA Public Key: (512 bit)
                Modulus (512 bit):
                    00:d1:e2:54:b1:26:b1:49:64:72:6d:eb:54:fe:0a:
                    fc:74:56:a8:86:f2:54:32:7e:09:fa:06:ae:94:2b:
                    de:a5:9d:3b:9d:c3:d9:ad:08:3b:ed:b8:96:a7:0d:
                    2f:65:61:49:7f:f0:b0:85:95:af:39:e2:64:82:4c:
                    ff:97:76:12:6b
                Exponent: 65537 (0x10001)
        X509v3 extensions:
```

```
X509v3 Subject Key Identifier:
    DD:92:3E:9E:A8:28:F0:85:FC:A6:4D:C1:1A:2A:BE:35:2D:F7:7A:55
X509v3 Authority Key Identifier:
    keyid:DD:92:3E:9E:A8:28:F0:85:FC:A6:4D:C1:1A:2A:BE:35:2D:F7:7A:55
    DirName:/C=US/ST=California/L=San Francisco/O=production/OU=web ...
    serial:EA:78:B1:33:90:2E:2B:A0

X509v3 Basic Constraints:
    CA:TRUE
Signature Algorithm: sha1WithRSAEncryption
    33:41:f4:22:72:aa:7b:e9:d2:07:a0:e7:aa:5d:21:89:66:84:
    8e:11:87:8f:1b:c1:b8:dd:6b:76:6d:24:55:eb:20:61:6d:89:
    15:90:78:8c:81:e1:48:e4:45:3d:fe:0e:fd:92:78:84:2c:bc:
    0c:6e:06:03:80:95:5f:5d:1b:41
```

One of the fields in the code snippet is called the Subject field. The Subject field stores information about the owner, which in our case is a device (or host). Traditionally, fields like Organization (O) and Organizational Unit (OU) are exactly as they sound; but in datacenter applications, they can be repurposed to provide richer identity.

The example shows one approach, where O is mapped to the environment, and OU is mapped to the role of the host. Since the certificate is signed and trusted, we can use this information to make authorization decisions. Leveraging X.509 fields in this way means that device access may be authorized without a call to an external service, so long as the server knows who/what it should be expecting.

Public and private components

As mentioned earlier, X.509 deals with key *pairs* rather than a single key. While it is overwhelmingly common that these are RSA key pairs, they don't necessarily have to be. X.509 supports many types of key pairs, and we have recently begun to see the popularization of other key types (such as ECDSA).

Private key storage

X.509 is incredibly useful for device authentication, but it doesn't solve all the problems. It still has a private key, and that private key must be protected. If the private key is compromised, the device's identity and privacy will be vulnerable as well. While other zero trust measures help guard against the damage this might cause (like user/application authentication or authorization risk analysis), this is considered a worst-case scenario and should be avoided at all costs.

Private keys can be encrypted when they are stored, requiring a password to decrypt. This is a good practice because it would require more than just disk access to successfully steal, but is only practical for user-facing devices. In the datacenter, encrypting the private key doesn't solve the problem because you still have to store the password, or somehow transmit it to the server, at which point the password becomes just as cumbersome as the private key itself.

Hardware security modules (HSMs) go a good distance in attempting to protect the private key. They contain hardware that can generate a public/private key pair and store the private key in secure memory. It is not possible to read the private key from the HSM. It is only possible to ask the HSM to do an operation with it on your behalf. In this way, the private key cannot be stolen as it is protected in hardware. We'll talk more about TPMs, a type of HSM, in the next section.

X.509 for device authentication

The application of X.509 to device authentication in a zero trust network is immense. It is a foundational cornerstone in proving device identity for just about every protocol we have and is instrumental in enabling end-to-end encryption. Every single device in a zero trust network should have an X.509 certificate.

There is one important consideration to make, however. We are using X.509 to authenticate a *device*, yet the heart of the whole scheme—the private key—is decidedly *software*-based. If the private key is stolen, the whole device authentication thing is a sham!

These certificates are often used as a proxy for true device authentication because the keys are so long and unwieldy that you would never write one down or memorize one. They are something that would be downloaded and installed, and because of that, they don't tend to follow users around—they more typically follow devices.

While it might be determined that the risk associated with the private key problem is acceptable, it still stands as a serious issue, particularly for zero trust. Fortunately, we can see some paths forward, and by leveraging TPMs it is possible to inextricably marry a private key to its hardware.

TPMs

A trusted platform module (TPM) is a special chip that is embedded in a compute device. Called a cryptoprocessor, these chips are dedicated to performing cryptographic operations in a trusted and secure way. They include their own firmware and are often thought of as a computer on a chip.

This design enables a small and lean hardware API that is easily audited and analyzed for vulnerability. By providing facilities for cryptographic operations, and excluding interfaces for retrieving private keys, we get the security we need without ever exposing secret keys to the operating system. Instead, they are bound to the hardware.

This is a very important property and the reason that TPMs are so important for device authentication in zero trust networks. Great software frameworks for identity and authentication (like X.509) do a lot for device authentication. But without a way to bind the software key to the hardware device it is attempting to identify, we cannot *really* call it device identity. TPMs solve this problem, providing the necessary binding.

Encrypting data using a TPM

TPMs generate and store what is known as a *storage root key*, or an SRK. This key pair represents the trust root for the TPM device. Data encrypted using its public key can be decrypted by the originating TPM *only*.

The astute reader might question the usefulness of this function in the application of bulk data encryption. We know asymmetric cryptographic operations to be very expensive, and thus not suitable for the encryption of relatively large pieces of data. Thus, in order to leverage the TPM for bulk data encryption, we must reduce the amount of data that the SRK is responsible for securing.

An easy way to do this is to generate a random encryption key, encrypt the bulk data using known-performant symmetric encryption (i.e., AES), and then use the SRK to encrypt the resulting AES key. This strategy, shown in Figure 5-2, ensures that the encryption key cannot be recovered, unless in the presence of the TPM that originally protected it.

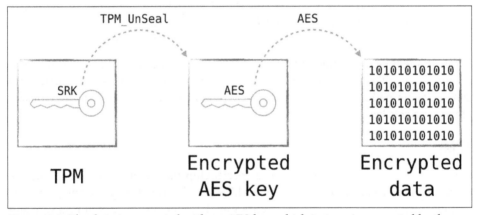

Figure 5-2. The data is encrypted with an AES key, which in turn is encrypted by the TPM

Most TPM libraries available for open consumption perform these steps for you, through the use of helper methods. It is recommended to inspect the internal operation of such methods before using them.

Intermediary keys and passphrases.   Many TPM libraries (such as TrouSerS) create intermediary keys when encrypting data using the TPM. That is, they ask the TPM to create a *new* asymmetric key pair, use the public key to encrypt the AES key, and finally use the SRK to encrypt the private key. When decrypting the data, you must first decrypt the intermediate private key, use it to decrypt the AES key, *then* decrypt the original data.

This implementation seems strange, but there are some relatively sane reasons for it. One reason is that the additional level of indirection allows for more flexibility in the distribution of secured data. Both the SRK and intermediate keys support passphrases, so the use of an intermediary key enables the use of an additional, perhaps more widely known, passphrase.

This may or may not make sense for your particular deployment. For the purposes of "This key should only be decryptable on this device only," it is OK (and more performant) to bypass the use of an intermediary key, if desired.

The most important application of TPM-backed secure storage is in protecting the device's X.509 private key. This secret key serves to authoritatively prove device identity, and if stolen, so is the identity. Encrypting the private key using TPM means that while the key might still be taken from disk, it will not be recoverable without the original hardware.

Key Theft Is Still Possible

Encrypting the device's private key and wrapping the key with the SRK does not solve all of the theft vectors. It protects the key from being directly read from disk, though an attacker with elevated privileges might still be able to read it from memory or simply ask the TPM to perform the operation for them.

The following two sections provide additional information on how to further validate hardware identity (beyond X.509 identity).

Platform configuration registers

Platform configuration registers (PCRs) are an important TPM feature. They provide storage slots into which hashes of running software is stored. It starts with the hash of the BIOS, then the boot record, its configuration, and so on. This sequence of hashes can then be used to attest that the system is in an approved configuration or state. Here is a truncated example of the first few registers stored in the TPM:

```
PCR-00: A8 5A 84 B7 38 FC ...        # BIOS
PCR-01: 11 40 C1 7D 0D 25 ...        # BIOS Configuration
PCR-02: A3 82 9A 64 61 85 ...        # Option ROM
PCR-03: B2 A8 3B 0E BF 2F ...        # Option ROM Configuration
PCR-04: 78 93 CF 58 0E E1 ...        # MBR
PCR-05: 72 A7 A9 6C 96 39 ...        # MBR Configuration
```

This is useful in a number of ways, including in ensuring that only authorized software configurations are allowed to decrypt data. This can be done by passing in a set of known-good PCR values when using the TPM to encrypt some data. This is known as "sealing" the data. Sealed data can only be decrypted by the TPM which sealed it, and only while the PCR values match.

Since PCR values cannot be modified or rolled back, we can use TPM sealing to ensure that our secret data is not only locked to the device, but also locked to a specific software configuration and version. This helps to prevent attackers from using device access to obtain the private key, since only the unmodified and approved software can unlock it.

Remote attestation

We have learned many ways we can use embedded device security to protect private keys and other sensitive device-related data. The unfortunate truth is that so long as a private key is stored *outside* of a physical TPM, it is still vulnerable to theft. This fact remains because all it takes to recover the private key is to convince the TPM to unlock it *once*. This action discloses the actual private key—something that is not possible when it is stored on the TPM.

Luckily, the TPM provides a way for us to uniquely identify it. It's another key pair called the *endorsement key* (EK), and each TPM has a unique one. The private component of an EK only ever exists on the TPM itself, and thus remains completely inaccessible by the operating system.

Remote attestation is a method by which the TPM generates something called a "quote," which is then securely transmitted to a remote party. The quote includes a list of current PCR values, signed using the EK. A remote party can use this to assert both host identity (since the EK is unique to the TPM) and software state/configuration (since PCRs cannot be modified). We'll talk more about how the quote can be transmitted in Chapter 8.

Why Not Just TPM?

You may find yourself wondering: why not use the TPM exclusively for device identity and authentication, and why include X.509 at all?

Currently, TPM access is cumbersome and non-performant. It can provide an X.509 certificate to confirm its identity, but it is limited in its interaction with the private key. For instance, the key used for attestation is only capable of signing data that originates in the TPM. For a protocol like TLS, this is a deal-breaker.

There have been some attempts to coerce the TPM attestation protocols into a more flexible form (like IETF draft draft-latze-tls-tpm-extns-02 (*http://bit.ly/2sYkGeA*), which defines a TLS extension for device authentication via TPM), though none of them have gained widespread adoption at the time of this writing.

There are a few open source implementations of remote attestation, including one in the popular IKE daemon strongSwan. This opens the doors for leveraging TPM data to not only authenticate an IPsec connection, but also authorize it by using PCR data to validate that the host is running authentic and unmodified software.

TPMs for device authentication

It is clear that TPMs present the best option for strong device authentication in mature zero trust networks. They provide the linchpin between software identity and physical hardware. There are, however, a couple limitations.

Many datacenter workloads are heterogeneous and isolated, like virtual machines or containers, both of which need to resort to TPM virtualization to allow the isolated workload to accomplish similar goals. While there are implementations available (such as vTPM for Xen), trust must still be rooted in a hardware TPM, and designing a secure TPM-based system that is capable of live migration is challenging.

Additionally, TPM support is still sparse despite its many uses and strengths. While TPM use would be expected in the context of device authentication in mature zero trust networks, it should not be considered a requirement. Adopting TPM support is no small feat, and there are much lower-hanging fruits in terms of zero trust adoption and migration.

Hardware-Based Zero Trust Supplicant?

The most common approach for supporting legacy devices in a zero trust network is to use an authentication proxy. The authentication proxy terminates the zero trust relationship and forwards the connection to the legacy host.

While it is possible to enforce policy between the authentication proxy and the legacy backend, this mode of operation is less than ideal and shares a handful of attack vectors with traditional perimeter networks. When dealing with legacy devices, it is desirable to push the zero trust termination point as close to the device as possible.

At the time of this writing, an authentication proxy is likely the best and most reasonable option, although it does seem that there is some room for a dedicated hardware device. This device can act as a zero trust supplicant, carrying a TPM chip, and plug directly into a legacy device's Ethernet port. Pairing the two in your inventory management system can allow for seamless integration between legacy devices and a zero trust network.

There are many applications that would significantly benefit from such a device. SCADA and HVAC systems, for instance, come to mind. While such a device is admittedly pure fantasy at present, it remains an interesting thought experiment.

Inventory Management

Authenticating a device's identity and integrity goes a long way in providing strong zero trust security, but being able to identify a device as belonging to the organization is only part of the challenge. There are lots of other pieces of information we need in order to calculate policy and make enforcement decisions.

Inventory management involves the cataloging of devices and their properties. Maintaining these records is equally important for both servers and client devices. It is sometimes more helpful to think of these as network entities rather than physical devices. While they indeed are commonly physical devices, they might also be logical entities on the network.

For instance, it is conceivable that a virtual machine or a container could be considered a "device," depending on your needs. They have lots of the same descriptive properties that a real server might have, after all. Lumping all of the virtual machine traffic from a single host into one policy gets us right back to the perimeter model. Instead, the zero trust model advocates that the workloads be tracked in order to drive the network policies they require. This inventory (or workload) database in this case can be specialized in order to accommodate the high rates of change that virtualized/containerized environments experience. So, while the traditional inventory management system and the workload scheduler might be different systems, they can still work together; for the purposes of this book, the scheduler service may act as an inventory management system of sorts, as shown in Figure 5-3.

It is not uncommon to have more than one inventory management system. As an example, many companies have both asset management and configuration management software. Both of these store device metadata that is useful to us; they just store different sets, collected in different ways.

 Configuration Management as an Inventory Database

Many configuration management systems, such as Chef or Puppet, offer modes in which data about the nodes they run on get persisted into a centralized database. Name, IP address, and the "kind" of server are examples of the type of information typically found in a CM-backed database. Using configuration management in this way is an easy first step toward developing an inventory database if you don't have one already.

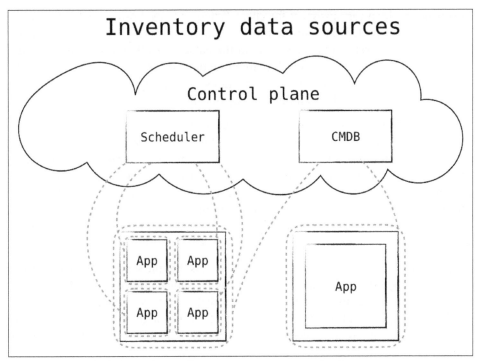

Figure 5-3. A scheduler and a configuration management database serve as inventory stores for the control plane

Knowing What to Expect

One of the great powers of a zero trust network is that it knows what to expect. Trusted entities can push expectations into the system, allowing all levels of access to be denied by default—only expected actions/requests are permitted.

An inventory database is a major component in realizing this capability. A huge amount of information about what to expect can be generated from this data; things like which user or application should be running on it, what locations we might expect it to be in, or even the kind of operating system are all pieces of information that can be used to set expectations.

In the datacenter, these expectations can be very strong. For instance, when provisioning a new server, we often know what IP address it will be assigned and what purpose it will serve. We can use that information to drive network ACLs and/or host-based firewalls, poking holes for that specific IP address only where necessary. In this way, we can have all traffic denied, allowing only the very specific flows we are expecting. The more properties that can be expected, the better.

This is not such an easy prospect for client-facing systems, however. Clients operate in new and unexpected ways all the time, and knowing exactly what to expect from them and when is very difficult. Servers in the datacenter often have relatively static and long-lived connections to a well-defined set of hosts or services. By contrast, clients tend to make many short-lived connections to a variety of services, the timing, frequency, and patterns of which can vary organically.

In order to address the wild nature of client-facing systems, we need a slightly different approach. One way to do this is to simply allow global access to the service and to protect it with mutually authenticated TLS, forcing the client to provide a device certificate before it can communicate with it. The device certificate can be used to look the device up in the inventory database and determine whether or not to authorize it. The advantage is that lots of systems support mutually authenticated TLS already, and specialized client software is not strictly required. One can provide reasonably strong security without too badly hindering accessibility or usability.

A significant drawback to this approach, however, is that the service is globally reachable. Requiring client certificates is a great way to mitigate this danger. However, we have seen from vulnerabilities like Heartbleed that the attack surface of a TLS server is relatively large. Additionally, the existence of the resources can be discovered by simply scanning for them, since we get to speak TCP to the resource before we authenticate with it.

How can we ensure that we don't engage clients that are not trusted? There has to be *some* untrusted communication, after all. What comes before the authentication?

Secure Introduction

The very first connection from a new device is a precarious one. After all, these packets must be admitted somewhere, and if they are not strongly authenticated, then there is a risk. Therefore, the first system that a new device contacts needs a mechanism by which it can authenticate this initial contact.

This arrangement is commonly known as *secure introduction*. It is the process through which a new entity is introduced to an existing one in a way that trust is transferred to it. There are many ways in which this can be effected; the method through which an operator passes a TOTP code to a provisioner in order to authorize a certificate request is a form of secure introduction.

The best (and perhaps only) way to do secure introduction is by setting an expectation. Secure introduction practically always involves a trusted third party. This is a system that is already introduced, and it holds the ability to introduce new systems. This trusted third party is the system that then coordinates/validates the specifics of the system to be introduced and sets the appropriate expectations.

Secure Introduction for Client Systems

Secure introduction of client-facing systems can be difficult due to the hard-to-predict nature of wild clients. When publicly exposing a client-facing endpoint is considered too risky, it is necessary to turn to more complicated schemes. The currently accepted approach is to use a form of signaling called pre-authentication, which announces a client's intentions just prior to taking action. We'll talk more about pre-authentication in Chapter 8.

What Makes a Good Secure Introduction System?

Single-use
Credentials and privileges associated with the introduction should be single use, preventing an attacker from compromising and reusing the key.

Short-lived
Credentials and privileges associated with the introduction should be short-lived, preventing the accumulation of valid but unused keys.

Third-party
Leveraging a third party for introduction allows for separation of duty, prevents the introduction of poor security practice, and alleviates operational headaches.

While these requirements might at first seem rigorous, they can be met through fairly simple means. A great example can be found in the way Chef implements host introduction. Originally, there was a single secret (deemed the "validation certificate") which was qualified to admit any host that possessed it as a new node. Thus, the introduction would involve copying this secret to the target machine (or baking it into the image), using it to register the new node, then deleting it.

This approach is neither single-use nor short-lived. Should the secret be recovered, it could be used by a malicious actor to steer application traffic to attacker-controlled hosts, or even trigger a denial of service.

Modern Chef takes a new approach. Instead of having a static validation certificate, the provisioning system (via Chef client utility "knife") communicates with the Chef server and creates a new client and associated client certificate. It then creates the new host, and passes in its client certificate. In this way, an expectation for the new client has been set. While these credentials are not short-lived, it remains as a superior approach.

Renewing Device Trust

It is important to accept the fact that no level of security is perfect—not even yours. Once this fact is acknowledged, we can begin to mitigate its consequences. The natural progression is that the longer a device is operating, the greater its chances of being compromised. This is why device age is a heavily weighted trust signal.

For this reason, rotation is very important. We earlier spoke at length about the importance of rotation, and devices are no different. Of course, this "rotation" is manifested in different ways depending on your definition of "device." If your infrastructure is run in a cloud, perhaps a "device" is a host instance. In this case, rotation is easy: just tear down the instance and build a new one (you *are* using configuration management, right?). If you're running physical hardware, however, this prospect is a little more difficult.

Reimaging is a good way to logically rotate a device. It is a fairly low-level operation, and will succeed in removing the majority of persistent threats seen in the wild today. One can trust a freshly reimaged device more than one that has been running for a year. While reimaging does not address hardware attacks or other low-level attacks like those shown in Figure 5-4, it serves as a reasonable compromise in places where physical rotation is more difficult. Datacenter and supply chain security partially mitigate this concern.

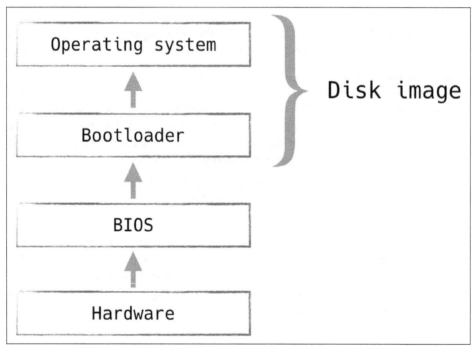

Figure 5-4. A disk image addresses the portions that house the vast majority of malware, but it's certainly not the whole picture

When it comes to managing client devices, the story changes quite a bit. Reimaging a client device is extraordinarily inconvenient for users. They customize the device (and its contents) over time in ways that are difficult to effectively or securely preserve. Oftentimes, when given a new device, they want to transfer the old image! This is not great news for people trying to secure client devices.

The solution largely depends on your use case. The trade-off between security and convenience will be very clear in this area. Everyone agrees that client devices *should* be rotated and/or reimaged every so often, but the frequency is up to you. There is one important relationship to keep in mind: the less often a device is rotated or reimaged, the more rigorous your endpoint security must be.

Without the relatively strong assurances of device security that we get with rotation, we must look for other methods to renew trust in a device that has been operating for a long time. There are two general methods through which this can be done: *local measurement* or *remote measurement*.

Local Measurement

Local measurement can be one of two types: *hardware-backed* or *software-backed*. Hardware-backed measurement is more secure and reliable, but limited in capability. Software-backed measurement is much less secure and reliable, but practically unlimited in its measurement capabilities.

One good option for hardware-backed local measurement is leveraging the TPM for *remote attestation*. Remote attestation uses a hardware device to provide a signed response outlining the hashes of the software currently running on that machine. The response is highly reliable and very difficult to reproduce. However, it generally only gives a picture of the low-level software or specifically targeted software. If an attacker has managed to get an unauthorized process running in user space, the TPM will not be very useful in its detection; thus, it has limited capability. See "Remote attestation" on page 76 for more information.

Software-backed local measurement involves some sort of agent installed on the endpoint which is used to report health and state measurements. This could be anything from a managed antivirus client to policy enforcement agents. These agents go to great lengths in order to attest and prove validity of the measurements they report, but even cursory thought quickly reaches the conclusion that these efforts are generally futile. Software-backed measurements lack the protection provided by hardware measurements, and an attacker with sufficient privilege can subvert systems like this.

Remote Measurement

Remote measurement is the best of the two options for one simple reason: it benefits from separation of duty. A compromised host can report whatever it wants to, possibly falsifying information in order to conceal the attacker. This is not possible with remote or passive measurement, since a completely different system is determining the health of the host in question.

Traditionally, remote measurement is performed as a simple vulnerability scan. The system in question will be periodically probed by a scanning device, which observes the response. The response gives some information away, like what operating system might be running on that device, what services might be active there, and maybe even what version of those services.

The scan results can be cross-referenced with known-bad signatures, like malicious software or vulnerable versions of legitimate software, producing a report like the one shown in Figure 5-5. Detection of known-bad signatures can then influence the trust of the device appropriately.

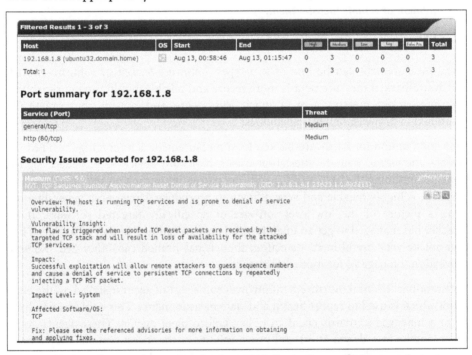

Figure 5-5. Greenbone web interface for OpenVAS (https://www.flickr.com/photos/ xmodulo/9499759166) showing three "medium" vulnerabilities for a scan target

There are a number of open source and commercial options available in the vulnerability scanning arena, including OpenVAS, Nessus, and Metasploit. These projects are all fairly mature and relied on by many organizations.

Unfortunately, vulnerability scanning comes with the same fundamental problem as local measurement: it relies on interrogation of the endpoint. It's the difference between asking someone if they robbed a bank, and watching them rob a bank. Sure, sometimes you can get the robber to admit that they did it, but a professional would never fall for that. Catching them in the act is much more effective. See "Network Communication Patterns" on page 90 for more about how to solve this dilemma.

Software Configuration Management

Configuration management is the process of tightly controlling and documenting all software changes. The desired configurations are typically defined as code or data, and checked into a revision control system, allowing changes to be audited, rolled back, and so on. There are many commercial and open source options available, the most popular of which being Chef, Puppet, Ansible, and CFEngine.

Configuration management software is useful in both datacenter and client deployments, and simply becomes required beyond a certain scale. Leveraging such software comes with many security wins, such as the ability to quickly upgrade packages after vulnerability announcements or to similarly assert that there are no vulnerable packages in the wild.

Beyond auditing and strict change control, configuration management can also be used as an agent for dynamic policy configuration. If a node can get a reliable and trusted view of the world (or part of it, at least), it can use it to calculate policy and install it locally. This functionality is practically limited to the datacenter though, since while dynamic, datacenter-hosted systems are decidedly more static and predictable than client systems. We'll talk more about this mode of zero trust operation later on.

CM-Based Inventory

We have mentioned several times the idea of using a configuration management database for inventory management purposes. This is a great first step toward a mature inventory management system and can provide a rich source of information about the various hosts and software running in your infrastructure.

We like to think that CM-based inventory management is a "freebie" in that configuration management is typically leveraged for the bevy of other benefits it brings. Using it as an inventory database most often comes about out of convenience.

Maintaining this view is important: configuration management systems aren't designed to act as inventory management systems...they're designed to act as configuration management systems! Using it as such will surely bring a few rough edges, and you will eventually outgrow it. This is not to say don't do it. It is better to actually realize a zero trust network by leveraging as much existing technology as possible than it is to never get there due to high barrier to entry.

Once we accept this fact, we can begin to leverage the wealth of data provided to us by the CM agents. Using Chef, for instance, we can calculate trust score and write policy against more than 1,500 host attributes. Here are some small snippets illustrating the kind of information the Chef agent collects and stores:

```
languages:
  c:
    gcc:
      description: gcc version 4.8.4 (Ubuntu 4.8.4-2ubuntu1~14.04)
      version:    4.8.4
  java:
    hotspot:
      build: 24.71-b01, mixed mode
      name:  Java HotSpot(TM) 64-Bit Server VM
    runtime:
      build: 1.7.0_71-b14
      name:  Java(TM) SE Runtime Environment
      version: 1.7.0_71
  perl:
... <SNIP> ...
dmi:
  bios:
    address:      0xE8000
    all_records:
      Address:              0xE8000
      BIOS Revision:        4.2
      ROM Size:             64 kB
      Release Date:         12/03/2014
      Runtime Size:         96 kB
      Vendor:               Xen
      Version:              4.2.amazon
      application_identifier: BIOS Information
  chassis:
    all_records:
      Asset Tag:            Not Specified
      Boot-up State:        Safe
... <SNIP> ...
  fqdn:           foo.bar
  hostname:       foo
  idletime:       2 days 09 hours 48 minutes 37 seconds
  idletime_seconds: 208117
  init_package:   init
  ipaddress:      192.168.1.1
  kernel:
    machine: x86_64
    modules:
      ablk_helper:
        refcount: 6
        size:     13597
... <SNIP> ...
  network:
    default_gateway:   192.168.1.254
```

```
default_interface: eth0
interfaces:
  eth0:
    addresses:
      192.168.1.1:
        broadcast: 192.168.1.255
        family:    inet
        netmask:   255.255.255.0
        prefixlen: 24
        scope:     Global
      22:00:0A:1E:55:AD:
        family: lladdr
    arp:
      192.168.1.2: fe:ff:ff:ff:ff:ff
      192.168.1.3: fe:ff:ff:ff:ff:ff
      192.168.1.254: fe:ff:ff:ff:ff:ff
    encapsulation: Ethernet
```

Searchable inventory

Some CM systems centrally store the data generated by their agents. Typically, this data store is searchable, which opens lots of possibilities for young zero trust networks. For instance, the agent can perform a search to retrieve the IP address of all web servers in datacenter A and use the results to configure a host-based firewall.

Audits and report generation are greatly enhanced through searchable inventory as well. This applies not only to datacenter hosts, but also to clients. By storing the agent data and making it searchable, you can ensure that you changed the CM code to upgrade that vulnerable package, and that the package did indeed update where it said it did.

Secure Source of Truth

One important thing to remember when using CM systems in the zero trust control plane is that the vast majority of the data available to CM systems is self-reported. This is critical to understand, since a compromised machine could potentially misrepresent itself. This can lead to complete compromise of the zero trust network if these facts are not considered during its design.

Thinking back to trust management, the trusted system in this case is the provisioner. Whether it be a human or some automated system, it is in the best position to assert the critical aspects of a device, which include the following:

- Device type
- Role
- IP address (in datacenter systems)
- Public key

These attributes are considered critical because they are often used in making authorization or authentication decisions. If an attacker can update the device role, for instance, perhaps they can coerce the network to expose protected services.

For this reason, restricting write access to these attributes is important. Of course, you can still use self-reported attributes for making decisions, but they should not be considered fact under any circumstance. It's useful to think of self-reported attributes as hints rather than truth.

Using Device Data for User Authorization

The zero trust model mandates authentication and authorization of both the device and the user or application. Since device authentication typically comes before user authentication, it must be done without information gained through user authentication. This is not the case for user authentication.

When user authentication occurs, device authentication has already succeeded, and the network has knowledge of the device identity. This position can be leveraged for all kinds of useful contextual knowledge, enabling us to do much stronger user authentication than was previously attainable.

One of the more common lookups one might make is to check whether we would expect this user, given the type of device or place of issue. For instance, you are unlikely to see an engineer's credentials being used from a mobile device that was issued to HR. So while the HR employee can freely access a particular resource using their own credentials, user authentication attempts using other credentials might be blocked.

Another good signal is user authentication frequency. If you have not seen a user log in from one of their devices in over a year, and all of a sudden there is a request from that device furnishing the user's credentials—well, I think it's fair to be a bit skeptical. Could it have been stolen?

Of course, there is also a good chance that the request is legitimate. In a case like this, we lower the trust score to indicate that things are a little fishy. The lower score can then manifest itself in many ways, like still being trusted enough to read parts of the internal wiki, but not enough to log into financial systems.

Being able to make decisions like this is a big part of the zero trust architecture and underscores the importance of a robust inventory management database. While inventory management is strictly required for device authentication reasons, the contextual advantage given to user authentication is invaluable.

Trust Signals

This section serves as a reference for various trust signals that are useful in calculating device trust score and writing policy.

Time Since Image

Over time, the likelihood that a device has been compromised increases dramatically. Endpoint security practices aim to decrease the risk associated with long-lived or long-running devices. Still, these practices are far from perfect.

Imaging a device ensures that the contents of the hard drive match a known good. While not effective against some lower-level attacks, it provides a reasonably strong assurance of trust. In the moments immediately following the image restore, a tremendous amount of trust exists in the device, as only the hardware or the restore system itself would be able to taint the process. Over time though, that trust wears off as the system goes through prolonged exposure.

Historical Access

Device authentication patterns, similar to user authentication patterns, are important in understanding risk and act as a nice proxy for behavioral filtering. Devices which have not been seen in a while are more suspicious than ones that come and go frequently. Maybe suspicious is the wrong word, but it's certainly unusual.

The request in question can also be tied to a resource, and it is wise to consider the device and the resource together in this context. For instance, a months-old device requesting access to a new resource is more suspicious than a request to a resource it has been accessing weekly for some time. This stands to say that the "first few" access attempts to a particular resource will be viewed with more skepticism than subsequent attempts.

Similarly, frequency can be analyzed to understand if a resource is being suspiciously over-utilized. A request from a device that has made 100 requests in the last day, but only 104 over the last month, is certainly more suspicious than one with 0 in the last day and 4 in the last month.

Location

While network location is typically something we aim to not make strong decisions on with regard to the zero trust model, it still provides reliable trust signaling in many cases.

One such case might be a sudden location change. Since we are talking about device authentication, we can set some reasonable expectations about the way that device moves around. For instance, a device authentication attempt from Europe might be pretty suspicious if we have authorized that same device in the US office just a couple hours prior.

It should be noted that this is a bit of a slippery slope when it comes to the zero trust model. Zero trust aims to eliminate positions of advantage within the network, so using network location to determine access right can be considered a little contradictory.

The authors recognize this and acknowledge that location-related data can be valuable while making authorization decisions. That said, it is important that this consideration not be binary. One should look for patterns in locations, and never make an absolute decision based solely on location. For instance, a policy which dictates that an application can only be accessed from the office is a direct violation of the zero trust model.

Network Communication Patterns

For devices that are connected to networks owned by the operator, there is an opportunity to measure communication patterns to develop a norm. Sudden changes from this norm are suspicious and can affect how much the system trusts such a device.

Network instrumentation and flow collection can quickly detect intrusions by observing them on the network. Making authorization decisions informed by this detection is very powerful. One example might be shutting down database access to a particular web server because that web server began making DNS queries for hosting providers on another continent.

The same applies to client devices. Consider a desktop that has never before initiated an SSH connection but is now frequently SSHing to internet hosts. It is fair to say that this change in behavior is suspicious and should result in the device being less trusted than it was previously.

Summary

This chapter focused on how a system can trust a device. This is a surprisingly hard problem, so a lot of different technologies and practices need to be applied to ensure that trust in a device is warranted.

We started with looking at how trust is injected into a device from the human operators. For relatively static systems, we can have a person involved in providing the critical credentials; but for dynamic infrastructure, that process needs to be delegated. Those credentials are incredibly valuable, and so we discussed how to safely manage them.

Devices eventually need to participate in the network, and so understanding how they authenticate themselves is important. We covered several technologies, such as

X.509 and TPMs, which can be used to authenticate a device on the network. Using these technologies along with databases of expected inventory can go a long way toward providing the checks and balances that give devices trust.

Trust is fleeting and degrades over time, so we talked about the mechanisms for renewing trust. Additionally, we discussed the many signals that can be continually used to gauge the trustworthiness of a device over time. Perhaps the most important lesson is that a device starts out in a trusted state and only gets worse from there. The rate at which its trust declines is what we'd like to keep a handle on.

The next chapter looks at how we can establish trust in the users of the system.

CHAPTER 6

Trusting Users

It's tempting to conflate user trust with device trust. Security-conscious organizations might deploy X.509 certificates to users' devices to gain stronger credentials than passwords provide. One could say that the device certificate strongly identifies the user, but does it? How do we know that the intended user is actually at the keyboard? Perhaps they left their device unlocked and unattended?

Conflating user identity with device identity also runs into problems when users have multiple devices, which is increasingly becoming the norm. Credentials need to be copied between several devices, putting them at increased risk of exposure. Devices might need different credentials based on their capabilities. In networks that have kiosks, this problem becomes even more difficult.

Zero trust networks identify and trust users separately from devices. Sometimes identifying a user will use the same technology that is used to identify devices, but we must be clear that these are two separate credentials.

This chapter will explore what it means to identify a user and store their identity. We will discuss when and how to authenticate users. User trust is often stronger when multiple people are involved, so we will discuss how to create group trust and how to build a culture of security.

Identity Authority

Every user has an identity, which represents how they are known in a larger community. In the case of a networked system, the identity of a user is how they are recognized in that system.

Given the large number of individuals in the world, identifying a user can be a surprisingly hard problem. Let's explore two types of identity:

- Informal identity
- Authoritative identity

Informal identity is how groups self-assemble identity. Consider a real-world situation where you meet someone. Based on how they look and act, you can build up an identity for that person. When you meet them later, you can reasonably assume that they are the same person based on these physical characteristics. You might even be able to identify them remotely—for example, by hearing their voice.

Informal identity is used in computer systems. Pseudonymous accounts—accounts that are not associated with one's real-world name—are common in online communities. While the actual identity of an individual is not necessarily known in these communities, through repeated interactions an informal identity is created.

Informal identity works in small groups, where trust between individuals is high and the risks are relatively low. This type of identity has clear weaknesses when the stakes are higher:

- One can manufacture a fictitious identity.
- One can claim the identity of another person.
- One can create several identities.
- Multiple individuals can share a single identity.

When a stronger form of identity is required, an authority needs to create *authoritative identity* credentials for individuals. In the real world, this authority often falls to governments. Government-issued IDs (e.g., a driver's license or passport) are distributed to individuals to represent their identity to others. For low-risk situations, these IDs alone are sufficient proof of one's identity. However, for higher risk situations, cross-checking the credentials against the government database provides a better guarantee.

Computer systems often need centralized authority for user identity as well. Like in the real world, users are granted credentials (of varying strength) which identify them in the system. Based on the degree of risk, cross-checking the credentials against a centralized database may be desired. We will discuss how these systems should function later.

Credentials can be lost or stolen, so it is important that an identity authority have mechanisms for individuals to regain control of their identity. In the case of government-issued identification, a person often needs to present other identifying information (e.g., a birth certificate or fingerprint) to a government authority to have their ID reissued. Computer systems similarly need mechanisms for a user to regain control of their identity in the case of lost or stolen credentials. These systems often require presenting another form of verification, say a recovery code or alternative authentication credential. The choice of required material to reassert one's identity can have security implications which we will discuss later.

Bootstrapping Identity in a Private System

Storing and authenticating user identity is one thing, but how do you generate the identity to begin with? Humans interacting with computer systems need a way to digitally represent their identity, and we seek to bind that digital representation as tightly to the real-world human as possible.

The genesis of a digital identity, and its initial pairing to a human, is a very sensitive operation. Controls to authenticate the human *outside* of your digital system must be strong in order to prevent an attacker from masquerading as a new employee, for instance. Similar controls might also be exercised for account recovery procedures where the user is unable to provide their current credentials.

Attacking Identity Recovery Systems

Users occasionally misplace or forget authentication material such as passwords or smart cards. To recover the factor (i.e., reset the password), the user must be authenticated by alternative and sometimes untraditional means. Attacks on such systems are frequent and successful. For example, in 2012, a popular journalist's Amazon account was broken into, and the attacker was able to recover the last four digits of the most recent credit card used. With this information, the attacker called Apple support and "proved" his/her identity using the recovered number. Be sure to carefully evaluate such reset processes—"secret" information is often less secret than it appears.

Given the sensitivity of this operation, it is important to put good thought and strong policy around how it is managed. It is essentially secure introduction for humans, and the good news is, we know how to do that pretty well!

Government-Issued Identification

It probably comes as no surprise that one of the primary recommendations for accomplishing human authentication is through the use of government-issued identification. After all, human authentication is precisely what they were designed for in the first place!

In some implementations, it may even be desirable to request multiple forms of ID, raising the bar for potential forgers/imposters. It goes without saying that staff must be properly trained in validating these IDs, lest the controls be easily circumvented.

Nothing Beats Meatspace

Despite our best efforts, human-based authentication schemes remain stronger than their digital counterparts. It's always a good idea to bootstrap a human's new digital identity in person. Email or other "blind" introductions are heavily discouraged. For instance, shipping a device configured to trust the user on first use (sometimes referred to as TOFU) is not uncommon. However, this method suffers from physical weakness since the package is vulnerable to interception or redirection.

Oftentimes, the creation of the digital identity is preceded by a lengthy human process, such as a series of interviews or the completion of a business contract. The result is that the individual has been previously exposed to already-trusted individuals who have learned some of his/her qualities along the way. This knowledge can be leveraged for further human-based authentication, as shown in Figure 6-1.

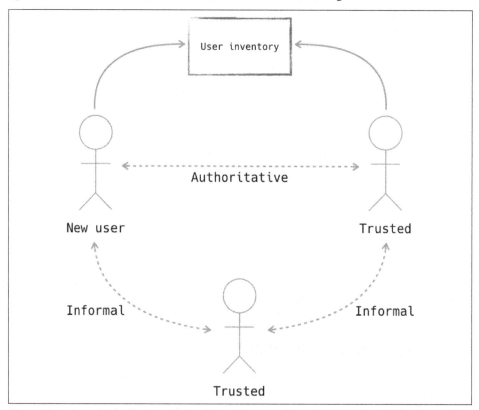

Figure 6-1. A trusted administrator relies on a trusted employee and a valid ID to add a new user to an inventory system

For instance, a hiring manager is in a good position to escort a new hire to helpdesk for human authentication, since the hiring manager is presumably already familiar with the individual and can attest to their identity. While this would be a strong signal of trust, just like anything else in a zero trust network, it should not be the only method of authentication.

Expectations and Stars

There are usually many pieces of information available prior to bootstrapping a digital identity. It is desirable to use as many pieces of information as is reasonable to assert that all of the stars line up as expected. These expectations are similar to ones set in a typical zero trust network; they are simply accrued and enforced by humans.

These expectations can range from the language(s) they speak to the home address printed on their ID, with many other creative examples in between. A thorough company may choose to even use information learned through a background check to set real-world expectations. Humans use methods like this every day to authenticate each other (both casually and officially), and as a result, these methods are mature and reliable.

Storing Identity

Since we need to bridge identity from the physical world to the virtual world, identity must be transformed into bits. These bits are highly sensitive and oftentimes need to be stored permanently. Therefore, we will discuss how to store this data to ensure its safety.

User Directories

To trust users, systems typically need centralized records of those users. One's presence in such a directory is the basis by which all future authentication will occur. Having all this highly sensitive data stored centrally is a challenge which unfortunately cannot be avoided.

A zero trust network makes use of rich user data to make better authentication decisions. Directories will store traditional information like usernames, phone numbers and organization role, and also extended information like expected user location or the public key of an X.509 certificate they have been issued.

Given the sensitive nature of the data being stored on users, it's best to not store all information together in a single database. Information about users isn't typically considered secret, but becomes sensitive when using such data to make authorization decisions. Additionally, having broad knowledge of all users in a system can be a privacy risk. For example, a system that stores the last known location of all users could be used to spy on users. Stored user data can also be a security risk, if that data can be leveraged to attack another system. Consider systems that ask users fact-based information as a means to further validate their identity.

Instead of storing all user information in a single database, consider splitting the data into several isolated databases. These databases should ideally only be exposed via a constrained API, which limits the information divulged. In the best case, raw data is never divulged, but rather assertions can be made about a user by the application that has access to the data. For example, a system that stores a user's previous known location could expose the following APIs:

- Is the user currently or likely to be near these coordinates?
- How frequently does the user change locations?

Directory Maintenance

Keeping user directories accurate is critical for the safety of a zero trust network. Users are expected to come and go over the lifetime of a network system, so good onboarding and offboarding procedures should be created to keep the system accurate.

As much as possible, it's best to integrate technical identity systems (LDAP or local user accounts) into organizational systems. For example, a company might have human resource systems to track employees that are joining or leaving the company. It is expected that these two sources of data are consistent with each other, but unless there is a system that has integrated the two or is checking their contents, the sets of data will quickly diverge. Creating automated processes for connecting these systems is an effort that will quickly pay dividends.

The case of two divergent identity systems raises an important point—which system is authoritative? Clearly one system must be the system of record for identity, but that choice should be made based on the needs of the organization. It doesn't much matter which system is chosen, only that one is authoritative and all other identity systems derive their data from the system of record.

Minimizing Data Stored Can Be Helpful

A system of record for identity does not need to contain all identity information. Based on our earlier discussion, it can be better to purposefully segment user data. The system of record needs to only store the information that is critical for identifying an individual. This could be as simple as storing a username and some personal information for the user to recover their identity should they forget it. Derivative systems can use this authoritative ID to store additional user information.

When to Authenticate Identity

Even though authentication is mandatory in a zero trust network, it can be applied in clever ways to significantly bolster security while at the same time working to minimize user inconvenience.

While it might be tempting (and even logical) to adopt a position of "It's not supposed to be easy; it's supposed to be secure," user convenience is among one of the most important factors in designing a zero trust network. Security technologies that present a poor user experience are often systematically weakened and undermined by their own users. A poor experience will disincentivize the user from engaging with the technology, and shortcuts to sidestep enforcement will be taken more often.

Authenticating for Trust

The act of authenticating a user is, essentially, the system seeking to validate that the user is indeed who they say they are. As you'll learn in the next section, different authentication methods have different levels of strength, and some are strongest when combined with others. Due to the fact that these authentication mechanisms are never absolute, we can assign some level of trust to the outcome of the operation.

For instance, you may need only a password to log into a subscription music service, but your investment account probably requires a password *and* an additional code. This is because investing is a sensitive operation: the system must trust that the user is authentic. The music service, on the other hand, is not as sensitive and chooses to *not* require an additional code, because doing so would be a nuisance.

By extension, a user may pass additional forms of authentication in order to raise their level of trust. This can be done specifically in a time of need. A user whose trust score has eroded below the requirements for a particular request can be asked for additional proof, which if passed will raise the trust to acceptable levels.

This is far from a foreign concept; it can be seen in common use today. Requiring users to enter their password again before performing a sensitive operation is a prime example of this concept in action. It should be noted, however, that the amount of trust one can gain through authentication mechanisms alone should not be unbound. Without it, consequences of poor device security and other undesirable signals can be washed out.

Trust as the Authentication Driver

Since authentication derives trust, and it is our primary goal to not frivolously drag users through challenges, it makes sense to use trust score as the mechanism that mandates authentication requirements. This means that a user should not be asked to further authenticate if their trust score is sufficiently high and, conversely, that a user should be asked to authenticate when their score is too low. This is to say that, rather than selecting particular actions which require additional authentication, one should assign a required score and allow the trust score itself to drive the authentication flow and requirements. This gives the system the opportunity to choose a combination of methods in order to meet the goal, possibly reducing the invasiveness by having context about the level of sensitivity and knowledge of how much each method is trusted.

This approach is fundamentally different from traditional authentication design approaches, which seek to designate the most sensitive areas and actions and authenticate them the heaviest, perhaps despite previous authentication and trust accumulation. In some ways, the traditional approach can be likened to perimeter security, in which sensitive actions must pass a particular test, after which no further protections are present. Instead, leveraging the trust score to drive these decisions removes arbitrary authentication requirements and installs adaptive authentication and authorization that is only encountered when necessary.

The Use of Multiple Channels

When authenticating and authorizing a request, using multiple channels to reach the requestor can be very effective. One-time codes provide an additional factor, especially when the code-generating system is on a separate device. Push notifications provide a similar capability by using an active connection to a mobile device. There are many applications of this idea, and they can take different forms.

Depending on the use case, one might choose to leverage multiple channels as an integral part of a digital authentication scheme. Alternatively, those channels might be used purely as an authorization component, where a requestor might be prompted to approve a risky operation. Both uses are effective in their own right, though user experience should (as always) be kept in mind when deciding when and where to apply them.

Channel Security

Communication channels are constructed with varying degrees of authentication and trust. When leveraging multiple channels, it is important to understand how much trust should be placed on the channel itself. This will dictate which channels are selected for use and when. For instance, physical rotating code devices are only as secure as the system used to distribute them or the identification check required to physically obtain one from your administrator. Similarly, a prompt via a corporate chat system is only as strong as the credentials required to sign in to it. Be sure to use a different channel than the one you are trying to authenticate/authorize in the first place.

Leveraging multiple channels is effective not because compromising a channel is hard, but because compromising many is hard. We will talk more about these points in the next section.

Caching Identity and Trust

Session caching is a relatively mature technology which is well documented, so we won't spend too much time talking about it, but it is important to highlight some design choices that are important for secure operation in a zero trust network.

Frequent validation of the client's authorization is critical. This is one of the only mechanisms allowing the control plane to effect changes in data plane applications as a result of changes in trust. The more frequently this can be done, the better. Some implementations authorize every request with the control plane. While this is ideal, it may not be a realistic prospect, depending on your situation.

Many applications validate SSO tokens only at the beginning of a session and set their own tokens after that. This mode of operation removes session control from the control plane and is generally undesirable. Authorizing requests with control plane tokens rather than application tokens allows us to easily revoke when trust levels fluctuate or erode.

How to Authenticate Identity

Now that we know when to authenticate, let's dig into how to authenticate a user. The common wisdom, which is also applicable in zero trust networks, is that there are three ways to identify a user:

Something they know
Knowledge the user alone has (e.g., a password).

Something they have
A physical credential that they user can provide (e.g., a token with a time-sensitive token).

Something they are
An inherent trait of the user (e.g., a fingerprint or retina).

We can authenticate a user using one or more of these methods. Which method or methods chosen will depend on the level of trust required. For high-risk operations, which request multiple authentication factors, it's best to choose methods that are not in the same grouping of something you know, something you have, or something you are. This is because the attack vectors are generally similar within a particular grouping. For example, a hardware token (something you have) can be stolen and subsequently used by anyone. If we pair that token with a second token, it's highly likely that both devices will be near each other and stolen together.

Which factors to use together will vary based on the device that the user is using. For example, on a desktop computer, a password (something you know) and a hardware token (something you have) is a strong combination that should generally be preferred. For a mobile device, however, a fingerprint (something you are) and passphrase (something you know) might be preferred.

Physical Safety Is a Requirement for Trusting Users

This section focuses on technological means to authenticate the identity of a user, but it's important to recognize that users can be coerced to thwart those mechanisms. A user can be threatened with physical harm to force them to divulge their credentials or to grant someone access under a trusted account. Behavioral analysis and historical trending can help to mitigate such attempts, though they remain an effective attack vector.

Something You Know: Passwords

Passwords are the most common form of authentication used in computer systems today. While often maligned due to users' tendency to choose poor passwords, this authentication mechanism provides one very valuable benefit: when done well, it is an effective method for asserting that a user's mind is present.

A good password has the following characteristics:

It's long
A recent NIST password standard states a minimum of 8 characters, but 20+ character passwords are common among security-conscious individuals. Passphrases are often encouraged to help users remember a longer password.

It is difficult to guess
Users tend to overestimate their ability to pick truly random passwords, so generating passwords from random number generators can be a good mechanism for choosing a strong password, though convenience is affected if it cannot be easily committed to memory

It is not reused
Passwords need to be validated against some stored data in a service. When passwords are reused, the confidentiality of that password is only as strong as the weakest storage in use.

Choosing long, difficult-to-guess passwords for every service or application a user interacts with is a high bar for users to meet. As a result, users are well served to make use of a password manager to store their passwords. Using this tool will allow users to pick much harder-to-guess passwords and thereby limit the damage of a data breach.

When building a service that authenticates passwords, it's important to follow best practices. Passwords should never be directly stored or logged. Instead, a cryptographic hash of the password should be stored. The cost to brute force a password (usually expressed in time and/or memory requirements) is determined by the strength of the hashing algorithm. The NIST periodically releases standards documents (*https://github.com/usnistgov/800-63-3*) that include recommended password procedures. As computers become more powerful, the current recommendations change, so it's best to consult industry best practices when choosing algorithms.

Something You Have: TOTP

Time-based one-time password, or *TOTP*, is an authentication standard where a constantly changing code is provided by the user. RFC 6238 (*https://tools.ietf.org/html/rfc6238*) defines the standard implemented in hardware devices and software applications. Mobile applications are often used to generate the code, which works well, since users tend to have their phones close by.

Whether using an application or hardware device, TOTP requires sharing a random secret value between the user and the service. This secret and the current time are passed through a cryptographic hash and then truncated to produce the code to be entered. As long as the device and the server roughly agree on the current time, a matching code confirms that the user is in possession of the shared key.

The storage of the shared key is critical, both on the device and on the authenticating server. Losing control of that secret will permanently break this authentication mechanism. The RFC recommends encrypting the key using a hardware device like a TPM, and then limiting access to the encrypted data.

Exposing the shared key to a mobile device places it in greater danger than it is on a server. The device could connect to a malicious endpoint that might be able to extract the key. To mitigate this vector, an alternative to TOTP is to send the user's mobile phone a random code over an encrypted channel. This code is then entered on another device to authenticate that the user is in possession of their mobile phone.

SMS Is Not a Secure Communication Channel

Sending the user a random code for authentication requires that the authentication code is reliably delivered to the intended device and is not exposed during transit. Systems have previously sent random codes as an SMS message, but the SMS system does make sufficient guarantees to protect the random code in transit. Using SMS for this system is therefore not recommended.

Something You Have: Certificates

Another method to authenticate users is to generate per-user X.509 certificates. The certificate is derived from a strong private key and then signed using the private key of the organization that provided the certificate. The certificate cannot be be modified without invalidating the organization's signature, so the certificate can be used as a credential with any service that is configured to trust the signature of the organization.

Since an X.509 certificate is meant for consumption by a computer, not by humans, it can provide much richer details when presented to a service for authentication. As an example, a system could encode metadata about the user in the certificate and then trust that data since it has been signed by a trusted organization. This can alleviate the need to create a trusted user directory in less mature networks.

Using certificates to identify users relies heavily on those certificates being securely stored. It is strongly preferred to both generate and store the private key component on dedicated hardware so as to prevent digital theft. We'll talk more about that in the next section.

Something You Have: Security Tokens

Security tokens are hardware devices that are used primarily for user authentication, but they have additional applications. These devices are not mass storage devices storing a credential that was provisioned elsewhere. Instead, the hardware itself generates a private key. This credential information never leaves the token. The user's device interacts with the hardware's APIs to perform cryptographic operations on behalf of the user, proving that they are in possession of the hardware.

As the security industry progresses, organizations are increasingly turning toward hardware mechanisms for authenticating user identity. Devices like smart cards or Yubikeys can provide a 1:1 assertion of a particular identity. By tying identity to hardware, the risk that a particular user's credentials can be duplicated and stolen without their knowledge is greatly mitigated, as physical theft would be required.

Storing a private key in hardware is by far the most secure storage method we have today. The stored private key can then be used as the backing for many different types of authentication schemes. Traditionally, they are used in conjunction with X.509, but a new protocol called *Universal 2nd Factor* (U2F) is gaining rapid adoption. U2F provides an alternative to full-blown PKI, offering a lightweight challenge-response protocol that is designed for use by web services. Regardless of which authentication scheme you choose, if it relies on asymmetric cryptography, you should probably be using a security token.

While these hardware tokens can provide strong protections against credential theft, they cannot guarantee that the token itself isn't stolen or misused. Therefore, it's important to recognize that while these tokens are great tools in building a secure system, they cannot be a complete replacement for a user asserting their identity. If we want the strongest guarantee that a particular user is who they claim to be, using a security key with addtional authentication factors (e.g., a password or biometric sensor) is still strongly recommended.

Something You Are: Biometrics

Asserting identity by recognizing physical characteristics of the user is called biometrics. Biometrics is becoming more common as advanced sensors are making their way into devices we use every day. This authentication system offers better convenience and potentially a more secure system, if biometric signals, such as the following, are used wisely.

- Fingerprints
- Handprints
- Retina scans
- Voice analysis
- Face recognition

Using biometrics might seem like the ideal authentication method. After all, authenticating a user is validating that they are who they say they are. What could be better than measuring physical characteristics of a user? While biometrics is a useful addition to system security, there are some downsides that should not be forgotten.

Authenticating via biometrics relies on accurate measurement of a physical characteristic. If an attacker is able to trick the scanner, they are able to gain entry. Fingerprints, being a common biometric, are left on everything a person touches. Attacks against fingerprint readers have been demonstrated—attackers obtain pictures of a latent fingerprint and then 3D print a fake one, which the scanner accepts.

Additionally, biometric credentials cannot be rotated, since they're a physical characteristic. They can also present an accessibility issue if, for example, an individual is born without fingerprints (a condition known as adermatoglyphia) or if they lost their fingers in an accident.

Finally, biometrics can present surprising legal challenges when compared against other authentication mechanisms. In the United States, for example, a citizen can be compelled by a court to provide their fingerprint to authenticate to a device, but they cannot be compelled to divulge their password, owing to their Fifth Amendment right against self-incrimination.

Out-of-Band Authentication

Out-of-band authentication purposefully uses a separate communication channel than the original channel the user used to authenticate that request. For example, a user logging into a website for the first time on a device might receive a phone call to validate the request. By using an out-of-band check, a service is able to raise the difficulty of breaking into an account, since the attacker would need control of the out-of-band communication channel as well.

Out-of-band checks can come in many forms. These forms should be chosen based on the desired level of strength needed for each interaction:

- A passive email can inform users of potentially sensitive actions that have recently taken place.
- A confirmation can be required before a request is completed. Confirmation could be a simple "yes," or it could involve entering a TOTP code.
- A third party could be contacted to confirm the requested action.

When used well, out-of-band authentication can be a useful tool to increase the security of the system. As with all authentication mechanisms, some level of taste is required to choose the right authentication mechanism and frequency, based on the request taking place.

Single Sign On

Given the large number of services users interact with, the industry would prefer to decouple authentication from end services. Having authentication decoupled provides benefits to both the service and the user:

- Users only need to authenticate with a single service.
- Authentication material is stored in a dedicated service, which can have more stringent security standards.
- Security credentials in fewer locations means less risk and eased rotations.

Single sign-on (SSO) is a fairly mature concept. Under SSO, users authenticate with a centralized authority, after which they will typically be granted a token of sorts. This token is then used in further communication with secured services. When the service receives a request, it contacts the authentication authority over a secure channel to validate the token provided by the client.

This is in contrast to decentralized authentication. A zero trust network employing decentralized authentication will use the control plane to push credentials and access policy into the data plane. This empowers the data plane to carry out authentication on its own, whenever and wherever necessary, while still being backed by control plane policy and concern. This approach is sometimes favored over a more mature

SSO-based approach since it does not require running an additional service, though it introduces enough complexity that it is not recommended.

SSO tokens should be validated against the centralized authority as often as possible. Every call to the control plane to authorize an SSO token provides an opportunity to revoke access or alter the trust level (as known to the caller).

A popular mode of operation involves the service performing its own sign in, backed by SSO authentication. The primary drawback of this approach is that it allows the control plane to authorize the request only once, and leaves the application to make all further decisions. Trust variance and invalidation is a key aspect of a zero trust network, so decisions to follow this pattern should not be taken lightly.

Existing Options

SSO has been around for a long time, and as such, there are many mature protocols/technologies to support it, including these popular ones:

- SAML
- Kerberos
- CAS

It is critical that authentication remain a control plane concern in a zero trust network. As such, when designing authentication systems in a zero trust network, aim for as much control plane responsibility as possible, and validate authorization with the control plane as often as is reasonably possible.

Moving Toward a Local Auth Solution

Local authentication that is extended out into remote services is another authentication mechanism that is increasingly becoming a possibility. In this system, users authenticate their presence with a trusted device, and then the device is able to attest to that identity with a remote service. Open standards like the FIDO Alliance's UAF standard use asymmetric cryptography and local device authentication systems (e.g., passwords and biometrics) to move trust away from a large number of services to relatively few user-controlled endpoints.

UAF, in a way, looks a lot like a password manager. However, instead of storing passwords, it stores private keys. The authenticating service is then given the user's public key and is thereby able to confirm that that the user is in possession of the private key.

By moving authentication into a smart local device, a number of benefits emerge:

- Replay attacks can be mitigated via a challenge-and-response system.

- Man-in-the-middle attacks can be thwarted by having the authentication service refuse to sign the challenge unless it originated from the same domain the user is visiting.
- Credential reuse is nonexistent, since per-service credentials can be trivially generated.

Authenticating and Authorizing a Group

Nearly every system has a small set of actions or requests that must be closely guarded. The amount of risk one is willing to tolerate in this area will vary from application to application, though there is practically no lower limit.

One of the risks you pass as you approach zero is the amount of trust in any single human being. Just like in real life, there are many times in which it is desirable to gain the consent of multiple individuals in order to authorize a particularly sensitive action. There are a couple ways that this can be achieved in the digital realm, and the cool part is, we can cryptographically guarantee it!

Shamir's Secret Sharing

Shamir's Secret Sharing is a scheme for distributing a single secret among a group of individuals. The algorithm breaks the original secret into n parts, which can then be distributed (Figure 6-2). Depending on how the algorithm was configured when the parts were generated, k parts are needed to recalculate the original secret value.

When protecting large amounts of data using Shamir's Secret Sharing, a symmetric encryption key is usually split and distributed instead of using the algorithm directly on data. This is because the size of secret that is being split needs to be smaller than some of the data used in the secret-sharing algorithm.

```
~ $ echo 'this is a secret' | ssss-split -n 5 -t 2
Generating shares using a (2,5) scheme with dynamic security level.
Enter the secret, at most 128 ASCII characters: Using a 128 bit security level.
1-4054162f42f328c2ecbff990e9e1996f
2-93285deac4d6406cde841b05b350f61f
3-22039b5646ca98093092ba897ac02cb0
4-35d0ca61c89c9130baf3de2f06322866
5-84fb0cdd4a80495554e57fa3cfa2f2c9
~ $ ssss-combine -t 2
Enter 2 shares separated by newlines:
Share [1/2]: 5-84fb0cdd4a80495554e57fa3cfa2f2c9
Share [2/2]: 4-35d0ca61c89c9130baf3de2f06322866
Resulting secret: this is a secret
```

Figure 6-2. An example ssss session

A Unix/Linux version of this algorithm is called ssss (*http://point-at-infinity.org/ssss/*). Similar applications and libraries exist for other operating systems or programming languages.

Red October

Cloudflare's Red October project (*https://github.com/cloudflare/redoctober*) is another approach to implementing group authentication to access shared data. This web service uses layered asymmetric cryptography to encrypt data such that a certain number of users need to come together to decrypt the data. Encrypted data isn't actually stored on the server. Instead, only user public/private key pairs (encrypted with a user chosen password) are stored.

When data is submitted to be encrypted, a random encryption key is generated to encrypt the data. This encryption key is then itself encrypted using unique combinations of user-specific encryption keys, based on an unlock policy that the user requests. In the simplest case, a user might encrypt some data such that two people in a larger group need to collaborate to decrypt the data. In this scenario, the original encrypted data's encryption key is therefore doubly encrypted with each unique pair of user encryption keys.

About DNS Root Zone Signing

The DNS Root Zone Signing Ceremony is an interesting example of a group authentication procedure. This ceremony is used to generate the root keys upon which all DNSSEC trust is based on. If the root key is compromised, the entire DNSSEC system's trustworthiness would be compromised, so the root key ceremony is built specifically to mitigate that risk.

The first ceremony occurred on June 16, 2010, and a new ceremony occurs every quarter. The ceremony utilizes seven actors, each with a different role. The ceremony mitigates the risk of compromise to a one-in-a-million chance, assuming a dishonesty rate of 5% among the actors in the ceremony. A strict procedural document is generated in order to organize the ceremony. HSMs, biometric scanners, and air-gapped systems are used to protect the digital key. In the end, a new public/private key pair is generated and signed, continuing the internet's trust anchor for another quarter.

You can read more about the signing ceremony on Cloudflare's website (*https://www.cloudflare.com/dns/dnssec/root-signing-ceremony/*), or you can view the materials for each ceremony on IANA's website (*https://www.iana.org/dnssec/ceremonies*).

See Something, Say Something

Users in a zero trust network, like devices, need to be active participants in the security of the system. Organizations have traditionally formed dedicated teams to focus on the security of the system. Those teams, more often than not, took that mandate to mean that they were solely responsible for the system's security. Changes needed to be vetted by them to ensure that the system's security was not compromised. This approach produces an antagonistic relationship between the security team and the rest of the organization, and as result, reduces security.

A better approach is to build a culture of collaboration toward the security of the system. Users should be encouraged to speak up if something they do or witness looks odd or dangerous, even if it's small. This sharing of knowledge will give much better context on the threats that the security team is working to defend against. Reporting phishing emails, even when users did not interact with them, can let the security team know if a determined attacker is attempting to infiltrate the network.

Devices which are lost or stolen should be reported immediately. Security teams might consider providing ways for users to alert them day or night in the event that their device has gone missing.

When responding to tips or alerts from users, security teams should be mindful of how their response to the incident affects the organization more broadly. A user who is shamed for losing a device will be less willing to report the loss in a timely manner in the future. Similarly, a late-night false alarm should be met with thanks to ensure that reporters don't second-guess themselves. As much as possible, try to bias the organization toward over-reporting.

Trust Signals

Historical user activity is a rich source of data for determining the trustworthiness of a user's current actions. A system can be built which mines user activity to build up a model of expected behavior. This system will then compare current behavior against that model as a method for calculating a trust score of a user.

Humans tend to have predictable access patterns. Most people will not try to authenticate multiple times a second. They also are unlikely to try to authenticate hundreds of times. These types of access patterns are extremely suspicious and are often mitigated via active methods like *CAPTCHAs* (automated challenges which only a human is able to answer) or locked accounts. Reducing false positives requires setting fairly high bars to be actively banned. Including this activity in an overall threat assessment score can help catch suspicious, but not obviously bad, behavior.

Looking at access patterns doesn't need to be restricted to authentication attempts. Users' application usage patterns can also reveal malicious intent. Most users tend to have fairly limited roles in an organization and therefore might only need to access a subset of data that is available to them. In an attempt to increase security, organizations will begin removing access rights from employees unless they definitely need the access to do their job. However, this type of restrictive access control can impact the ability of the organization to respond quickly to unique events. System administrators are a class of users which are given broad access, thereby weakening this approach as a defense mechanism. Instead of choosing between these two extremes, we can score the user's activity in aggregate and then use their score to determine if they are still trusted to access a particularly sensitive resource. Having hard stops in the system is still important—it's the less clear cases where the system should trust users, but verify their trustworthiness via logged activity.

Lists of known bad traffic sources, like the one provided by Spamhaus, can be another useful signal for the trustworthiness of a user. Traffic that is originating from these addresses and is attempting to use a particular user's identity can point toward a potentially compromised user.

Geolocation can be another useful signal for determining trust of a user. We can compare the user's current location against previously visited locations to determine if it is out of the ordinary. Has the user's device suddenly appeared in a new location in a timeframe that they couldn't reasonably travel? If the user has multiple devices, are they reporting conflicting locations? Geolocation can be wrong or misleading, so systems shouldn't weight it too strongly. Sometimes users forget devices at home or geolocation databases are simply incorrect.

Summary

This chapter focused on how to establish trust in users in a system. We talked about how identity is defined and the importance of having an authority to reference when checking the identity of a user in the system. Users need to be entered into a system to have an identity, so we talked about some ideal ways to bootstrap their identity.

Identity needs to be stored somewhere, and that system is a very valuable target for attackers. We talked about how to store the data safely, the importance of limiting the breadth of data being stored in a single location, and how to keep stored identity up to date as users come and go.

With authoritative identity defined and stored, we turned our attention to authenticating users that claim to have a particular identity. Authentication can be an annoyance for users, so we discussed when to authenticate users. We don't want users to be inundated with authentication requests, since that will increase the likelihood that they accidentally authenticate against a malicious service. Therefore, finding the right balance is critical.

There are many ways that users can be authenticated, so we dug into the fundamental concepts. We discussed several authentication mechanisms that are in use today. We also looked at some authentication mechanisms that are on the horizon as system security practices are responding to threats.

Oftentimes, increasing trust in a system of users involves creating procedures where multiple users play a role to accomplish a goal. We discussed group authentication and authorization systems like "two person rules," which can be used to secure extremely sensitive data. We also talked about building a culture of awareness in an organization by encouraging users to report any suspicious activity.

Finally, zero trust networks can leverage user activity logs to build a profile of users to compare against when evaluating new actions. We enumerated some useful signals which can be used to build that profile.

The next chapter looks at how trust in applications can be built.

CHAPTER 7

Trusting Applications

Marc Andreessen, a notable Silicon Valley investor, famously declared that "software is eating the world." In many ways, this statement has never been truer. It is the software running in your datacenter that makes all of the magic happen, and as such, it is no secret that we wish to trust its execution.

Code, running on a *trusted* device, will be faithfully executed. A trusted device is a prerequisite for trusting code, which we covered in Chapter 5. However, even with our execution environment secured, we still have more work to do to trust that the code that's running on a device is trustworthy.

As such, trusting the device is just half of the story. One must also trust the code and the programmers who wrote it. With the goal being to ensure the integrity of a running application, we must find ways to extend this human trust from the code itself all the way to its actual execution.

Establishing trust in code requires that:

- The people producing the code are themselves trusted
- The code was faithfully processed to produce a trustworthy application
- Trusted applications are faithfully deployed to the infrastructure to be run
- Trusted applications are continually monitored for attempts to coerce the application with malicious actions

This chapter will discuss approaches to securing each of these steps, with a focus on the inheritance of trust from human to production application.

Understanding the Application Pipeline

The creation, delivery, and execution of code within a computer system is a very sensitive chain of events. These systems are an attractive target for adversaries due to their ability to gain greater access. Attack vectors exist at every step, and subversion at these stages can be very difficult to detect. Therefore, we must work to ensure that every link of this chain (shown in Figure 7-1) is secured in a way that makes subversion detectable.

This process is similar to *supply chain security*, the collective efforts of governments around the world to enhance security. Ensuring that military equipment is securely built/sourced is critical in ensuring the effectiveness of the fighting force, and software creation and delivery is no different.

Supply Chain Criticality

In 2007, the Israeli government conducted an airstrike against a suspected nuclear facility in Syria. One of many mysteries surrounding this strike is the sudden failure (*https://en.wikipedia.org/wiki/Operation_Orchard*) of Syrian radar systems, providing the Israelis with cover. The failure of these radar systems, which were supposedly state of the art, is now widely believed to be attributable to a hardware kill switch hidden in a commercial chip used by the radar equipment. While never fully verified, stories like this one highlight the importance of secure supply chains, whether it be hardware or software.

In support of a secure software delivery chain, every step of the process should be fully auditable with cryptographic validation occurring at each critical point. Generally speaking, these steps can be broken down into four distinct phases:

- Source code
- Build/compilation
- Distribution
- Execution

Let's start with trusting the source code itself.

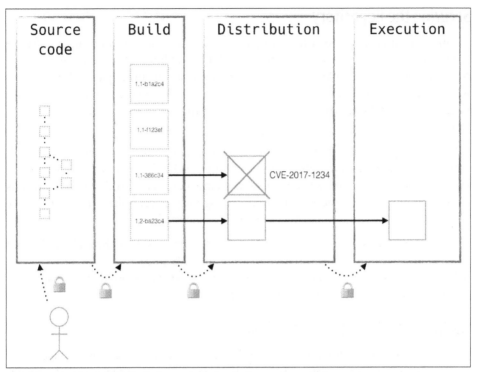

Figure 7-1. A build pipeline depends on both the security of the engineers creating source and configuring the system, as well as the security of the components of the pipeline

Trusting Source

Source code is the first step in running any piece of software. To put it very simply, it's difficult to trust source code that is written by an untrusted human. Even with careful code auditing, it is still possible for a malicious developer to purposefully encode (and hide!) a vulnerability in plain sight. In fact, there is even a well-known competition (*http://www.underhanded-c.org/*) dedicated to this dark art. While even well-meaning developers can inadvertently add weakness to an application, a zero trust network will focus on identifying malicious use instead of removing trust from those users.

Setting the trusted developer problem aside for a minute, we still face the problem of securely storing and distributing the source code itself. Typically, source code is stored in a centralized code repository, against which many developers interact and commit work. These repositories must also fall under tight control, particularly if they are being used directly by systems that build/compile the code in question.

Securing the Repository

Maintaining traditional security approaches when it comes to securing a software repository is still effective, and does not prohibit the addition of more advanced security features. This includes basic principles such as the principle of least access, whereby users are only given as much access to the repository as is required to complete the task at hand. In practice, this usually manifests itself as heavily limited/restricted write access.

While this approach is still valid and recommended, the story has changed a little bit with the introduction of distributed source control. With the code repository living in multiple places, it is not always possible to secure a single, centralized entity. In this circumstance, however, there remains an analog for this centralized repository—the system storing the code from which the build system reads.

In this case, it is still highly desirable to protect this system through traditional means; however, the problem becomes more difficult since code can enter the distributed repository in any number of ways. The logical extension, then, is that securing the build source repository alone is not enough.

Authentic Code and the Audit Trail

Many version control systems (VCS), particularly those which are distributed, store source history using cryptographic techniques. This approach, called content addressable storage, uses the cryptographic hash of the content being stored as the identifier of that object in a database, rather than its location or coordinates. It's possible to see how a source file could be hashed and stored in such a database, thereby ensuring that any change in the source file results in a new hash. This property means that files are stored immutably: it's impossible to change the contents of the files once stored.

Some VCS systems take this storage mechanism a step further by storing the history itself as an object in the content addressable database. Git, a popular distributed VCS project, stores the history of commits to the repository as a directed acyclic graph (DAG). The commits are objects in the database, storing details like the commit time, author, and identifiers of ancestor commits. By storing the cryptographic hashes of ancestor commits on each commit itself, we form a Merkle tree, which allows one to cryptographically validate that the chain of commits are unmodified (Figure 7-2).

If a commit in the DAG were to be modified, its update will affect all the descendant commits in the graph, changing each commit's content, and by extension, its identifier. With the source history distributed to many contributors, the system gains another beneficial property: it's impossible to change the history without other contributors noticing.

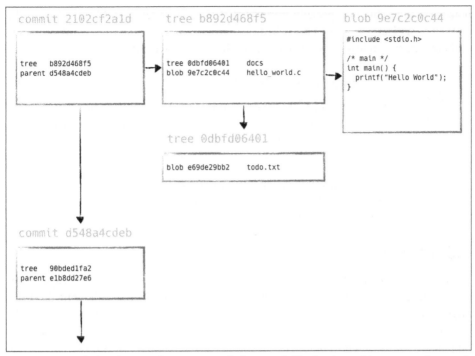

Figure 7-2. Git's database makes unwanted changes difficult, since objects are referenced using a hash of their contents

Storing the DAG in this manner gives us tamper-proof history: it's impossible to change the history subversively. However, this storage does nothing to ensure that new commits in the history are authorized and authentic. Imagine for a moment that a trusted developer is persuaded to pull a malicious commit into their local repository before pushing it to the official repository. This commit is now in the repository by leaning on the trusted developer's push access. Even more concerning, the authorship metadata is just plain text: a malicious committer can put whatever details they want in that field (a fact that was used amusingly to make commits appear to be authored by Linus Torvalds on GitHub (*http://www.jayhuang.org/blog/pushing-code-to-github-as-linus-torvalds/*)).

To guard against this attack vector, Git has the ability for commits and tags to be signed using the GPG key of a trusted developer. *Tags*, which point to the head commit in a particular history, can be signed using a GPG key to ensure the authenticity of a release. Signed commits allow one to go a step further and authenticate the entire Git history, making it impossible for an attacker to impersonate another committer without first stealing that committer's GPG key.

Signed source code clearly provides significant benefit and should be used wherever possible. It provides robust code authentication not only to just humans, but machines too. This is especially important if CI/CD systems build and deploy the code automatically. A fully signed history allows build systems to cryptographically authenticate the code as trusted before compiling it for deployment.

In the Beginning, There Was Nothing

Many repositories begin with unsigned commits, transitioning to signed commits later on. In this brownfield case, the first commit to be signed is essentially endorsing all commits that came before it. This is important to understand, as you may wish to perform an audit at this time. Having said that, the overhead or difficulty of performing such an audit should not dissuade or delay the transition to signed code; the audit, if you choose to do one, can be performed in due time.

Code Reviews

As we learned in Chapter 6, it can be dangerous to concentrate powerful capabilities onto a single user. This is no different when considering source code contributions. Signed contributions enable us to authenticate the developer committing the code, but does not ensure that the code being committed is correct or safe. Of course, we do place a nontrivial amount of trust in the developer, though this does not mean that said developer should unilaterally commit code to sensitive projects.

To mitigate this risk, most mature organizations implement a code review process. Under code review, all contributions must be approved by one or more additional developers. This simple process drastically improves not just the quality of the software, but also reduces the rate at which vulnerabilities are introduced, whether they be intentional or accidental.

Trusting Builds

Build servers are frequently targeted by persistent threats, and for good reason. They have elevated access, and produce code that is executed directly in production. Detecting artifacts that have been compromised during the build stage can be very difficult, so it is important to apply strong protections to these services.

The Risk

In trusting a build system, there are generally three things that we want to assert:

- The source code it built is the code we intended to build.
- The build process/configuration is that which we intended.
- The build itself was performed faithfully, without manipulation.

Build systems can ingest signed code and produce a signed output, but the function(s) applied in between (i.e., the build itself) is generally not protected cryptographically—this is where the most significant attack vector lies.

This particular vector is a powerful one, as shown in Figure 7-3. Without the right processes and validation, subversion of this kind can be difficult or impossible to detect. For instance, imagine a compromised CI/CD system that ingests signed C code, and compiles it into a signed binary, which is then distributed and run in production. Production systems can validate that the binary is signed, but would have no way of knowing if additional malicious code has been compiled in during the build process. In this way, a seemingly secure system can successfully run malicious code in production without detection. Perhaps even worse, the consumers are fooled into thinking the output is safe.

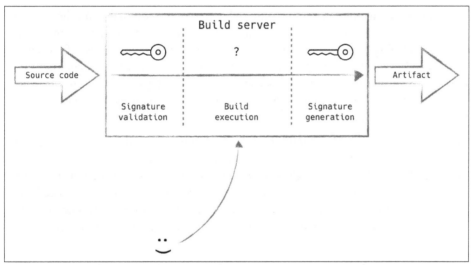

Figure 7-3. The build configuration and its execution is not protected cryptographically, in contrast to the source code and the generated artifact. This break in the chain poses great threat, and is a powerful attack vector.

Due to the sensitive nature of the build process, outsourcing the responsibility should be carefully evaluated. Things like reproducible builds can help identify compromises in this area (more on that in a bit), but can't always prevent their distribution. Is this really something you want a third-party provider to do for you? How much do you trust them? Their security posture should be weighed against your own chance of being a high value target.

Host Security Is Still Important

This section focuses on securing various steps of the software build process, but it is important to note that the security of the build servers themselves is still important. We can secure the input, output, and configuration of the build, but if the build server is compromised then it can no longer be trusted to faithfully perform its duties. Reproducible builds, immutable hosts, and the zero trust model itself can help in this regard.

Trusted Input, Trusted Output

If we think of the build system as a trusted operation, it's clear that we need to trust the input of that operation in order to produce trusted output.

Let's start with trusting the input to the build system. We discussed mechanisms for trusting the source control systems earlier. The build system, as a consumer of the version control system, is responsible for validating the trustworthiness of the source. The version control system should be accessed over an authenticated channel, commonly TLS. Additionally, for extra security guarantees, tags and/or commits should be signed and the build system should validate those signatures—or chain of signatures—before starting a build.

The build configuration is another important input to the build system. Attacking the build configuration could allow an attacker to direct the build system to link against a malicious library. Even seemingly safe optimization flags can be malicious in security critical code, where timing attack mitigation code can be accidentally optimized away. Putting this configuration under source control, where it can be versioned and attested to via signed commits, helps to ensure that the build configuration is also a trusted input.

With the input sufficiently secured, we can turn our attention to the output of the build process. The build system needs to sign the generated artifacts so downstream systems can validate their authenticity. Build systems typically also generate cryptographic hashes of the build artifacts to guard against corruption or malicious attempts to replace the binaries once produced. Securing the build artifacts and hashes, and then distributing them to downstream consumers, completes the trusted output of the build system.

Reproducible Builds

Reproducible builds (*https://reproducible-builds.org/*) are the best tool we have in guarding against subversion of the build pipeline. In short, software supporting reproducible builds is compiled in a deterministic way, ensuring that the resulting binary is exactly the same for a given source code, no matter who built it. This is a very powerful property, as it allows multiple parties to examine the source code and produce identical builds, thus gaining confidence that the build process used to generate a particular binary was not tampered with.

This can be done in a number of ways, but it generally involves a codified build process, and enables developers to set up their own build environment to produce binaries that match the distributed versions bit-for-bit. With reproducible builds, one can "watch" the output of a CI/CD system, and compare its output to results compiled locally. In this way, malicious interference or code injection during the build process can be easily detected. When combined with signed source code, we arrive at a fairly robust process that is able to authenticate both the source code and the binary produced by it.

Virtualized Build Environments Enable Reproducible Builds

Having reproducible builds sounds easy on paper, but reproducing a built binary so it's byte for byte identical is a very hard problem. Distributions have historically built packages inside a virtual filesystem (a chroot jail) to ensure that all dependencies of the build are captured in the build configuration. Virtual machines or containers can be useful tools to ensure that the build environment is fully insulated from the host running the build.

Decoupling Release and Artifact Versions

Immutable builds are critical in ensuring the security of a build and release system. Without it, replacing a known good version is possible, opening up the door for attacks that target the underlying build artifact. This would enable an attacker to masquerade a "bad" version as a "good" version. For this reason, artifacts generated by build systems should have Write Once Read Many semantics.

Given the immutable artifact requirement, a natural tension arises with the versioning of those artifacts. Many projects prefer to use meaningful version numbers (e.g., semantic versioning) in their releases to communicate the potential impact to downstream consumers with an upgrade of their software. This desire to attach meaning to the version number can be difficult to incorporate into a build system that needs to ensure that every version is immutable.

For example, when working toward a major release, a project might have a misconfigured build that causes the build system to produce incorrect output. The maintainers now face a choice. They could republish the release using a patch-level bump, or they might decide to bend the rules and republish the same version using a new build artifact. Many projects choose the latter option, preferring the benefit of a clearer marketing story than the more correct reversion. This is a bad habit to get into when considering the masquerade just described.

It's clear from this example that in either case, two separate build artifacts were produced, and the version number associated with the build artifact is a separate choice for the project. Therefore, when creating a build system, it's better to have the build system produce immutable versions independent of the publicly communicated version. A later system (the distribution system) can manage the mapping of release versions to build artifact versions. This approach enables us to maintain immutable build artifacts without sacrificing usability or introducing bad security practices.

Trusting Distribution

The process of choosing which build artifacts to deliver to downstream consumers is called distribution. The build system produces many artifacts, some of which are meant for downstream consumption. Therefore, we need to ensure that the distribution system maintains control over which artifacts are ultimately delivered.

Promoting an Artifact

Based on our earlier discussion on immutable build artifacts, promotion is the act of designating a build artifact as the authoritative version without changing the contents of that artifact. This act itself should be immutable: once a version is assigned and released, it cannot be changed. Instead, a new artifact needs to be produced and released under an incrementally higher version number.

This constraint presents a chicken-and-egg scenario. Software typically includes a way to report its version number to the user, but if the version number isn't assigned until later in the build process, how does one add that version information without changing the build artifact?

A naive approach would be to subtly change the artifact during the promotion process, for example, by having the version number stored in a trivially modified location in the build artifact. This approach, however, is not preferred. Instead, release engineers should make a clear separation between the publicly released version number and the build number, which is an extra component of the release information. With this model, many build artifacts are produced which use the same public release version, but each build is additionally tagged with a unique build number (Figure 7-4). The act of releasing that version is therefore choosing the build artifact that will be signed and distributed. Once such a version is released, all new builds should be configured to use the next target version number.

Figure 7-4. This Firefox public release version is 51.0.1, but the package name retains a build ID

Of course, this promotion must be communicated to the consumer in a way that they can validate they are in possession of the promoted build, and not some intermediary and potentially flawed build. There are a number of ways to do this, and it is largely a solved problem. One solution is to sign the promoted artifacts with a release-only key, thus communicating to the consumers that they have a promoted build. Another way to do this is to publish a signed manifest, outlining the released versions and their cryptographic hashes. Many popular package distribution systems, such as APT, use this method to validate builds obtained from their distribution systems.

Distribution Security

Software distribution is similar to electricity distribution, where electricity is generated by a centralized source, and carried over a distribution network in order to be delivered to a wide consumer base. Unlike electricity, however, the integrity of the produced software must be protected while it transits the distribution system, and allow the consumer to independently validate its integrity. There are a number of widely adopted package distribution and management systems, practically all of which have implemented protections around the distribution process and allow consumers to validate the authenticity of packages received through them. Throughout this section, we will use the popular package management software *Advanced Packaging Tool* (APT) as an example of how certain concepts are implemented in real life, though it is important to keep in mind that there are many options available to you— APT is merely one.

Integrity and Authenticity

There are two primary mechanisms used to assert integrity and authenticity in software distribution systems: *hashing* and *signing*. Hashing a software release involves computing and distributing a cryptographic hash representing the binary released, which the consumer can validate to ensure that the binary has not been changed since it left the hands of the developer. Signing a release involves the author encrypting the hash of the release with their private key, allowing consumers to validate that the software was released by an authorized party. Both methods are effective, and are not necessarily mutually exclusive. In order to better understand how these methods can be applied in a distribution system, it is useful to look at the structure and security of an APT repository.

An APT repository contains three types of files: a `Release` file, a `Packages` file, and the packages themselves. The packages file acts as an index for all of the packages in the repository. It stores a bit of metadata on every package the repository contains, such as filenames, descriptions, and checksums. The checksum from this index is used to validate the integrity of the downloaded package before it is installed. This provides integrity, assuring us that the contents have not changed in flight. It is, however, mostly only effective against corruption, since an attacker can simply modify the index hashes if the goal is to deliver modified software. This is where the `Release` file comes in.

The `Release` file contains metadata about the repo itself (as opposed to the `Packages` file, which stores metadata about the packages contained within it). This includes things like the name and version of the OS distribution the repo is meant for. It also includes a checksum of the `Packages` file, allowing the consumer to validate the integrity of the index, which in turn can validate the integrity of the packages we download. That's great, except still an attacker can simply modify the `Release` file with the updated hash of the `Packages` file and be on their way.

So, we introduce cryptographic signatures (Figure 7-5). A signature provides not only integrity for the contents of the signed file (since a hash is included in the signature), but also authenticity, since successful decryption of the signature proves that the generating party was in the presence of the private key.

Using this principle, the maintainer of the software repo signs the `Release` file with a private key, to which there is a well-known and well-distributed public key. Any time the repo is updated, package file hashes are updated in the index, and the index's final hash is updated in the `Release` file, which is then signed. This chain of hashes, the root of which is signed, provides the consumer with the ability to authenticate the software they are about to install.

In the event that you're unable to sign a software release in some way, it is essential to fall back to standard security practices. You will need to ensure that all communication is mutually authenticated—this means traffic to, from, and in between any distribution repository. Additionally, you'll need to ensure that the storage the repository leverages is adequately secured, be it AWS S3 or otherwise.

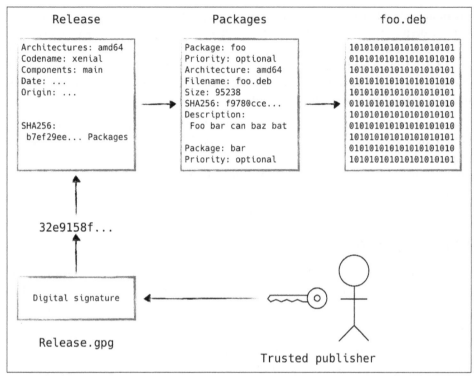

Release   Packages   foo.deb

```
Architectures: amd64
Codename: xenial
Components: main
Date: ...
Origin: ...


SHA256:
  b7ef29ee... Packages
```

```
Package: foo
Priority: optional
Architecture: amd64
Filename: foo.deb
Size: 95238
SHA256: f9780cce...
Description:
  Foo bar can baz bat

Package: bar
Priority: optional
```

```
1010101010101010101
0101010101010101010
1010101010101010101
0101010101010101010
1010101010101010101
0101010101010101010
1010101010101010101
0101010101010101010
0101010101010101010
1010101010101010101
```

32e9158f...

Digital signature

Release.gpg

Trusted publisher

Figure 7-5. The maintainer signs the Release file, which contains a hash of the Packages index, which contains hashes of the packages themselves

Trusting a Distribution Network

When distributing software with a large or geographically disparate consumer base, it is common to copy the software to multiple locations or repositories in order to meet scaling, availability, or performance challenges. These copies are often referred to as mirrors. In some cases, particularly when dealing with publicly consumed software, the servers hosting the mirrors are not under the control of the organization producing the software. This is obviously a concern, and underscores the requirement of a software repo to be authenticated against the author (and not the repo owner).

Referring back to APT's hashing and signing scheme, it can be seen that we *can*, in fact, authenticate the Release file against the author using its signature. This means that for every mirror we access, we can check the Release signature to validate that the mirror is in fact a faithful copy of the original release.

One might think that by signing the Release file, software can be distributed through untrusted mirrors safely. Additionally, repositories are often hosted without TLS under the assertion that the signing of the release is sufficient for protecting the distribution network. Unfortunately, both of these assertions are incorrect.

There are several classes of attacks that open up when connecting to an untrusted mirror, despite the fact that the artifact you're obtaining is ultimately signed. For instance, a downgrade to an older (signed) version can be forced, as the artifact served will still be legitimate. Other attack vectors can include targeting the package management client itself. In the interest of protecting your clients, always make sure they are connecting to a trusted distribution mirror.

The dearth of TLS-protected repositories presents another vulnerability to the distribution of software. Attackers that are in a position to modify the unprotected response could perform the same attacks that an untrusted mirror could. Therefore, the best solution to this problem is moving package distribution to TLS-protected mechanisms. By adding TLS, clients can validate that they are in fact connecting to a trusted repository and that no tampering of the communication can occur.

Humans in the Loop

With a secure pipeline crafted, we can make considered decisions on where humans are involved in that pipeline. By limiting human involvement only to a few key points, the release pipeline stays secure while also ensuring that attackers are not able to leverage automation in the pipeline to deliver malicious software.

The ability to commit code to the version control system is a clear spot where humans are involved. Depending on the sensitivity of the project, requiring humans to only check in signed commits provides strong confidence that the commit is authentic.

Once committed, humans needn't be involved in the building of software artifacts. Those artifacts should ideally be produced automatically in a secured system. Humans should, however, be involved in the process of choosing which artifact is ultimately distributed. This involvement could be implemented using various mechanisms: copying an artifact from the build database to the release database or tagging a particular commit in source control, for example. The mechanism by which humans certify a releasable binary doesn't much matter, as long as that mechanism is secured.

It's tempting when building secure systems to apply extreme measures to mitigate any conceivable threat, but the burden placed on humans should be balanced against the potential risk. In the case of software that is widely distributed, the private signing key should be well guarded, since the effort of rotating a compromised key would be extreme. Organizations that release software like this will commonly use "code signing ceremonies," where the signing key is stored on a hardware security module (HSM) and unlocked using authorization from multiple parties, as a mitigation against the theft of this highly sensitive key. For internal use–only software, the effort to rotate a key might be reasonably less, so more lax security practices are reasonable.

An organization might still prefer a code signing ceremony for particularly sensitive internal applications—a system that stores credit card details, for example.

Humans and Code Signing Keys

Bit9 is a software security firm that develops an application enabling *application whitelisting*. They had many high-profile clients, from government agencies to Fortune 100 companies. In 2013, an attack against their corporate network was able to recover one of Bit9's private code signing keys, which was then used to sign and install malware into a handful of its customers. It is widely believed that this was done in order to bypass the strong security provided by Bit9's software itself, and underscores the importance of securing code signing keys. If you carry high risk, as Bit9 did, it might be a good idea to employ a code signing ceremony.

Trusting an Instance

Understanding what is running in your infrastructure is important when designing a zero trust network. After all, how can you know what to expect on your network if you don't know what to expect on your hosts? A solid understanding of the software (and versions) running in your datacenter will go a long way in both breach detection and vulnerability mitigation.

Upgrade-Only Policy

Software versions are important constructs in determining exactly which version of the code you have and how old it is. Perhaps most importantly, they are used heavily in order to determine what vulnerabilities one might be exposed to, given the version they are running.

Vulnerability announcements/discoveries are typically associated with a version number (online service vulnerabilities being the exception), and generally include the version numbers in which the vulnerability was fixed. With this in mind, we can see that it might be desirable to induce a version downgrade in order to expose a known vulnerability. This is an effective attack vector as the software being coerced to run is frequently authorized and trusted, since it is a perfectly valid release, albeit an older one.

If the software is built for internal distribution, perhaps the distribution system serves only the latest copy. Doing this prevents a compromised or misconfigured system from pulling down an old version that may contain a known vulnerability. It is also possible to enforce this roll-forward mentality in hardware. Apple iOS famously uses a hardware security chip to validate software updates and to ensure that only signed software built *after* the currently installed software can be loaded.

Authorized Instances

The importance of knowing what's running is more nuanced than simply understanding what is the latest version to have been deployed. There are many edge cases that arise, such as a host that has fallen out of the deployment system; one that has been previously authorized but is now "rogue" by way of no longer receiving updates. In order to guard against cases like this, it's critical that running instances be individually authorized.

It is possible to use techniques described in Chapter 4 to build dynamic network policy in an effort to authorize application instances, but network policy is often host/device oriented rather than application oriented. Instead, we can leverage something much more application-centric in the pursuit of authorizing a running instance: secrets.

Most running applications require some sort of secret in order to do their job. This secret can manifest itself in many ways: an API key, an X509 certificate, or even credentials to a message queue are common examples. Applications must obtain the secret(s) in order to run, and furthermore, the secret must be *valid*. The validity of a secret (as obvious as it sounds) is the key to authorizing a running application, as with validation comes *invalidation*.

Attaching a lifetime to a secret is extremely effective in limiting its abuse. By creating a new secret for every deployed instance and attaching a lifetime to the secret, we can assert that we know precisely what is running, since we know precisely how many secrets we have generated, whom we gave them to, and their lifetimes. Allowing secrets to expire mitigates the impact of "rogue" instances by ensuring they will not operate indefinitely.

Of course, someone must be responsible for generating and injecting these secrets at runtime, and this is no small responsibility. The system carrying this responsibility is ultimately the system that is authorizing the instance to run. As such, it makes sense for this responsibility to fall in the hands of the deployment system, since it already carries similar responsibility.

Trusted Third Parties in Instance Authorization

Rather than giving your deployment system direct access to secrets, it is possible to leverage a trusted third party, allowing the deployment system to instead assign policy dictating which secrets the running instance can access. Hashicorp's Vault, for instance, has a feature called *response wrapping* in which an authorized party can request a secret to be generated and stored for later retrieval. In the context of a deployment system, the deploy itself could contact Vault and direct the creation of secrets on behalf of the authorized instances, injecting a one-time-token into the runtime which the application can use to retrieve the generated secrets, as shown in Figure 7-6.

In such a system, the deployment service notifies the secret management service of the impending changes, authorizing the new application instances. During the deploy itself, the deployment service injects key(s), which the new instances use to identify themselves to the secret management system, which is expecting their request. The secret management system then provisions unique time-bound credentials, returns them to the application, and further continues to manages their lifecycle.

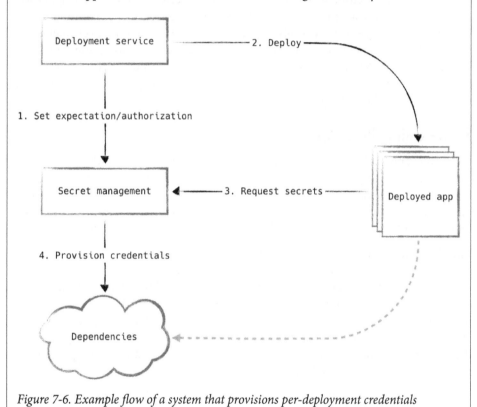

Figure 7-6. Example flow of a system that provisions per-deployment credentials

It doesn't take much thought to realize the power of a system which can create and (potentially) retrieve secrets. With great power comes great responsibility. If allowing an autonomous system to generate and distribute secrets comes with too much risk for your organization, you might consider including a human at this step. Ideally, this would manifest as a human-approved deployment in which a TOTP or other authenticating code is provided. This code will, in turn, be used to authorize the creation/ retrieval of the secrets by the deployment system.

Runtime Security

Trusting that an application instance is authorized/sanctioned is only one half of the concern. There is also the need to validate that it can run safely and securely through its lifecycle. We know how to deploy an application securely, and validate that its deployment is authorized, but will it remain an authorized and trustworthy deployment for the entirety of its life?

There are many vectors which can compromise perfectly authorized application instances, and it might be no surprise to learn that these are the most commonly used vectors. For instance, it is typically easier to corrupt an existing government agent than it is to masquerade as one or attempt to become one. For this reason, individuals with outstanding debt are commonly denied security clearance. They might be fully trusted at the time they are granted clearance, but how susceptible are they to bribery if they are in debt? Can they be trusted in this case?

Secure Coding Practices

Most (all?) application-level vulnerabilities start with a latent bug, which an attacker can leverage to coerce the trusted application to perform an undesirable action. Fixing each bug in isolation will result in a game of whack-a-mole, where developers fix one security-impacting bug only to find two more. Truly mitigating this exposure requires a shift in mindset of the application developers to secure coding practices.

Injection attacks, where user-supplied data is crafted to exploit a weakness in an application or related system, commonly occur when user data is not properly validated before being processed. This type of attack is mitigated by introducing several layers of defenses. Application libraries will carefully construct APIs that avoid trusting user-supplied data. Database querying libraries, for example, will provide APIs to allow the programmer to separate the static query from variables that are provided by the user. By instituting a clear separation between logic and data, the potential for injection attacks is greatly reduced.

Having clear APIs can also support automated scans of application software. Security-aware organizations are increasingly running automated analysis tools against their source code to detect and warn application developers of insecure coding practices. These systems warn about using insecure APIs, for example, by highlighting database queries that are constructed using string concatenation instead of the API discussed earlier. Beyond warning about insecure APIs, application logic can be traced to identify missing checks. For example, these tools might confirm that every system transaction includes some authorization check, which mitigates vulnerabilities that allow attackers to reference data that they should not be allowed to access. These examples represent only a handful of the capabilities possessed by code analysis tools.

Proactively identifying known vulnerabilities is useful, but some vulnerabilities are too subtle to deterministically detect. As a result, another mitigation technique in use is fuzzing. This practice sends random data to running applications to detect unexpected errors. These errors, when exposed, are often the sort of weaknesses that attackers use to gain a foothold in the system. Fuzzing can be executed as part of a functional testing suite early in the build pipeline, or even continuously against production infrastructure.

There are entire books written on secure coding practices, some of which are dependent on the type of application being created. Programmers should familiarize themselves with the appropriate practices to improve the security of their applications. Many organizations choose to have security consultants inspect their applications and development practices to identify problems.

Isolation

Isolating deployed applications by constraining the set of resources they can access is important in a zero trust network. Applications have traditionally been executed inside a shared environment, where a user's applications are running in an execution environment with very few constraints on how those applications can interact. This shared environment creates a large amount of risk should an application be compromised, and presents challenges similar to the perimeter model.

Application isolation seeks to constrain the damage of a potentially compromised application by clearly defining the resources that are available to the application. Isolation will constrain capabilities and resources that the operating system provides:

- CPU time
- Memory access
- Network access
- Filesystem access
- System calls

When implemented at its best, every application is given the least amount of access necessary to complete its work. A well-constrained application that becomes compromised will quickly find that no additional leverage in the larger system is gained. As a result, by isolating applications, the potential damage from a compromised application is greatly reduced. In a multiprocess environment (e.g., a server running several services), other still-safe services are protected from attempts to move laterally on that system.

Application isolation can be accomplished using a number of different technologies:

- SELinux, AppArmor
- BSD jails

- Virtualization/containerization
- Apple's App Sandbox
- Windows' Isolated Applications

Isolation is generally seen as breaking down into two types: *virtualization* and *shared kernel* environments. Virtualization is often considered more secure, since the application is contained inside a virtual hardware environment, which is serviced by a hypervisor outside the VM's execution environment. Having a clear boundary between the hypervisor and the virtual machine creates the smallest surface area of the two.

Shared kernel environments, like those used in containerized or application policy systems, provide some isolation guarantees, but not to the same degree as a fully virtualized system. A shared kernel execution environment uses fewer resources to run the same set of applications, and is therefore gaining favor in cost-conscious organizations. As virtualization tries to address the resource-efficiency problem, by providing more direct access to the underlying hardware, the security benefits of the virtualized environment begin to look more like the shared kernel environment. Depending on your threat model, you may choose to not share hardware at all.

Active Monitoring

As with any production system, careful monitoring and logging is of the utmost importance, and is particularly critical in the context of security. Traditional security models focus their attention on external attack vectors. Zero trust networks encourage the same level of rigor for internal activity. Early detection of an attack could be the difference between complete compromise and prevention altogether.

Apart from the general logging of security events throughout the infrastructure such as failed or successful logins, which is considered passive monitoring, there exists an entire class of active monitoring as well. For instance, the fuzzing scans we previously discussed can take time to turn up new vulnerabilities—perhaps more time than you're willing to spend early on in the release pipeline. An active monitoring strategy advocates that the scans also be run against production, continuously.

Don't Do That in Production!

Occasionally, the desire to take certain actions in production can be met with resistance for fear of impacting availability or stability of the overall system. Security scans frequently fall into this bucket. In reality, if a security scan can destabilize your system, then there is a greater underlying problem, which might even be a vulnerability in and of itself. Rather than avoiding potentially dangerous scans in production, ask why they might be risky, and work to ensure that they can be run safely by resolving any system deficiencies contributing to the concern.

Of course, fuzzing is just one example. Automated scanning can be a useful tool for ensuring consistent behavior in a system. For example, a database of anticipated listening services could be compared against an automated scan of actual listening services so deviations can be addressed. Not all scanning will result in such clear action, however. Scanning of installed software, for example, will typically be used to drive prioritization of upgrades based on the threats a network is exposed to or expects to see.

Effective system scanning requires multiple types of scanner, each of which inspects the system in a slightly different manner:

- Fuzzing (i.e., afl-fuzz)
- Injection scanning (i.e., sqlmap)
- Network port scanning (i.e., nmap)
- Common vulnerability scanning (i.e., nessus)

So, what to do when all this monitoring actually discovers something? The answer typically depends on the strength of the signal. Traditionally, suspicious (but not critical) events get dumped into reports and periodically reviewed. This practice is by far the least effective, as it can lead to report fatigue, with reports going unnoticed for weeks at a time. Alternatively, important events can page a human for active investigation. These events have a strong enough signal to warrant waking someone up. In most cases, this is the strongest line of defense.

Applications Monitoring Applications

One novel idea in the context of application security monitoring is the idea that applications participating in a single cluster or service can actively monitor the health of their peers, and gain consensus with others on their sanity. This might manifest itself as TPM quotes, behavioral analysis, and everything in between. By allowing applications to monitor each other, you gain a high signal-to-noise ratio while at the same time distributing the responsibility throughout the infrastructure. This approach most effectively guards against side-channel attacks, or attacks enabled through multitenancy, since these vectors are less likely to be shared across the entire cluster.

In highly automated environments, however, a third option opens up: active response. Strong signals that "something is wrong" can trigger automated actions in the infrastructure. This could mean revoking keys belonging to the suspicious instance, booting it out of cluster membership, or even signaling to datacenter management software that the instance should be moved offline and isolated for forensics.

Of course, as with any high-level automation, one can do a lot of damage very quickly when utilizing active responses. It is possible to introduce denial-of-service attacks with such mechanisms, or perhaps more likely, shut down a service as a result of operator error. When designing active response systems, it is important to put a number of fail-safes in place. For instance, an active response that ejects a host from a cluster should not fire if the cluster size is dangerously low. Being thoughtful about building active response limitations such as this goes a long way in ensuring the sanity of the active response process itself.

Summary

This chapter dove into how applications in a zero trust network are secured. It might seem counter-intuitive that a zero trust network needs to be concerned with application security. After all, the network is untrusted so untrustworthy applications existing on the network should be expected. However, while the network works to detect and identify malicious application activity, that goal is made impossible if deployed applications are not properly vetted before being authorized to run. As a result, most of this chapter focused on how to securely develop, build and deploy applications in a zero trust network, and then monitor the running instances to ensure that they stay trustworthy.

The chapter introduced the concept of a trusted application pipeline, which is the mechanism by which software written by trusted developers is transformed into built applications that are then deployed into infrastructure. This pipeline is a highly valuable target for would-be attackers, and so it deserves special attention. We dug into secure source code hosting practices, sound practices for turning source code into trusted artifacts, and securely selecting and distributing those artifacts to downstream consumers. The application pipeline can be visualized as a series of immutable transformations on input from earlier in the pipeline, so we explored how to meet the goals of that pipeline without introducing too much friction in the process.

Human attention is a scarce but important resource in a secure system. With the rate of software releases ever increasing, it's important to mindfully consider when humans are best introduced in the proces. We discussed where to put humans in the loop to ensure that the pipeline remains secure.

Once applications are built, the process of securing their continued execution in a production environment shifts a bit. Old trusted applications may in the future become untrusted as vulnerabilities are discovered, so we discussed the importance of an upgrade-only policy when running applications. Secrets management is often a difficult task for security engineers, where changing credentials is often very burdensome. With a smooth credential provisioning process, however, a new opportunity emerges to frequently rotate credentials, using the credentialing process itself as a mechanism for ensuring only authorized applications continue to run in a production environment.

We ended the chapter with a section discussing good application security hygiene. Learning secure coding practices, deploying applications in isolated environments, and then monitoring them aggressively is the final leg in a trustworthy production environment.

With all the components of a zero trust network explored, the next chapter focuses on how network communication itself is secured.

CHAPTER 8

Trusting the Traffic

Authenticating and authorizing network flows is a critical aspect of a zero trust network. In this chapter, we're going to discuss how encryption fits into the picture, how to bootstrap flow trust by way of secure introduction, and where in your network these security protocols best fit.

Zero trust is not a *complete* departure from everything we know. Traditional network filtering still plays a significant role in zero trust networks, though its application is nontraditional. We'll explore the role filtering plays in these networks toward the end of this chapter.

Encryption Versus Authentication

Encryption and authenticity often go hand in hand, yet serve distinctly separate purposes. Encryption ensures confidentiality—the promise that only the receiver can read the data you send. Authentication enables a receiver to validate that the message was sent by the thing it is claiming to be.

Authentication comes with another interesting property. In order to ensure that a message is in fact authentic, you must be able to validate the sender and that the message is unaltered. Referred to as *integrity*, this is an essential property of message authentication.

Encryption is possible without authentication, though this is considered a poor security practice. Without validation of the sender, an attacker is free to forge messages, possibly replaying previous "good" messages. An attacker could change the ciphertext, and the receiver would have no way of knowing. There are a number of vectors opened by the omission of authentication, so the recommendation is pretty much the same across the board: use it.

Authenticity Without Encryption?

Message authenticity is a stated requirement of a zero trust network, and it is not possible to build one without it. But what about encryption?

Encryption brings confidentiality, but it can also be an occasional nuisance. Troubleshooting becomes harder when you can't read packet captures without complicated decryption processes. Intrusion detection becomes difficult to impossible if the network traffic can't be inspected. There are, in fact, some legitimate reasons to avoid encryption.

That said, be absolutely certain that you do not care about data confidentiality if you choose to not use encryption. While keeping data unencrypted is convenient for administrators, it is never legitimate if the data actually requires confidentiality. For instance, consider the scenario shown in Figure 8-1.

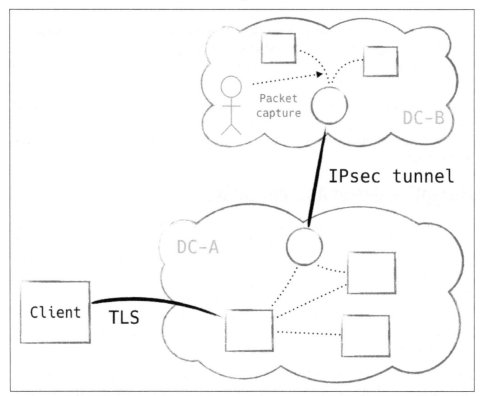

Figure 8-1. Confidentiality within the datacenter is just as important as outside the datacenter

This is an exceedingly common architecture. Note that it only encrypts traffic in certain areas, leaving the rest open (perhaps for the benefit of system administrators).

Clearly, however, this data requires confidentiality, as it is encrypted in transit between sites.

This is a direct contradiction of the zero trust architecture, as it creates privileged zones in the network. Thus, citing good reasons to not encrypt traffic is a very slippery slope. In practice, systems that truly do not require confidentiality are rare.

In addition to all of this, authentication is still required. There are few network protocols which provide strong authentication but not encryption, and all of the transport protocols we discuss in this book provide authentication as well as encryption. If you look at it this way, encryption is attained "for free," leaving few good reasons to exclude it.

Bootstrapping Trust: The First Packet

The first packet in a flow is oftentimes an onerous one. Depending on the type of connection, or point of the device lifecycle, this packet can carry with it very little trust.

We generally know what flows to expect inside the datacenter, but in client-facing systems, it's anyone's guess. These systems must be widely reachable, which greatly increases risk. We can use protocols like mutually authenticated TLS to authenticate the device before it is allowed to access the service; however, the attack surface in this scenario is still considerable, and the resources are also publicly discoverable.

So how do you allow only trusted connections, silently dropping all others, without answering a single unauthenticated packet? This is known as the *first packet problem*, and it is mitigated through a method called *pre-authentication* (Figure 8-2).

Pre-authentication can be thought of as the authorizing of an authentication request by setting an expectation for it. It is often accomplished by encrypting and/or signing a small piece of data and sending it to the resource as a UDP packet. The use of UDP for pre-authentication is important because UDP packets do not receive a response by default. This property allows us to "hide," exposing ourselves only once we passively receive a packet encrypted with the right key.

Upon the passive receipt of a properly encrypted pre-authentication packet, we know we can expect the sender to begin authentication with us, and we can poke granular firewall holes allowing only the sender the ability to speak with our TLS server. This mode of pre-authentication operation is also known as *Single Packet Authorization* (SPA).

SPA is not a fully suited device authentication protocol. It merely helps to mitigate the first packet problem. Without downplaying the importance of the properties we gain by using pre-authentication, it must not be substituted for a more robust mutually authenticating protocol like TLS or IKE.

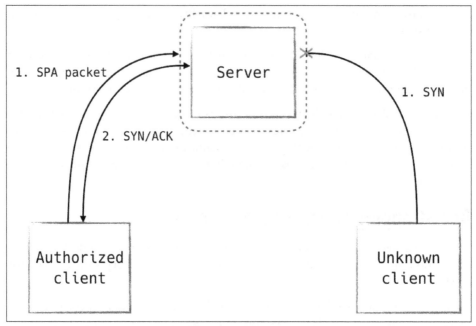

Figure 8-2. A client in possession of the pre-authorization key can send a signed packet in order to set an expectation for a TCP connection. Without it, no acknowledgments are sent.

fwknop

fwknop (*http://www.cipherdyne.org/fwknop/*) is a popular open source SPA implementation. It supports a wide variety of operating systems, and integrates directly with host firewalls to coordinate the creation of tightly scoped and short-lived exceptions.

Short-lived exceptions

When fwknop receives a valid SPA packet, its contents are decrypted and inspected. The decrypted payload includes protocol and port numbers which the sender is requesting access to. fwknop uses this to create firewall rules permitting traffic from the sender to those particular ports—rules that are removed after a configurable period of time. The default value is 30 seconds, but in practice, you may only need just a few seconds.

As mentioned, the rule which fwknop creates is tightly scoped. It permits only the sender's IP address and only the destination ports requested by the sender. The destination ports which may be requested can be restricted via policy on a user-by-user basis. Additionally, it is possible for the sender to specify a source port, restricting the scope of the rule even further.

SPA payload

The fwknop SPA implementation has seven mandatory fields and three optional fields included in its payload. Among these are a username, the access request itself (which port, etc.), a timestamp, and a checksum:

- 16 bytes of random data
- Local username
- Local timestamp
- fwknop version
- SPA message type
- Access request
- SPA message digest (SHA-256 by default)

Once the client has generated the payload, it is encrypted, an optional HMAC is added, and the SPA packet is formed and transmitted.

Payload encryption

Two modes of encryption are supported: *AES* and *GnuPG*. The former being symmetric and the latter being asymmetric, two options are provided in order to cater to multiple use cases and preferences.

Personal applications or small installations might prefer AES since it does not require any GnuPG tooling. AES is also more performant with regard to data volume and computational overhead. It does have some downsides though, practically all of which originate from the fact that it is a symmetric algorithm.

Symmetric encryption comes with difficult key distribution problems, and beyond a certain scale, these challenges can grow to be untenable. Leveraging the GnuPG encryption mode solves most of these problems and is the recommended mode of operation, despite being less performant than its counterpart.

HMAC

fwknop can be configured to add an *HMAC* to the end of its payload. A *hashed message authentication code* (HMAC) prevents tampering by guaranteeing that the message is authentic. This is important because otherwise an attacker could arbitrarily modify the ciphertext, and the receiver would be forced to process it.

You may have noticed that there is a message digest which is calculated and stored along with the plain text. This digest helps to mitigate attacks in which the ciphertext is modified, but is also less than ideal, as this method (known as *authenticate-then-encrypt* or *AtE*) is vulnerable to a few niche classes of attacks. Adding an HMAC to the encrypted payload prevents these attacks from being effective.

In addition, decryption routines are generally much more complex than HMAC routines, meaning they are more likely to suffer from a vulnerability. Applying an HMAC to the ciphertext allows the receiver to perform a lightweight integrity check, helping to ensure that we are only sending trusted data to the decryption routines.

It is strongly recommended to configure fwknop to use HMAC.

A Brief Introduction to Network Models

Networking stacks have many different responsibilities in transmitting data over a network. As such, it would be easy for a networking stack to become a jumbled mess of code. Therefore, the industry long ago decided to spend the effort to clearly define a set of standardized layers in a networking stack. Each layer is responsible for some portion of the job of transmitting data over the wire. Lower layers deliver functionality and guarantees to higher layers in the stack.

Building up these layers isn't just useful for organizing code. These layer definitions are often used to describe where new technology operates in the stack. For example, you might have heard of a layer 7 or layer 4 load balancer. A load balancer distributes traffic load across a set of backend machines, but the layer at which it operates greatly determines its capabilities. A layer 7 load balancer, for example, can make decisions about where to route traffic based on details in an HTTP request like the requested path or a particular header. HTTP operates at layer 7, so this data is available to inspect. A layer 4 load balancer, by contrast, does not consider layer 7 data and therefore can only pass traffic based on simpler connection details like the source IP and port.

There are many different network models. Most of these models can be roughly mapped to equivalents in other network models, but sometimes the boundaries can be a bit fuzzy. For this book, we will only focus on two network models: the *OSI* network model and the *TCP/IP* network model. Understanding the boundaries of these two models will help in later discussions about where zero trust responsibilities should be handled in the network model.

Network Layers, Visually

The idea of a layer might be strange at first, though a simplistic way to understand the concept is by comparing them to Russian nesting dolls. Each layer typically contains the next, encapsulated by it in a section known as the *payload* (Figure 8-3).

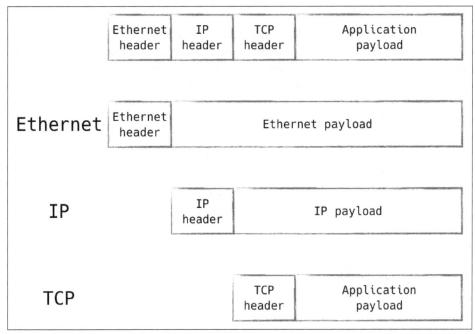

Figure 8-3. Lower network layers transport higher-layer traffic in their payload fields, creating a nested structure inside a single packet

OSI Network Model

The OSI network model was published in 1984 after being merged from two separate documents started several years earlier. The model is published by two separate standards bodies: the International Organization for Standardization (ISO) published ISO 7498, while the Telecommunications Standardization Sector of the International Telecommunication Union (ITU-T) published X.200.

The model itself is extracted from the experiences building several networks at the time, ARPANET being the most well known. The model defines seven distinct layers (explained in the following sections), each of which owns a portion of the responsibilities for transmitting data.

Layer 1—Physical Layer

The physical layer is defined as the interface between a network device and the physical medium over which network transmission occurs. This can include things like pin layout, line impedance, voltage, and frequency. The parameters of the physical layer (sometimes referred to as a PHY) depend on the kind of medium used. Twisted pair, coaxial cabling, and radio waves are examples of mediums in common use today.

Layer 2—Data Link Layer

The data link layer is responsible for the transmission of data over the physical layer. This layer only considers data transmission between directly connected nodes. There is no concept of transmission between interconnected networks. Ethernet (802.3) is the most well-known protocol operating at this layer.

Layer 3—Network Layer

The network layer is responsible for transmitting data packets between two interconnected nodes. At this layer, packets might need to transverse multiple layer 2 segments to reach their destination, so this includes concepts to allow routing data to its destination by inspecting a destination address. IP is often said to operate at this layer, but the boundaries can be a bit fuzzy, as we will explore later.

Layer 4—Transport Layer

The transport layer builds upon the simple packet transmission capabilities of layer 3, usually as an intermediary protocol designed to augment layer 3 with many desirable services:

- Stateful connections
- Multiplexing
- Ordered delivery
- Flow control
- Retransmission

These services might look similar to the services that a protocol like TCP provides. In fact, TCP is a layer 4 protocol; however, in a way similar to IP, this association can be a bit awkward.

Not all of these services need to be provided by a protocol operating at this level. UDP, for example, is a layer 4 protocol which offers only one of these services (multiplexing). It remains a layer 4 protocol because it is an intermediary protocol which is directly encapsulated by layer 3.

Layer 5—Session Layer

The session layer isn't commonly discussed in most networks. This layer provides an additional layer of state over connections, allowing for a communication resumption and communication through an intermediary. Several VPN (PPTP, L2TP) and proxy protocols (SOCKS) operate at this layer.

Layer 6—Presentation Layer

The presentation layer is the layer that application developers will most commonly interact with. This layer is responsible for handling the translation between application data (often represented as structural data) and transmittable data streams. In addition to this serialization responsibility, this layer is often responsible for cross-cutting concerns like encryption and compression. TLS is a well-known protocol operating at this layer, though it operates at layer 6 only after the session is established (which happens at layer 5—the process of changing from a lower layer to a higher layer is sometimes referred to as an *upgrade*).

Layer 7—Application Layer

The application layer is the highest layer in the OSI model. This layer provides the high-level communication protocols that an application uses to communicate on the network. Some common protocols at this layer are DNS, HTTP, and SSH.

TCP/IP Network Model

The TCP/IP network model is another important network model. This model deals with the protocols most often found on the internet today.

Unlike the OSI model, the TCP/IP model does not try to define strict layers with clear boundaries. In fact, RFC 3439 (*https://www.ietf.org/rfc/rfc3439.txt*), which documents the "philosophical guidelines" that internet architects use has a section entitled "Layering Considered Harmful." Still, the model is said to define the following rough layers, from lowest to highest:

- Link layer
- Internet layer
- Transport layer
- Application layer

These layers can be roughly mapped to the OSI model, but the mappings are only best effort. The application layer roughly covers layers 5–7 in the OSI model. The transport layer roughly maps to layer 4, though its introduction of the concept of a port gives it some layer 5 characteristics. The internet layer is similarly generally associated with layer 3. The abstraction is leaky, however, as higher-level protocols like ICMP (which are transmitted via IP) concern themselves with details of how traffic is routed around the internet.

Where Should Zero Trust Be in the Network Model?

With a better understanding of network layer models, we can now take a look at where to best apply zero trust controls in the network stack.

There are two predominant network security suites: *TLS* and *IPsec*. TLS (Transport Layer Security, to which SSL is a predecessor) is the most common of the two. Many application layer protocols support TLS to secure traffic. IPsec is an alternative proto-col, more commonly used to secure things like VPNs.

Despite having "transport" in its name, TLS does not live in the transport layer of the TCP/IP model. It is found in the application layer (somewhere between layer 5 and 6 in the OSI model), and as such, is largely an application concern.

TLS as an Infrastructure Concern

Perimeter networks frequently abstract TLS away from applica-tions, shifting the responsibility from the application to the infra-structure. In this mode, TLS is "terminated" by a dedicated device at the perimeter, forwarding the decrypted traffic to a backend ser-vice. While this mode of operation is not possible in a zero trust network, there remain a handful of strategies for deploying TLS as an infrastructure concern while still conforming to the zero trust model. More on that later.

IPsec, by contrast, is generally considered part of the internet layer in the TCP/IP model (layer 3 or 4 in the OSI model, depending on interpretation). Being further down the stack, IPsec is usually implemented in a host's kernel. IPsec was developed for the IPv6 specification. It was originally a requirement for IPv6, but was eventually downgraded to a recommended status.

With two alternatives to secure network transit, the question becomes, is one prefer-red over the other? Zero trust's goal is secure communication for all traffic. The best way to accomplish this goal is to build systems that provide secure communication by default. IPsec, being a low-level service, is well positioned to provide this service.

Using IPsec, host-to-host communication can be definitively secured. Being integra-ted deep in the network stack, IPsec can be configured to only allow packet transmis-sion once a secure communication channel has been established. Furthermore, the receiving side can be configured to only process packets that have been sent securely. In this system, we have essentially created a "secure virtual wire" between two hosts over which only secured traffic can flow. This is a huge benefit over traditional secu-rity initiatives that add secure communication one application at a time.

Simply securing communications between two devices is not sufficient to build a zero trust network. We need to ensure that each individual network flow is authorized. There are several options for meeting this need:

- IPsec can use a unique security association (SA) per application (see RFC 4301, section 4.4.1.1 (*https://tools.ietf.org/html/rfc4301#section-4.4.1.1*)). Only author-ized flows are then allowed to construct these security policies.

- Filtering systems (software firewalls) can be layered on top of IPsec. We will discuss the role of filtering in zero trust later in this chapter.
- Application-level authorization should be used to ensure that communications are authorized. This could use standard authorization techniques, such as access tokens or X.509 certificates, while delegating strong encryption and authentication responsibilities to the IPsec stack.
- For a truly "belt and suspenders" system, mutually authenticated TLS could be layered on top of the existing IPsec layer. This defense-in-depth approach provides two layers of encryption (mTLS and IPsec), protecting communication should one of them being compromised, at the expense of complexity and increased overhead.

Client and Server Split

While IPsec has a number of beneficial properties, its lack of popularity presents real-world obstacles for its use in systems today. The issues one will see can be broken down into three areas:

- Network support issues
- Device support issues
- Application support issues

Network support issues

Network support can hamper the use of IPsec in the wild. IPsec introduces several new protocols, two of which (ESP and AH) are new IP protocols. While these protocols are fully supported in simple LAN networks, on some networks, getting these packets transmitted can be quite a challenge. This could be due to misconfigured firewalls, NAT traversal, or routers being purposefully configured to not allow traffic to flow. For example, Amazon Web Services, a large public cloud provider, does not allow ESP or AH traffic to be transmitted on its networks. Public hotspots like those found at businesses or libraries also often have spotty support for IPsec traffic.

To mitigate these issues, IPsec includes support for encapsulating traffic in a UDP frame (depicted in Figure 8-4). This encapsulation allows an inhospitable network to transmit the traffic, but it adds extra complexity to the system.

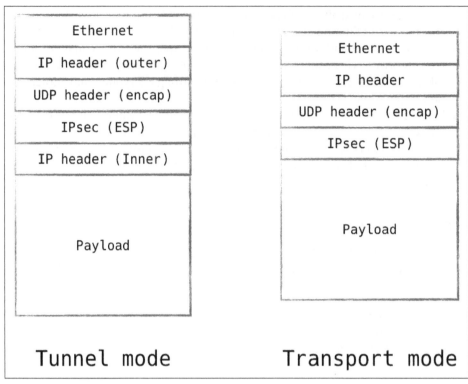

Ethernet	
IP header (outer)	Ethernet
UDP header (encap)	IP header
IPsec (ESP)	UDP header (encap)
IP header (Inner)	IPsec (ESP)
Payload	Payload

Tunnel mode   **Transport mode**

Figure 8-4. IPsec supports encapsulating ESP packets in a UDP packet, making it look like normal UDP traffic

Device support issues

Device support can also be a major factor in rolling out an IPsec-protected network. The IPsec standard is complex, with many configuration options and cipher suites. Both hosts in the relationship need to agree to a common protocol and cipher suite before communication can flow. Cipher suites in particular frequently need to be adjusted as compromises are revealed. Finding that a stronger cipher suite has not been implemented is a real issue in IPsec systems. To be fair, TLS needs to handle these same issues; but due to the nature of having IPsec implemented in the system's kernel, progress on newer protocols and cipher suites is naturally slower.

IPsec also requires active configuration of the devices in the relationship. In a client/server system with varying device capabilities, configuring the client devices can be rather challenging. Desktop operating systems can usually be configured to support the less popular protocol. Mobile operating systems, however, are less likely to fully support IPsec in a way that conforms to the zero trust model.

Application support issues

IPsec places additional requirements on the system configuration versus typical TLS-based security. A system wanting to make use of IPsec needs to configure IPsec policy, enable kernel support for the desired cipher suites, and run an IKE daemon to facilitate the negotiation of IPsec security associations. When compared to a library-based approach for TLS, this extra complexity can be daunting. This is doubly so when many applications already come with built-in TLS support, which seemingly offers a turnkey solution for network security.

It should be noted that while the library approach seems more attractive on first glance, in practice it presents quite a bit of hidden complexity. Being a library, applications need to expose configuration controls to the TLS library. Applications frequently support the more common server TLS, but neglect to expose configuration for presenting a client certificate that is required to create a mutually authenticated TLS connection. Additionally, system administrators may need to adjust configuration in reaction to recently exposed vulnerability. With a large set of applications, finding the application-specific configuration that needs to be adjusted can hamper the rollout of a critical fix.

The web browser is frequently the common access point into organizational systems. Its support for modern TLS is generally very good (assuming organizations stay up to date on the latest browser versions). This common access point mitigates the issue of configuration, as there is a small set of target applications that need to be adjusted.

On the server side, many organizations are turning toward a model where network communication is secured via a local daemon. This approach centralizes configuration in a single application and allows for a base layer of network security to be supplied by the system administrator. In a way, it looks very similar to the IPsec model, but implemented using TLS instead.

A pragmatic approach

Given all the pluses and minuses of the two approaches, a pragmatic solution seems available to system administrators.

For client/server interactions, mutually authenticated TLS seems to be the most reasonable approach to network security. This approach would typically involve configuring a browser to present client certificates to server-side access proxies which will ensure that the connection is authenticated and authorized. Of course, this restricts the use of zero trust to browser-based applications.

For server/server interactions, IPsec seems more approachable. The server fleet is generally under more controlled configuration, and the network environment is more well known. For networks which don't support IPsec, UDP encapsulation can be used to avoid network transit issues.

Microsoft Server Isolation

For environments which fully employ Microsoft Windows with Active Directory, a feature called *server isolation* is particularly attractive. By leveraging Windows Firewall, Network Policy, and Group Policy, server isolation provides a framework through which IPsec configuration can be automated. Furthermore, server isolation can be tied to Active Directory security groups, providing fine-grained access control which is backed by strong IPsec authentication.

While complications surrounding IPsec transit over public networks still exist, server isolation is perhaps the most pragmatic approach for obtaining zero trust semantics in a Windows-based environment.

Since the IPv6 standard includes IPsec, the authors hope that it will become a more viable solution for both types of network communication as network adoption progresses.

The Protocols

We learned about mutually authenticated TLS and IPsec in the previous section, as well as when you might use one versus the other. In this section, we'll discuss the two protocols in detail. It is very important to understand the inner workings of these protocols as you deploy them, since there are many configuration controls in them. Both are complicated in their own right, and insecure configurations are common.

IKE/IPsec

Internet Key Exchange (IKE) is a protocol which performs the authentication and key exchange components of IPsec. It is typically implemented as a daemon and uses a pre-shared key or an X.509 certificate to authenticate a peer and create a secure session. Inside this secure session, another key exchange is made. The results of this second key exchange are then used to set up an IPsec security association, the parameters of which are leveraged for bulk data transfer. Let's take a closer look.

IKEv1 Versus IKEv2

There are two versions of IKE, and most software suites support both. For all new deployments, it is strongly recommended to use IKEv2. It is both more flexible and more reliable than its predecessor, which was overly complicated and less performant. For the purposes of this book, we will be talking about IKEv2 exclusively.

IKE and IPsec

There is frequent confusion around the relationship between IKE and IPsec. The reality is that IPsec is not a single protocol; it is a collection of protocols. IKE is often considered part of the IPsec protocol suite, though its design makes it feel complimentary as opposed to a core component. IKE can be thought of as the control plane of IPsec. It handles session negotiation and authentication, using the results of the negotiation to configure the endpoints with session keys and encryption algorithms.

Since the core IPsec protocols are embedded in the IP stack, IPsec implementations are typically found in the kernel. With key exchange being a relatively complex mechanism, IKE is implemented as a user space daemon. The kernel holds state defining active IPsec security associations, and traffic selectors defining which packets IPsec policy should be applied to. The IKE daemon handles everything else, including the negotiation of the IPsec security association (SA) itself (which is subsequently installed into the kernel for use).

Authentication credentials

IKEv2 supports both pre-shared keys and X.509 public/private key pairs. In addition, it supports the Extensible Authentication Protocol (EAP). Supporting EAP means that IKEv2 supports a bevy of other authentication methods (including support for multifactor authentication) by proxy. We will avoid analyzing EAP directly, however, as the ecosystem is very large.

It goes without saying that X.509 certificates are the preferred method of authentication for IKE. While pre-shared keys are supported, we strongly recommend against them. They present major distribution and generation challenges, but most importantly, they are meant for *humans* to *remember.*

X.509 certificates are not meant for humans; they're meant for devices. They carry with them not only proof of trust, but also signed metadata and a way to strongly encrypt data using its identity. These are powerful properties, and the reason certificates are the undisputed champion of device authentication credentials.

IKE SA_INIT and AUTH

All IKEv2 exchanges begin with a pair of packets named IKE_SA_INIT. This initial exchange handles cryptographic suite selection, as well as a Diffie–Hellman exchange. The Diffie–Hellman key exchange provides a method for two systems to negotiate a session key without ever transmitting it.

The resulting session key is used to encrypt fields in the next pair of messages: the IKE_AUTH packets. In this step, the endpoints exchange certificates and generate what is known as a CHILD_SA. The CHILD_SA contains the IPsec parameters for a security association between the two endpoints, and the IKE daemon then programs these parameters into the kernel. From this point forward, the kernel will encrypt all traffic matching the selectors.

Cipher suite selection

Cipher choice with IPsec is slightly less trivial than TLS. This is because IPsec is implemented in the kernel, making cipher support a little more stringent than it would be if it were simply a software package. As a result, a wide variety of devices and operating system versions will complicate IPsec deployments.

RFC 6379 (*https://tools.ietf.org/html/rfc6379*) sets forth what is known as the *Suite B Cryptographic Suite*. It was authored by the US National Security Agency, and is (at the time of this writing) a widely accepted standard when it comes to selecting IPsec cipher suites.

Much like TLS, IKE cipher suites include algorithms for key exchange, bulk encryption, and integrity. Unlike TLS, it does not include authentication, as IKE takes care of that outside of the crypto suite selection.

RFC 6379 is fairly prescriptive with regard to these choices. All of the suites defined in Suite B leverage varying strengths of the AES encryption algorithm and the ECDH key agreement protocol. They leverage GCM and SHA for integrity. For the majority of use cases, Suite B is recommended.

There are a couple instances in which Suite B might not be appropriate. The first is that not all IPsec implementations support elliptic curve cryptography, which is mandated. The second is concern around the security of popularized elliptic curve implementations, as many believe that state actors have interfered with them in order to subvert the security they aim to provide.

In consideration of either of these cases, equivalent-strength DH is recommended as a good alternative.

IPsec security associations

IPsec security associations (SAs) are the end result of an IKE negotiation and describe what is sometimes referred to as a "relationship" with the remote endpoint. They are unidirectional, so for a relationship between two endpoints, you will normally find two SAs (inbound and outbound).

An IPsec SA is uniquely identified by an SPI (Security Parameter Index, not to be confused with an IKE SPI) and has a limited lifetime. As traffic traverses the IP stack, the kernel finds packets matching the selector(s) and checks to see if there is an active security association for the selector in question. If there is an entry, the kernel encrypts the packet according to the parameters defined in the SA, and transmits it. If there is no entry, the kernel will signal the IKE daemon to negotiate one.

An IPsec SA has four distinct states in its lifecycle: larval, mature, dying, and dead.

A *larval* SA is one that is still being negotiated by the IKE daemon and has only part of its state installed. Once the negotiation is complete, the SA progresses to the *mature* state, in which it begins encrypting traffic. As the SA nears the end of its lifetime, a new SA is negotiated and installed with the same policy. The original SA progresses to the *dying* state, and all relevant traffic switches over to the new SA. After some time, the old SA expires and is marked as *dead*.

IPsec tunnel mode versus transport mode

IPsec supports two modes of operation, *tunnel mode* and *transport mode* (Figure 8-5). Tunnel mode is by far the most widely deployed variant. When IPsec operates in tunnel mode, an SA is formed with the remote endpoint which is used to encapsulate IP packets and secure it en route to the endpoint. This encapsulation covers the entirety of the IP packet, including the IP header. This means that in tunnel mode, the IPsec endpoint can be different than the endpoint for which the IP traffic is destined, since a new IP header will be exposed once the protected traffic is unpacked.

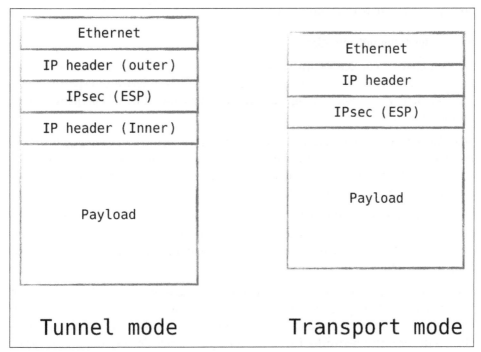

Figure 8-5. IPsec tunnel mode allows traffic from one network to be tunneled into another

This is why it is called tunnel mode. It is frequently used in VPNs, where one wishes to make a secure connection to a remote network, enabling administrators to tunnel flows destined for that network through the secure channel. This brings an interesting realization though in the world of zero trust networks: tunnel mode, by its very nature, strongly implies that the traffic will become *unprotected* at some point in time. Security is ensured between the sender and a network intermediary, but after that all bets are off. It is the opinion of the authors that, for this reason, the use of tunnel mode contradicts the zero trust architecture.

Transport mode, on the other hand, offers practically identical security guarantees, just minus the tunnel part. Instead of encapsulating an entire IP packet, it encapsulates only the IP payload. This is useful for direct host-to-host IP communication. Rather than establishing a security association with an intermediary network device, transport mode establishes a security association directly with the endpoint to which the traffic is addressed, ensuring security is applied end to end. This property allows transport mode to fit nicely into the zero trust model.

While transport mode is the obvious choice for a full-blown zero trust datacenter architecture, it is important to remain realistic. Zero trust migrations are difficult, and IPsec tunnel mode is still a tool which can be leveraged along the journey to a homogeneous zero trust architecture.

IKE/IPsec for device authentication

When it comes to device security in a zero trust network, we are looking to provide not only authentication for the device, but also device-to-device transport security. This is exactly what IPsec is designed to do, and the reason that it is perhaps the best protocol for the job.

Since IPsec is implemented directly on top of IP, it can handle most application traffic, not just TCP or UDP. Additionally, since it is implemented in the kernel, the applications being protected need no knowledge of the underlying security. They simply run as they would normally, and the traffic gets encrypted "for free."

This encryption and authenticity may come "for free" from the perspective of the application, but that is certainly not the case for the device! As you can see, the configuration of IPsec is nontrivial, and managing the multitude of policies can be challenging (or impossible without automation).

Another consideration is how widely supported IPsec is as a network protocol. Not all public networks (e.g., coffee shops) support IPsec and may even actively block it. Difficulty in configuration and lack of universal support make IPsec less desirable for client-side zero trust networks. However, those pain points don't typically exist inside the datacenter, where IPsec remains a front contender with regard to device security protocols.

Mutually Authenticated TLS

Commonly referred to by the name of its predecessor, Transport Layer Security (TLS) is the protocol most commonly used to secure web traffic. It is a mature and well-understood protocol, is widely deployed and supported, and is already trusted with some of the most sensitive tasks, like banking transactions. It is the "S" in HTTPS.

When TLS is used to secure web sessions, the client validates that the server certificate is valid, but the server rarely validates the client. In fact, the client rarely presents a certificate at all! The "mutual" prefix for TLS is meant to denote a TLS configuration in which client certificate validation is required (and thus, mutually authenticated).

While a lack of client authentication may be acceptable for services that are being published to the general public, it is not acceptable for any other use case. Mutual authentication is a requirement for security protocols conforming to the zero trust model, and TLS is no exception.

The basics of a TLS handshake are fairly straightforward, as shown in Figure 8-6. A client initiates the session with a ClientHello message sent to the server, which includes a compatibility list for things like cipher suites and compression methods. The server chooses parameters from the compatibility list and replies with a Server-Hello defining the selections it made, followed by the server's X.509 certificate. It also requests the client's certificate at this time.

The client then generates a secret key and uses the server's public key to encrypt it. It sends the server this encrypted secret key, as well as its client certificate, and a small bit of proof that it is in fact the owner of that certificate. The secret key generated by the client is ultimately used to derive several additional keys, including one which acts as a symmetric session key. So, once the client sends these details off, it has enough information to set up its side of the encrypted session. It signals the server that it is switching to session encryption, the server validates the client, sends a similar message in return, and the session is fully upgraded.

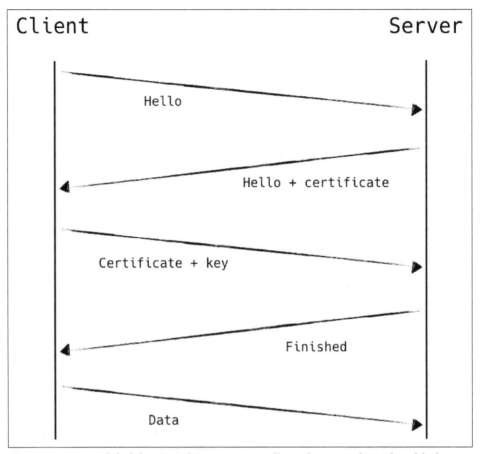

Figure 8-6. A simplified diagram showing a mutually authenticated TLS handshake using RSA key exchange

Cipher suite negotiation and selection

TLS supports many different kinds of authentication and encryption. A cipher suite is a named combination of these components. There are four primary components in a TLS cipher suite:

- Key exchange
- Authentication
- Bulk encryption
- Message authenticity

Choosing the right set of supported cipher suites is important in ensuring your TLS deployments remain secure. Many cipher suites are known to be weak. At the same time, the strongest cipher suites are poorly supported among clients in the wild.

Who gets to say. During the TLS handshake, the client presents its list of supported cipher suites in order of preference. The server gets to choose one from this list, assuming that there is shared support at all, in which case the session will fail to establish. While the client gets to communicate its cipher preferences to the server, it is ultimately the server which is allowed to choose. This is important because it preserves the client/server, consumer/operator relationship.

With this, the overall security of the system is limited to the strongest negotiable cipher suite of the weakest client. Historically, many online resources support weak cipher suites in a bid to maintain backward compatibility with older clients. Knowing this, there have been many attacks against cipher suite negotiation, including downgrade attacks which enable an attacker to actively weaken the encryption algorithm used by a client.

As a result, it is recommended that servers support only the strongest set of cipher suites that is reasonable. In the case of datacenter deployments, this list might be limited to only a few approved suites, as there is strict control over the "clients." This is not always reasonable for true client-facing deployments, however.

Negotiation as a Weakness

Cipher suite negotiation is, for the stated reasons, considered an anti-pattern in modern cryptographic protocols. Newer protocols and frameworks such as Noise aim to eliminate protocol negotiation. Work in this area is highly active at the time of this writing, and the authors look forward to widespread adoption of cryptographic protocols which lack weaknesses such as this one.

Key exchange. The TLS key exchange describes the process for securely generating an encryption key over an insecure channel. Sometimes described as a key agreement or exchange protocols, these protocols use mathematical functions to agree on keys without ever transmitting them in the clear (or in most cases, at all).

There are three primary key exchange/agreement protocols in popular use with TLS. They are, in rough order of preference: *ECDHE*, *DHE*, and *RSA*.

ECDHE is based on a Diffie–Hellman exchange, using elliptic curves to agree on a key. Elliptic curve cryptography is very strong, efficient, and is based on a mathematical problem which remains difficult to solve. It is the ideal choice for security and performance considerations.

DHE is also based on a Diffie–Hellman exchange, except it uses modular arithmetic to agree on a key, rather than elliptic curves. In order for these exchanges to be strong, they require larger keys than ECDHE. This is because the math involved for regular DHE is well solved, and we are getting better and better at solving those problems. So, while DHE can provide security similar to that of ECDHE, it is less performant in doing so.

RSA key exchange is based on the same asymmetric operations that prove identity for digital signatures (e.g., X.509 certificates). It uses the public key of the server to encrypt the shared secret for transmission. This key exchange protocol is widely supported, although it has two primary limitations: it requires use of RSA-based authentication, and it does not provide perfect forward secrecy.

Quantum Vulnerability

The security of practically all public key cryptography in popular use today is based on the assumption that factoring large numbers is a hard, computationally expensive problem. This assumption, however, is invalid when considering quantum computation. Classical computing must rely on a technique known as the *general number field sieve* in order to derive the factors of large numbers. It's an algorithm that is relatively inefficient. *Shor's algorithm*, on the other hand, is a quantum algorithm that is exponentially more efficient than the general number field sieve. It can be used to rapidly break most asymmetric key exchanges, given a sufficiently powerful quantum computer.

Quantum-resistant protocols are under active development at the time of this writing. While none is quite ready for production, the looming quantum threat should not deter one from implementing public key cryptography today. It remains the best tool we have, and cryptographers are working hard to define a clear path forward. For more information, check out the Post-Quantum Cryptography conference (*https://pqcrypto.org/*).

Perfect Forward Secrecy. *PFS*, or *perfect forward secrecy*, is a cryptographic property in which the disclosure of a private key does not result in the compromise of previously negotiated sessions. This is a valuable property because it ensures that an eavesdropper cannot record your session data for later decryption. The RSA key exchange does not support PFS because the session key is directly encrypted and transmitted using the private key. DHE or ECDHE must be used in order to obtain PFS.

Mind Your Curves. Cryptography experts have called into question the security of many elliptic curve-based key agreement implementations. While the math and fundamental principles are sound, a standardized set of curves are typically used as the input for these functions. These standard curves rely on a set of constants, which must remain secure in order to maintain the integrity of cryptographic operations performed with the resulting curves.

It is these constants which have been questioned. It is believed by some of the brightest minds in the industry that the constants which are widely available for these purposes have been manipulated by state actors and are compromised. If this is true, it stands to reason that any elliptic curve crypto implementation leveraging these well-known constants has in fact been secretly subverted.

For this reason, some experts recommend use of DHE key agreement over ECDHE, despite its better math and performance properties. This is problematic in some places, since not all clients fully support DHE (most famously, Internet Explorer does not support DHE in combination with RSA authentication). The recommended course of action in this case is to curate server-side cipher suites to prefer DHE negotiation where available, falling back to ECDHE when necessary.

Authentication. There are three common authentication methods, one of which is on it's way out: *RSA*, *DSA*, and *ECDSA*.

RSA authentication is overwhelmingly the most common, in use in over 99% of web-based TLS resources. Generally speaking, RSA is a safe bet so long as a sufficiently-sized key is used. This caveat raises the concern that the we are getting better at solving the mathematical problem at the heart of the RSA algorithm, requiring key sizes to increase in order to keep up with advances. Despite this, RSA remains the most popular and most often recommended authentication method.

DSA authentication is no longer recommended. While it is (for the most part) a sound technology at its core, a series of other problems have artificially weakened it, including adoption and opinionated standardization. ECDSA, on the other hand, is the newer cousin of DSA and uses elliptic curves to facilitate public/private key pairs.

ECDSA is frequently touted as the future. It applies all the benefits of elliptic curve cryptography to the authentication component, including smaller key size and better performance and mathematical properties. It is presumed, however, that ECDSA authentication is susceptible to the use of malicious elliptic curves, as described in "Mind Your Curves" on page 158.

When making a decision between RSA and ECDSA authentication, the brokenness of widely published elliptic curves should be carefully considered. Identity compromise can be catastrophic. Additionally, ECDSA is not nearly as widely supported as RSA is. With the acknowledgment of these two points, it is fair to say that RSA authentication is still a good choice at the time of this writing, despite the existence of a technologically superior algorithm (ECDSA).

Separation of duty

For the purposes of a zero trust network, it is a good idea to separate the encryption duties from the application itself (Figure 8-7). The resource we are securing in this case is the device, and as such, it makes a lot of sense for this piece to be independent of the workload itself.

Doing this also alleviates a number of pain points, including zero-day mitigation, performance penalties, and auditing. For protocols like IPsec, this separation of duty is part of the design, but this is not the case for TLS. Historically, applications speak TLS directly, loading and configuring shared TLS libraries for remote communication.

We have seen this pattern's rough spots time and time again. Shared libraries become littered throughout the infrastructure, being consumed by a multitude of projects, all with independent versions and configurations. Some languages have more flexible libraries than others, limiting your ability to enforce the latest and greatest. Above all, it is very difficult to ensure that all these applications are indeed consuming TLS the right way, and remain up to date with regard to known vulnerabilities.

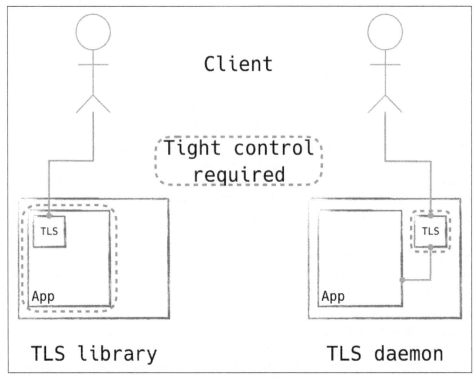

Figure 8-7. Traditional applications include TLS libraries and perform those duties themselves. Using a local TLS daemon instead means better control and consistent performance.

To address the problem, it is useful to move the handling of TLS configuration to the control plane. Connections to the service are brokered by the TLS daemon then locally forwarded to the application. The TLS daemon is configured with system certificates, trust authorities, and endpoint information—that's about it.

In this way, we can ensure that all software receives device authentication and security with TLS, regardless of its support for it. Additionally, since zero trust networks whitelist flows, we can ensure that application traffic is protected by limiting whitelisted flows to known TLS endpoints.

Bulk encryption

All the TLS intricacies and components discussed up to this point apply primarily to the initial TLS handshake. The TLS handshake serves two primary purposes: authentication and the creation of session keys.

TLS handshakes are computationally expensive due to the mathematical operations required to make and validate them. This is a distinct trade-off between security and performance. While we strongly desire this level of security, the performance impact is prohibitively expensive if we apply these operations to all communications.

Asymmetric cryptography is extraordinarily important in the process of secure introduction and authentication, but its strength can be matched by symmetric cryptography so long as identity or authentication is not a concern. Symmetric encryption uses a single secret key instead of a public/private key pair, and is less computationally expensive than asymmetric cryptography by orders of magnitude. This is where the concept of a TLS handshake and session keys comes in.

Some very smart mathematicians and cryptographers realized that we can use the strong yet expensive operations to securely generate a single secret—one which can be shared between the parties (Figure 8-8). The key exchange component of TLS is that which generates this shared key and ensures that both parties have knowledge of it.

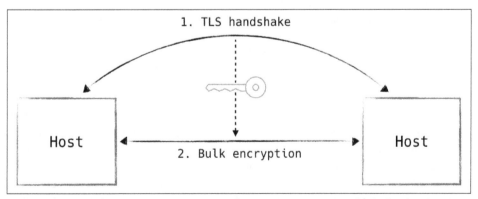

Figure 8-8. TLS handshake generates a symmetric encryption key for bulk transfer. IPsec uses a similar mechanism.

This shared key is then used as the input for a symmetric encryption algorithm, which is applied to all session traffic following the handshake. This methodology ensures that the entire session benefits from the strength of asymmetric cryptography without inheriting any of the performance implications associated with asymmetric encryption schemes.

When it comes to choices for bulk encryption algorithms, TLS supports many, but the recommendation is pretty well aligned across the board: just use AES. It checks all the desirable boxes, including the fact that it is unpatented, widely implemented in hardware, and practically universally implemented in software. It is very performant, heavily vetted/scrutinized, and remains unbroken to the best of public knowledge. Many people say "AES is good enough," and while that might be a tough pill to swallow when it comes to security protocols, such a statement has never been so close to the truth.

Message authenticity

When communicating securely, message authenticity is an important if not required property. Encryption provides confidentiality, but without message authenticity, how do you ensure the integrity of that message? Without an error during decryption, it is difficult or impossible to distinguish a tampered message from an authentic one.

Some encryption modes (such as AES-GCM) provide message confidentiality and authenticity guarantees simultaneously. However, these guarantees are only applicable during bulk encryption; there are several TLS exchanges which are not protected by the bulk transfer specifications, and the message authenticity scheme protects those as well.

Explicit Authenticity Sometimes Required

Since some bulk encryption algorithms provide message integrity assurances, it is not always necessary to perform explicit authenticity checks on every packet. Instead, TLS will prefer built-in assurances for bulk transfers and rely on explicit authenticity checks for all packets not associated with the bulk transfer (for instance, TLS control messages).

As far as choice goes, the options are limited to MD5 and the SHA family of hashes. The former has been cryptographically broken for quite some time now, leaving the SHA family as the only reasonable choice for ensuring message integrity under TLS. There are even concerns when using the weaker SHA variant, SHA-1, as it is now considered vulnerable in the face of ever-increasing compute power. As such, it is recommended to choose the strongest SHA hash which can be reasonably deployed, given hardware and software constraints.

It is additionally recommended to use bulk encryption with built-in authenticity wherever possible, as it is generally more performant and secure than relying on a disjoint authenticity mechanism. TLS version 1.3 mandates the use of authenticated encryption.

Mutually authenticated TLS for device authentication

Just like any other protocol used for device authentication, TLS comes with its ups and downs.

The first is that, due to its position in the network stack, TLS is protocol-dependent. It is most commonly implemented as a TCP-based protocol, though a UDP-based variant dubbed DTLS is also available. The presence of DTLS highlights the deficiency of the position of TLS in the stack. With this, TLS suffers diminishing returns when used to secure IP protocols other than those which it natively supports, like TCP or UDP.

Another thing to consider is the automation requirement. TLS is commonly deployed as an infrastructure service in perimeter networks by leveraging intermediaries which are typically positioned at the perimeter. This mode of operation, however, is unsuitable for a zero trust network as long as the intermediary and the upstream endpoint are separated by a computer network. In a zero trust network, applications leveraging a TLS-speaking intermediary must be on the same host as the intermediary itself. As a result, protecting datacenter zero trust networks with TLS requires additional automation to configure applications to speak through this layer of external security. It does not come "for free" like other protocols such as IPsec.

All of that said, it remains today's best choice for protecting client-facing zero trust networks. TLS is very widely supported in both software and transit (i.e., intermediary networks worldwide), and can be relied upon for straightforward and trustworthy operation. Most web browsers support mutually authenticated TLS natively, which means that resources can be protected using zero trust principles without the immediate need for specialized client-side software.

Filtering

Filtering is the process by which packets are admitted or rejected by systems on a network. When most people think of filtering, they typically envision a firewall, a service or device which sits between the network and application to filter traffic going to or coming from that device. Firewalls do provide filtering, but they can provide other services like network address translation (NAT), traffic shaping, and VPN tunnel services. Filtering can be provided by other systems not traditionally considered, like routers or managed switches. It's important to remember that filtering is a simple service which can be applied at many points in a networked system.

Filtering can be quite frustrating for users without a security mindset since it blocks desired network communication. Wouldn't it be better to get rid of that nuisance and assume the user knows what they want? Unfortunately, well-meaning users can trivially expose services that on further inspection they would rather not expose. During the early days of always-on internet connections, users' computers routinely made the accident of exposing file sharing and chat services on the public internet. Filtering provides a type of checks and balances for network communication, forcing users to consider whether a particular connection should really cross a sensitive boundary.

Many of the zero trust concepts so far have focused on advanced encryption and authentication systems. This is because these aspects of network security are not nearly as pervasive in network designs as they should be. However, we should not downplay the importance of network filtering. It is still a critical component of a zero trust architecture, and so we will explore it in three parts:

Host filtering
Filtering of traffic at the host

Bookended filtering
Filtering of traffic by a peer host in the network

Intermediary filtering
Filtering of traffic by devices in between two hosts

Host Filtering

Host filtering deputizes a network endpoint to be an active participant in its own security. The goal is to ensure that every host is configured to filter its own network traffic. This is different than traditional network design, where filtering is delegated to a centralized system away from the host.

Centralized filtering is most often implemented using a hardware firewall. These firewalls make use of *application-specific integrated circuits (ASICs)* to efficiently process packets flowing through the device. Since the device is often a shared resource for many backend systems, these ASICs are critical for it to accomplish the task of filtering the aggregate traffic of all those systems. Using ASICs brings raw performance at the expense of flexibility.

Software firewalls, like those found in modern operating systems, are much more flexible than their hardware counterparts. They offer a rich set of services like defining policies based on time of day and arbitrary offset value. Many of these software firewalls can be further extended with new modules to offer additional services.

Unlike the early days of the internet, all modern desktop and server operating systems now offer some form of network filtering via a host-based firewall:

Linux
 IPtables

BSD systems
 Berkley Packet Filter (BPF)

macOS
 Application firewall and additional host firewalls available via the command line

Windows
 Windows Firewall service

Perhaps surprisingly, neither iOS nor Android ships with a host-based firewall. Apple's iOS Security Guide notes that it considers a firewall unnecessary since the attack surface area is reduced on iOS "by limiting listening ports and removing unnecessary network utilities such as telnet, shells, or a web server." Google does not publish an official security guide. Android, perhaps owing to its ability to run non-Play Store approved software, does have third-party firewalls available to install if a user chooses to do so.

Zero trust systems assume the network is hostile. As a result, they filter network traffic at every point possible, often using on-host firewalls. Adding an on-host firewall reduces the attack surface of a host by filtering out undesirable network traffic. While software-based firewalls don't have the same throughput capabilities as hardware-based systems, the fact that the filtering is distributed across the system (and therefore sees a portion of the aggregate traffic) often results in little performance degradation in practice.

Using on-host filtering is simple to get started with. Configuration management systems have very good support for managing on-host firewalls. When writing the logic to install services, it's easiest to capture the allowed connections right alongside its installation and configuration routines. Filtering in a remote system, conversely, is more difficult since the exceptions are separated from the application that needs them.

On-host firewalls also offer opportunities for novel uses of programmable filtering. Single packet authorization (SPA), which we discussed earlier in this chapter, is a great example of this idea. SPA programmatically manages the on-host firewall to reduce the attack surface of a service on a host. This is advantageous because on occasion, carefully crafted malicious packets can be constructed to exploit a weakness in network services. For example, a service might require authentication and authorization before processing a request, but the authentication logic could have a buffer overflow error which an attacker can use to implement a remote code execution vulnerability. By introducing a filtering layer, we can hide the more complex service interface behind a simpler system which manages firewall rules.

There are of course issues when using on-host firewalls exclusively for network filtering. One such issue is the chance for a co-located firewall to be rendered meaningless should a host become compromised. An attacker who is able to gain access to a host and elevate their privilege could remove the on-host firewall or adjust its configuration. Needless to say, this is a big deal, as it removes a layer of defense in the system. This concern is why filtering has traditionally been handled by a separate device, away from potentially risky hosts.

This approach highlights the benefits of isolation in security design, which on-host filtering could benefit from. As the industry moves toward isolation techniques like virtualization and containerization, it becomes clear that these technologies present an opportunity to further isolate on-host filtering. Without these technologies, the only form of isolation that is available is local user privilege. On a Unix-based system, for example, only the root user is able to make adjustments to the firewall configuration. In a virtualized system, however, one could implement filtering outside the virtual machine, which provides strong guarantees against attacks on the filtering system. In fact, this is how Amazon's security group feature is implemented, as shown in Figure 8-9.

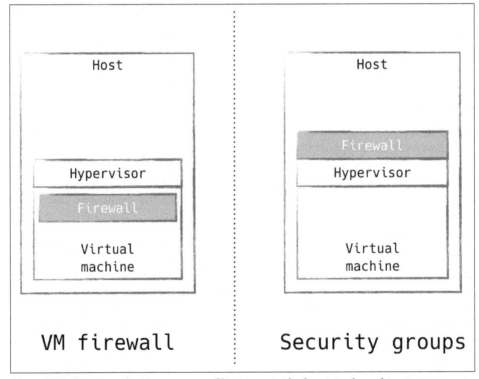

Figure 8-9. EC2 Security Groups move filtering outside the virtual machine to improve isolation

Another issue with on-host filtering is the cost associated with pushing filtering deep into the network. Imagine a scenario where a large percentage of traffic is filtered away by on-host filtering. By applying filtering nearest to the destination system, the network incurs extra cost to transmit those packets, only for them to be ultimately thrown away. This situation also raises the possibility of a denial-of-service attack forcing internal network infrastructure to route large volumes of useless traffic, as well as overwhelming the comparatively weaker software firewalls. For this reason, while on-host firewalls are the best place to start thinking about filtering, they present a risk if they are the only place filtering occurs. We will discuss ways to push filtering out into the network in "Intermediary Filtering" on page 169.

Bookended Filtering

Bookended filtering is the act of applying policy not just on the receipt of a packet, but while sending them too. This mode of filtering is not commonly found in traditional networks. It brings some interesting advantages to network design, which we will now explore.

Egress (the opposite of ingress) is a term used to describe network traffic that is leaving a host. This type of filtering is commonly used to manage communication from a private network out to public networks, but it is rarely used within a private network. There are a few reasons this is the case:

- Ingress filtering is easier to reason about, since listening services can be enumerated when building firewall rules. Egress filtering requires more bookkeeping to capture how hosts intend to communicate.
- Ingress filtering is generally considered good enough to stop undesirable communication in the network.
- Egress filtering requires knowledge of every expected flow, something not usually found in traditional networks.

Bookended filtering uses egress filtering within the zero trust network to further harden the system. We can see how this hardening is beneficial with the example shown in Figure 8-10. Let's consider a system where a database server has ingress filter rules set up to allow access from application servers. A well-meaning administrator is investigating some network connectivity issues. In the process of their investigation, the admin loosens the database's ingress filtering to rule out the possibility that it was causing the issue. Crucially, this administrator forgets to revert their change after disproving that theory. This error removes a layer of defense in the system for some time. Worse yet, discovering this lost defense can be difficult because the expected communication (from the app servers to the database server) continues to work.

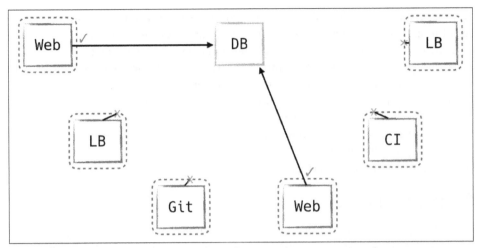

Figure 8-10. Bookended filtering can provide protection in unexpected circumstances

In this scenario, a network that has pervasive bookended filtering is protected even when this critical misconfiguration is in the system. In a way, it's similar to herd immunity—the collective benefit that a community provides to unvaccinated members when the vast majority of members are vaccinated against a disease. Instead of preventing illness, bookended filtering protects misconfigured systems from the potential impact of that misconfiguration.

Building bookended filtering into a system isn't as hard as it might seem, given the right conditions. Communication flows need to be captured in a way that can be consumed programmatically. The best way to capture these flows is by defining fine-grained ingress rules. These ingress rules should allow access to a service based on each client's server role instead of broadly opening access to a service. By capturing this detail, we have constructed a dependency graph from which egress rules can be calculated and applied throughout the system.

Like we discussed in host filtering, egress filtering is best applied when it is isolated from the applications running within the system. The same insights apply here: prefer implementing filtering on the other side of a virtualized or containerized environment to have the most robust filtering mechanisms. Looking beyond the filtering implementation, it's important to consider the isolation of the data used to build egress filtering rules. It might seem attractive to calculate that data from a dynamic data source such as a service discovery system, but bookended filtering is most effective when the flow database is isolated from the running system. Instead use a slowly changing database, especially one that requires a human to review changes.

Project Calico

Project Calico (*https://www.projectcalico.org/*) is a virtual network system for dynamically scheduled workloads. A *workload* is a generic term that applies to any application which needs to be run in a datacenter. This application could be inside a container or a virtual machine. Calico takes the lessons learned in operating the internet and brings them into the datacenter to create a simpler network which can scale efficiently as the size of one's network grows.

Calico is not a full zero trust solution, but it does echo some of the ideas of zero trust networks. Calico distributes filtering throughout the network, which is enforced on the host machines. These hosts are dynamically reconfigured based on changes in a database which describes the entire network. This design looks very similar to the host filtering we discussed earlier.

Calico also includes the bookended (*http://docs.projectcalico.org/v2.0/reference/architecture/data-path*) filtering concepts we discussed. This means that hosts on both ends of a connection are filtering traffic based on their knowledge of which connections should be allowed. This double enforcement of network communication is seen as a secondary defense in the network fabric.

Intermediary Filtering

Intermediary filtering is the idea that devices other than the sender or receiver can and should participate in filtering traffic in a zero trust network. This at a minimum means perimeter filtering can play a role in a zero trust network, and at the maximum, intermediary devices within the network's fabric.

As we discussed in "Host Filtering" on page 164, filtering traffic only at the destination incurs an extra cost on the network when the ratio of undesirable traffic is very high. High throughput filtered traffic will most often originate from internet ingress traffic. Ideally, we want to filter traffic as soon as possible to reduce the impact and the cost of filtering. For this application, filtering at the perimeter systems that sit between the zero trust network and the internet is ideal. These devices typically need to be hardware based to efficiently filter the packets coming into the system.

Perimeter filters can also be an important check and balance in a zero trust network. The perimeter filters should be a combination of global rules and coarse-grained host policy. By keeping global rules separate from host policy, invariants about the external network configuration are defined.

Exceptions to this policy should be traceable back to host infrastructure that relies on those exceptions, and the actions taken to instantiate them. The best implementation derives these exceptions from the host policies themselves. By tying the host policy to the exception policy, the system will be more consistent as hosts come and go from the network. These exceptions, however, must be verified to be as narrowly scoped as possible. A review process should be exercised for all policy changes in order to guard against overly broad exceptions which can compromise the system's security.

UPnP Considered Harmful

Deriving perimeter policies from host policies should not be conflated with UPnP, a technology used to reconfigure consumer firewalls. UPnP is rightly criticized because any application on the network can reconfigure the perimeter. In the zero trust model, there is a chain of trust between the host policies and the exceptions that are created at the perimeter.

It might seem odd that we're discussing perimeter filtering in such a positive light, given the failings of the perimeter model. The key detail to understand here is that zero trust networks don't throw out *all* perimeter concepts. Instead, they encourage administrators to start at the host and work their way outward. Perimeter devices eventually play a role in this way, with denial-of-service mitigation being by far the most notable application.

An exciting idea in zero trust networks is to use the host policy database to dynamically program the network fabric itself. This would result in a *software-defined network* (SDN) that does not blindly route packets to the destination, but actively manages switching and routing policy based on which flows are expected and allowed. This results in a few benefits:

- Potentially malicious traffic is kept away from hosts, reducing the attack surface.
- Software firewalls on the hosts are augmented by the network itself, adding additional layers of defense in the network.

Like the perimeter filtering discussed earlier, filtering in the network fabric should be seen as an enhancement to the base layer of host-based filtering. It must not act as a replacement for it.

Forwarding and Routing Authorization

As we discuss filtering, there is a theme that arises—zero trust networks leverage relatively slowly changing details of the network to distribute enforcement, resulting in a network that is more secure. This observation opens up an interesting opportunity: can we propagate enforcement into the network infrastructure, effectively elevating those pipes from a simple packet transmitting system to a smart network fabric?

Imagine an SDN controller which only installed flow instructions based on the result of a strong authentication and authorization process. A client wishing to access a network resource can signal the control plane, providing the network access request along with the appropriate credentials. After successful request authorization, the network is installed and available, but only for the specific flow which was authorized.

Summary

This chapter focused on how traffic gains trust in a zero trust network. We teased apart the distinctions between encryption and authenticity—two concepts that are related but distinct. Zero trust networks require authenticity in communication, and most networks also gain value in having their traffic encrypted.

We explored the first packet problem in network communications. Modern authentication systems are fairly complicated systems, which results in a large surface area for attacks. We talked about hiding those services behind a single packet authorization system, which is a relatively simple service that can be used to hide a more complex authentication system like TLS.

We then talked about two competing protocols for encryption and authentication of network traffic: TLS and IPsec. We discussed how these systems differ and gave clear guidance that mutually authenticated TLS is best suited for client/server interactions or in heterogeneous environments, while IPsec seems well suited inside the datacenter (particularly so when Network Address Translation is not present).

Zero trust networks still need packet filtering capabilities, which they deploy throughout the network. We described three types of filtering that can be deployed in such a network: host, bookended, and intermediary filtering. Each type of filtering adds additional robustness to the network and can be deployed in the network using system automation and a shared database of expected network communication.

The next chapter takes all the concepts we have learned thus far and lays out a plan for creating your own zero trust network.

CHAPTER 9

Realizing a Zero Trust Network

This chapter will help readers develop a strategy for taking the knowledge in previous chapters and applying it to their system. Zero trust networks are very likely to be built around existing systems, so this chapter will focus on how to make that transition successfully.

It's important to remember that zero trust is not a product that can be bolted onto the network. It is a set of architectural principles which are applied based on the needs and constraints of the network. Therefore, this chapter cannot provide a checklist of changes to be made, but rather a framework for how to approach realizing in a zero trust network in your own system.

Choosing Scope

Before setting out to build a zero trust network, it is important to choose the proper scope for the effort. A very mature zero trust network will have many interacting systems. For a large organization, constructing these systems might be feasible, but for smaller organizations, the number and complexity of those systems may make a zero trust network seem out of reach.

It's important to remember that the zero trust architecture is an ideal to work toward instead of a list of requirements that must be met completely from day one. This is no different than perimeter-based networks. Less mature networks may initially choose a simple network design to reduce the complexity of administration. As the network matures and the risk of a breach increases, the network will need to be redesigned to further isolate systems.

While the zero trust network design is an ideal, not all features of the design have equal value. Determining which components are required and which are nice to have will go a long way in ensuring the success of a zero trust implementation.

What's Actually Required?

Limiting the scope of a zero trust network necessarily requires prioritizing the set of properties that were presented earlier in this book. This RFC-style prioritization list is the authors' opinion on how that work should be prioritized:

- All network flows MUST be authenticated before being processed.
- All network flows SHOULD be encrypted before being transmitted.
- Authentication and encryption MUST be performed by the endpoints in the network.
- All network flows MUST be enumerated so that access can be enforced by the system.
- The strongest authentication and encryption suites SHOULD be used within the network.
- Authentication SHOULD NOT rely on public PKI providers. Private PKI systems should be used instead.
- Devices SHOULD be regularly scanned, patched, and rotated.

RFC-Style Prioritized Lists

RFC documents are the lingua franca of proposed changes to internet infrastructure. In these documents, language and structure is clearly defined to allow readers to more quickly understand the changes proposed in this document.

One aspect of that language which is very useful in prioritization discussion is the standard terms defined in RFC 2119 (*https://www.ietf.org/rfc/rfc2119.txt*). This RFC defines a set of terms (MUST/MUST NOT, SHOULD/SHOULD NOT, MAY/MAY NOT) which, when used, carry greater weight than their normal usage in common literature.

This book's prioritized list uses these terms with a similar intention to their definitions in RFC 2119 (*https://www.ietf.org/rfc/rfc2119.txt*). While architectural characteristics don't have quite the same requirements as protocol designs, the use of these standard terms is intended to echo the usage presented in that RFC.

For completeness, here are the intended definitions of these standard terms when used in this book:

MUST
> This term is used for a requirement that is required for the implemented system to be considered compatible with the zero trust design.

MUST NOT
> This is the opposite of MUST. A system intending to implement the zero trust design is required to not have this characteristic.

SHOULD

> This term denotes an architectural characteristic that is desired in a zero trust network, but given cost constraints can be deprioritized. When deprioritizing this feature, system administrators should be aware that they are trading the security of their systems for reduced cost in implementing them. When at all possible, system administrators should avoid compromising on these characteristics because the benefit of not compromising on them is considered worth the upfront cost of their implementation.

SHOULD NOT

> This is the opposite of SHOULD.

MAY

> This term is used for architectural characteristics of a zero trust network that bring value, but are considered nice-to-haves. System administrators should plan on implementing these aspects once they have built a system that satisfies the MUST and SHOULD definitions. It is important to note that these additional features bring additional value to the network by hardening it, so they should not be considered a net loss.

With this prioritized list of design requirements for building a zero trust network, let's dig into why particular requirements were categorized the way they were.

All network flows MUST be authenticated before being processed

In a zero trust network, all packets received by the system are immediately suspicious. As such, they must be rigorously inspected before allowing the data within them to be processed. Strong authentication is the primary mechanism by which we accomplish this.

Authentication is absolutely required in order to gain confidence about the provenance of network data. It is, perhaps, the single most important component of a zero trust network. Without it we have nothing, and are forced to place trust in the network.

All network flows SHOULD be encrypted before being transmitted

A key lesson of this book is that a network link cannot be trusted to reliably convey data or signals from one system to another. The physical accessibility of a network link to unsafe actors makes it trivial for that network to be compromised. Moreover, even in a physically secure network, bad actors can digitally infiltrate a system and passively probe the network for valuable data.

By encrypting data on a device before transmitting it on the network, we reduce the attack surface of that communication to the trustworthiness of the device itself, namely application and physical device security.

Authentication and encryption MUST be performed by the application-layer endpoints

Since zero trust networks recognize the threat that trusting network links pose to the security of a system, it is important that secure communications be established between application-layer endpoints. Adding middleware components that handle these responsibilities (like VPN concentrators or TLS-terminating load balancers) can leave upstream network communications exposed to physical and virtual threats.

As a result, a system that claims to be zero trust is required to implement encryption and authentication at every application-layer endpoint on the network.

All network flows MUST be enumerated so that access can be enforced by the system

Zero trust networks depend on data that defines the expected characteristics of the network. Therefore, defining every expected network flow is critical to safeguarding the network.

We should be careful to note that enumerating flows does not require onerous change management controls to provide value. A simple process for defining expected flows brings enormous value in terms of network enforcement and change auditing.

Without the list of expected network flows, zero trust systems are unable to highlight unexpected communications which need attention from administrators or should be denied.

It is the strongly held opinion of the authors that deferring the effort to enumerate flows will ultimately result in a task list that is considered infeasible. The authors feel that the best way to keep this database of expected flows up to date is to distribute the responsibility of defining those flows into the organization. When distributing this responsibility, organizations should take caution to educate teams on best practices for change management to guard against internal threats to the system. One such threat is allowing a single person to update the flow database without any oversight. A simple review system can mitigate this threat.

Flow Data as the Source of Truth

Building a database of expected flows is best accomplished by making the flow database the data source for allowing that access. By setting up this dependency (and disallowing external modification), the flow database will be consistent with the actual allowed access.

When capturing flows, following these rules will improve the quality of the data:

- Capture the intended use of a flow along with the policy details (e.g., LB access—from LB hosts to web application).
- Prefer narrowly defined flows over broad access.

The strongest authentication and encryption suites available SHOULD be used within the network

Zero trust networks assume a hostile network environment, so strong authentication and encryption suites are an important component in the security of a zero trust network.

Which suites offer strong security unfortunately changes, so this book cannot offer specific choices that will stand the test of time. Readers should refer to security standards like the NIST encryption guidelines to pick strong cipher suites.

System administrators should always aim for the strongest suites possible, but device and application capabilities might limit the types of suites that are available. In these cases, administrators should be aware that by reducing the strength of these suites, security is being compromised in their network.

Authentication SHOULD NOT rely on public PKI providers—private PKI systems should be used instead

Public PKI systems provide trust assurances to unmanaged endpoints in a secure communication. A certificate authority signs certificates used in establishing secure communications. The endpoint receiving that signed certificate is able to verify its authenticity by comparing the signing material against the list of trusted certificate authorities already present on the system. By seeding systems with a list of trusted public certificate authorities, endpoints can establish secure communication channels with systems they have not previously communicated with.

Given the benefit that the public PKI system provides to build secure communication channels, why do zero trust networks prefer private PKI systems? The reason, perhaps unsurprisingly given zero trust's focus on managing trust, is that trusting a third party places the system at increased risk. There are several risks that the public PKI system brings to a zero trust network.

One concern is the number of public certificate authorities that are considered trusted. As internet traffic has grown, the number of trusted public CAs has grown with it. Each one of those trusted CAs has the ability to sign a fraudulent certificate that incorrectly asserts the trustworthiness of a malicious system. Certificate pinning can help with this risk by giving an endpoint the knowledge of which certificate to expect for a given endpoint, but certificate pinning requires that the endpoint have prior knowledge of the expected certificate, which presents a new challenge.

Using a public CA also presents another threat. State actors have become more aggressive in using judicial powers to force organizations to act against the trust guarantees that they provide to their customers. These requests have increasingly used laws which prohibit involved parties from disclosing their actions. Given this aggressive stance, allowing state actors into the trust mechanisms of a zero trust network should give system administrators pause.

Based on these concerns, zero trust networks should prefer privately held PKI systems. Endpoints should be configured to only allow certificates signed by the private PKI system. We discussed PKI in greater detail in Chapter 2.

Devices SHOULD be regularly scanned, patched, and rotated

We learned in Chapter 5 that the security of devices is critical for building a zero trust network. Administrators need to build with the assumption that trusted devices on the network are compromised, and therefore build defenses into device management to mitigate this threat.

To that end, devices should be regularly scanned to capture the software that's running or installed on the device at a given point in time. Scanning can be used to discover and prevent known malicious software from running on the device, but administrators should operate under the assumption that malware prevention software (e.g., antivirus software) will always be imperfect. Rather than focusing all energy on stopping malicious software from running, administrators should focus on building forensics capabilities so they can analyze the impact of an inevitable malware attack.

Keeping devices fresh is also very important. System administrators should have a plan for regularly installing the latest security patches. Additionally, a regular device rotation policy will help ensure that devices don't accrue cruft, which can compromise the security of that system.

Prefer Reimaging over Long-Term Scanning and Patching

Device trustworthiness degrades over time due to the increased risk that a device could have been compromised. Regularly reimaging devices, while disruptive, ensures that the trust in the fleet remains high. Aim to reimage servers once a quarter and personal devices every two years.

Building a System Diagram

Building a system diagram is an important first step toward realizing a zero trust network. Having a clear picture of how both internal and external network communication is occurring will be useful when designing system communication channels.

System diagrams, such as the one shown in Figure 9-1, are often maligned for being horribly out of date. These diagrams are typically built by hand, which requires a large amount of human effort. Given the speed at which the diagrams fall out of date, there is a commonly held opinion that system diagrams simply aren't worth the investment. This viewpoint, however, misses the benefit of having a human-focused view of how the system should be constructed. While an engineer could read code or interrogate existing systems to determine how the system is constructed, this doesn't give any insight into whether that state was desired or accidental.

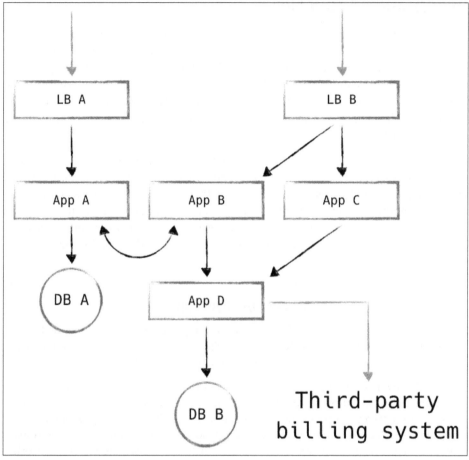

Figure 9-1. A diagram like this is a good starting point for building a zero trust network. Directionality is important.

So if system diagrams are useful, but often out of date, the natural question is how much time and effort should we put into their creation. A good path forward for an existing network is to first observe the communication that is flowing through the network. You can capture this communication using tools that log flows. Once flow information is captured, producing a system diagram will be an exercise in categorizing classes of communication.

In the next section, we will talk about tools for capturing and categorizing network flows, as well as a strategy for breaking down this large effort into smaller chunks of work.

Understanding Your Flows

A *network flow* is a time-bound communication between a source system and a destination. A single flow could be be directly mapped to an entire conversation when using a bidirectional transport protocol (e.g., TCP). For unidirectional transport protocols (e.g., UDP), a single flow might only capture half of a network conversation. This is because while two UDP flows might be logically related, an observer on the network may be unable to make that association without a deep understanding of the application data.

Capturing all the flow activity in an existing production network is a logical first step for a system that wants to move to a zero trust model. Logging flows in a network over a long period of time is a noninvasive way to discover what network connections exist and should be considered in the new security model. Without this up-front information gathering, efforts to move to a zero trust model will result in frequent network communication issues, causing the project to be deemed too invasive and disruptive.

Ways to Discover Flows

There are many different mechanisms for logging and analyzing network flows. Which system is used will largely depend on the type of network being run (physical or virtual) and the level of access that an administrator has over the endpoints.

Physical networks have rich capabilities for accessing the raw packets that are flowing over the network. Business-class switches will generally have the ability to mirror packets to a second port on the switch (known as a SPAN or mirror port). This approach is relatively safe to enable on a lightly loaded switch, but it will mask some types of errors in the network. TAP devices, which are placed inline in the network link, will guarantee that all data is transmitted to a monitoring device. For the purposes of discovering logical flows in the network, either approach will work.

Virtualized networks might have the ability to inspect network traffic, but they generally operate on a coarser level. Amazon Web Services, for example, has a feature that logs every flow in a network, which can be used to analyze traffic on its systems (Figure 9-2).

Figure 9-2. Some cloud providers have flow logging features built in; this is a screenshot of the AWS flow log feature (used with permission from Roy Feintuch (http://bit.ly/aws-feintuch))

While discovering flows via the network fabric gives perfect visibility into the traffic that is flowing, tying that analysis back to individual applications is difficult without some endpoint monitoring system. In the case where control of endpoints is feasible, discovering network flows on the endpoints themselves can provide a more detailed view of the source of traffic in the system. Software firewalls operating in log-only mode can be a useful tool to discover flows in the system without impacting communication.

On Linux endpoints, there are several approaches to discovering and cataloging network flows, which Harald Welte's paper "Flow-based network accounting with Linux" (*https://www.kernel.org/doc/ols/2005/ols2005v2-pages-273-278.pdf*) captures.

With all network flows logged, the next goal is to categorize flows based on higher-level system connections. These connections should be defined at the logical systems level instead of the individual IP/port level. The connections being defined with this exercise are very valuable data. With the definitions in hand, one is able to better enforce known connections and gain awareness of changes to the communication patterns within a network. Since many operations of secure network can be derived from this database of connections, it's clear that capturing this mapping is very useful.

For a very large network, capturing and categorizing all network flows could be an enormous undertaking. The natural question is whether capturing all network connections is a requirement for transitioning to a zero trust network. Fortunately, a zero trust network can be incrementally realized within an existing perimeter-based system. One can leverage the existing perimeter or network boundaries to build a zero trust network on either side of the boundary. The zero trust model can then spread from zone to zone as in Figure 9-3, enhancing the network security of the existing system while maintaining the operational security measures already in place.

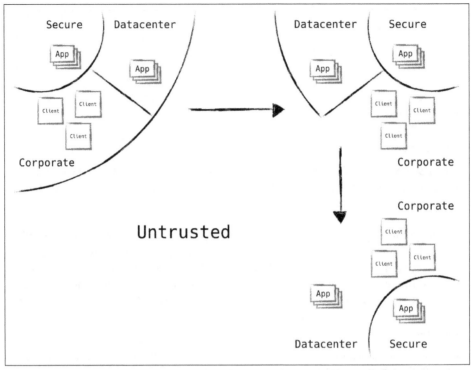

Figure 9-3. Zero trust adoption can move zone by zone, giving an easy migration path away from the traditional perimeter architecture

Controller-Less Architecture

A fully mature zero trust network will have at its core several control plane systems which provide critical security services. While having these systems is ideal, it is possible to iterate toward the idealized deployment while using common infrastructure systems initially. We will explore some of these systems now.

"Cheating" with Configuration Management

Many operationally mature organizations use configuration management tools to manage their infrastructure. When using these systems, the desired configuration state is captured and version controlled. After examining the current state of the system, the configuration management system uses this desired configuration to calculate modifications that will bring the system to the desired state. Using a configuration management tool brings a number of benefits over planned changes executed by humans:

- Changes to the system are applied consistently across the entire fleet.
- The configuration data can be stored in a version control system, which provides a useful record of what changes were made and why.
- Configuration drift is less likely to occur, since its state is policed by the configuration management system.

The first way that configuration management is often deployed is to manage the configuration of individual computers. The systems are started from a known blank slate (usually just the initial installation of the operation system) and then reconfigured to the desired state based on that machine's role in the infrastructure. Having this process automated makes it easy to replace infrastructure.

While using configuration management for this task brings a lot of value, these tools can also be used as a general-purpose automation framework. For instance, they can be used to configure cryptographic primitives between infrastructure hosts, or to poke tightly scoped holes in host-based firewalls. In this way, configuration management (or CM) systems can be used to drive a subset of the functions that are normally offered by a mature zero trust control plane.

Similarly, CM systems can also be used to build up useful abstractions in the network. Most CM tools support mechanisms for extending the set of available resources or actions. Using this extension point, it's possible to build more complex resources into the system. For example, one could define the concept of a service resource which would capture all the standard infrastructure that should be used to make the service available on the network.

CM Is a Temporary Stepping Stone

Configuration management systems are best deployed in a manner where the system reaches a stable configuration. With this ideal in mind, using a configuration management system to make frequent changes to the system would seem counterproductive. We shouldn't dismiss this concern, as it has some validity to it. Instead, we should be mindful that leveraging a configuration management system to build a zero trust network is just a stepping stone to the ideal solution, which would move those responsibilities to a dedicated controller.

Application Authentication and Authorization

A typical organization makes use of many services, the client-side delivery of which is increasingly browser-based. Since a zero trust network does not infer trust based on the network address of a connection, every service needs to handle authentication and authorization.

A simple solution is to to store username and passwords in each application. This approach, however, is heavily discouraged, primarily due to management complexity.

Instead of having each application implement its own authentication systems, it is far better to have applications integrate with an identity provider system which can provide centralized authentication and authorization checks. SAML (Security Assertion Markup Language) is one technology that can be used to integrate an application with an identity provider. OAuth2 is another.

This is not to say that an application should have no authorization responsibilities at all. To the contrary, it is expected that some application-level authorization exist, particularly when considering things like varying user permissions. The overhead of account management, user authentication, and high-level authorization/access can be offloaded while still allowing room for application-centric authorization.

When authenticating with an identity provider, multifactor authentication must be used to ensure that the user credentials cannot be easily stolen. We discussed multifactor authentication in Chapter 6.

Authenticating Load Balancers and Proxies

Many service architectures call for the use of a load balancer to distribute requests to a set of backend hosts. Oftentimes these load balancers represent the boundary between a client-facing system and a datacenter system. This can create confusion around how to properly apply zero trust controls in such a system, since client-facing zero trust semantics can be fairly different than server-side systems.

In Chapter 7, we spoke about how to manage application authentication and authorization as an analog to user authentication and authorization. In backend systems, the best way to authorize an application is to inject ephemeral credentials at runtime, whether that be an API key, short-lived certificate, or otherwise. Each credential uniquely represents a running application instance.

In a load-balanced system, the load-balancing software itself can be viewed as a server-side application. Each software instance is started with ephemeral credentials identifying the instance to upstream hosts. This is in addition to device authentication, which occurs between the load balancer and upstream system using techniques discussed in Chapter 5.

With this architecture, the load balancer can then handle user and client device authentication and authorization responsibilities, leveraging identity providers if desired. Information from the resulting authentication and authorization process (such as username) can then be sent along with the original request to the backend hosts. In this way, the zero trust architecture can be preserved as data crosses client-server boundaries and enters the datacenter.

Prefer Security Tokens over TOTP

When multifactor authentication was first deployed in organizations, users were given simple devices which continuously generated time-based tokens. With the prevalence of today's smart phones, most users prefer to use a multifactor application on their smart phone to generate codes.

Protocols which use security tokens, like U2F, are increasingly prefered over time-based token systems due to their protection against phishing attacks. It's a bonus that these systems are generally also easier for users to work with. When possible, prefer security tokens over TOTP systems. We discussed these technologies in Chapter 6.

Relationship-Oriented Policy

Zero trust advocates for a control plane that injects the results of authorization decisions into the network to allow trusted communication to occur. In that model, each network flow is individually authenticated and authorized. Enforcement is obtained by reconfiguring or signaling the network fabric to allow authorized communication.

In a scaled-down zero trust network, which lacks these control plane systems, we are forced to scale back that ambition. Instead of building a network that uses dynamic injection and signaling, we can build a system that defines policies at the relationship level.

In relationship-oriented network policy, communication between two devices is defined and controlled via traditional network filtering mechanisms like firewalls and required TLS connections. These policy enforcement mechanisms can seem very similar to a perimeter-based model. The key difference in the relationship-oriented model is that the policy is tightly scoped to communicating devices instead of communicating network segments. This approach is sometimes referred to as *microperimeterization*.

By capturing and enforcing which devices should be communicating with each other, we build a database of expected communication which will be of great value in the future when dynamic policy systems are deciding whether to allow a network flow.

Policy Distribution

Distributing policy (as opposed to just enforcement) throughout the network is a common characteristic of a scaled-down version of zero trust. Given the fine-grained policy decisions we expect in the network, automation is critical to making the network operable.

In a mature zero trust network, policy interpretation is fully handled by control plane systems, which can dynamically reconfigure network infrastructure and devices, or give authorization responses to signaling enforcement components.

In a controller-less deployment, however, we must use a different mechanism. Configuration management systems can be used to fill this void in the network control plane.

Devices can be dynamically configured to implement their own enforcement of expected network communication. Configuring an on-host software firewall which is calculated from the relationship policy database can provide per-host enforcement that is less difficult to operate than a centralized, physical firewall. Communications can be similarly authorized by hosts via mechanisms like mutually authenticated TLS, again controlled by configuration management software.

The key realization here is that by using existing configuration management systems, we are able to build a virtual control plane which can distribute enforcement responsibilities into the network fabric. While this approach is pragmatic, it isn't without its downsides:

- Requiring hosts to enforce policy risks having that policy removed or altered should the host be compromised. In compatible environments, pushing this responsibility across an isolation boundary (e.g., a hypervisor, the host OS in containerized systems, or network security groups) provides better protection.
- Changes via configuration management systems often have a longer period of inconsistency while policy is being rolled out into the system.

Defining and Installing Policy

Security policies need to be captured in a format that's separate from the individual devices that are used to implement those policies. There are a few reasons for storing this data outside the implementing systems:

- Having the policy captured separately allows for auditing of the implementation against the desired policy.
- The policy definitions can be reused when switching underlying enforcement systems. For example, configuring a new vendor's system is made easier if the policy is captured in a non–vendor-specific format.

A separate database that captures intended policy can quickly fall out of date unless mechanisms are put in place to ensure that it is consistent with the implementation. The best way to ensure this happens is to generate implementation configuration from this policy database using configuration management systems.

Some system administrators may choose to capture policy directly in configuration management code. In less mature networks, this approach is considered sufficient, since the configuration management system will consistently apply the policies defined on the target devices. As the network matures, administrators may find that moving the definitions out to data allows for them to be used in more locations. For example, host-based and managed network firewalls could be configured from a shared policy database if that data is extracted from configuration management code.

Defining variable trust policies is too difficult to attempt in less mature networks. System administrators should instead focus on defining and capturing known policies.

When building up policies, especially in an existing network, it is helpful to have mechanisms for testing proposed policies. The gold standard is a system which can take proposed policy changes and report on traffic which would be denied by the enforcement of those policy changes. Building up this policy preview system requires quite a few components: a database of logged production flows, a policy simulator, and a system to identify differences in current production policy and proposed policy. For many organizations, that level of sophisticated policy simulation is simply out of reach.

A simpler approach to safely introducing policy changes can be achieved using the following rollout procedure:

1. Take a subset of the desired policy, which we will call the proposed policy.
2. Deploy the proposed policy in a logging-only fashion.
3. Collect production traffic over a sufficient period of time.
4. Investigate traffic which would be rejected should the proposed policy be enforced.
5. Enforce the proposed policy.
6. Repeat this process until all desired policy has been deployed.
7. When all the desired policy is in place, enable a policy which rejects traffic by default.

This "log then enforce" procedure will provide ample time to discover unforeseen issues in the production environment. In addition to this approach, a phased rollout, where policy is enforced over a subset of the production footprint, can also help identify issues without affecting the entire production system.

Zero Trust Proxies

Zero trust proxies are application-level proxy servers which can be used to secure a zero trust network. Proxies are deployed as infrastructure to handle authentication, authorization, and encryption responsibilities. The manner in which these proxies are deployed is critical to ensure the safety of a zero trust network.

Zero trust proxies can operate in two different modes: *reverse proxy* or *forward proxy*. Depending on the situation, one or both of these proxy modes may be used, as shown in Figure 9-4.

In reverse proxy mode, the proxy is receiving connection requests from zero trust-enabled clients. The proxy receives the initial connection, validates that the connection should be allowed, and then passes the request to the application for processing.

In forward proxy mode, a non-zero–trust-aware component needs to make a network request to another zero trust system on the network. Since the non-zero–trust-aware component is unable to work with the control plane to initiate the request properly, it communicates through the authentication proxy to handle that responsibility.

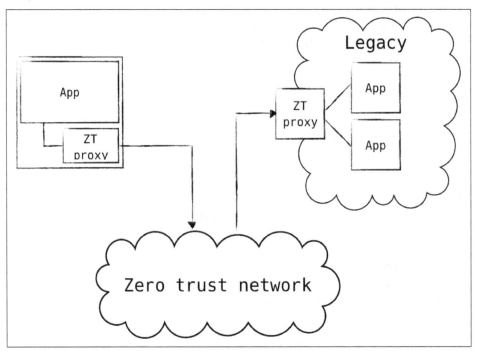

Figure 9-4. Co-located forward proxies can be used to connect to zero trust resources from legacy systems, while co-located or centralized reverse proxies can allow access to legacy services by zero trust clients.

Proxies can be used to build a zero trust network, but the proxies should be deployed on the same device that the workload is running on. When a zero trust network is built in this manner, all workload communication is forcibly routed through the proxy before being emitted on the network. Isolating this responsibility in a proxy brings advantages over incorporating it in individual applications, which we covered in Chapter 8.

Placing proxies on dedicated devices is not recommended for building a zero trust network. Trying to isolate zero trust responsibilities in an external proxy goes against the model which seeks to secure all traffic, including traffic between proxies/load balancers and backend services.

Building a zero trust network can be especially difficult for system administrators who do not have complete control of all devices or services on the network. For example, a network might have vendor-supplied components which need to be secured without changing the device itself.

Zero trust proxies can help bridge the gap in this situation. Placing such a proxy between the unmodifiable component and the zero trust network can allow that component to participate in the network, though with a lesser guarantee of its security.

It is critical that the non-zero–trust-aware component be completely isolated. This isolation must ensure that all network communication to and from that component can only occur through its authentication proxy. If possible, direct mechanical connection should be preferred.

Client-Side Versus Server-Side Migrations

When realizing a zero trust network, deciding on whether client-to-server interactions or server-to-server interactions should be undertaken first is ultimately dependent on the needs of the organization and the level of effort required to meet the goal.

Client-to-server interactions are usually the first to be focused on. Oftentimes, the clients are physically mobile and accessing services from uncontrolled networks. Additionally, with these devices being mobile, the physical security of the device is reasonably called into question. Building zero trust capabilities at this access point therefore brings a lot of value.

There are, however, real hurdles to building zero trust at the client/server layer. Organizations don't necessarily have existing automation systems installed on client machines to allow the zero trust network to be built. Additionally, the types of devices in use on the clients can be much more diverse, which means that the required automation has to be compatible with more systems.

Server-to-server interactions can be an easier initial target for zero trust networks. These systems frequently have existing automation tools installed. They also tend to have a less diverse set of providers in use. Finally, they are often the systems which are housing sensitive data, and so are an attractive target for would-be attackers.

Ultimately, the decision of where to start should focus on which target is the weakest link in the system's network defenses. Building a threat model can help determine which systems are the most exposed. With that knowledge, choosing where to invest time and resources is easier.

Case Studies

Since the exact architecture of a zero trust network is dependent on the details of a particular organization's network, it can be hard to see how all the pieces fit together. To help visualize how these principles manifest themselves in different situations, we are going to explore the experiences of a couple organizations that have successfully transitioned to a zero trust model.

Google's BeyondCorp effort focused on bringing zero trust architecture to the client-to-server interactions that their highly distributed and mobile workforce uses every day.

PagerDuty's Cloud Agnostic Network focuses on server-to-server and cross-cloud interactions which needed to be secured from both external and internal threats.

Case Study: Google BeyondCorp

Betsy Beyer

Starting in November 2014, Google published a series of articles in ;login: describing a new and groundbreaking security model it was deploying to its entire corporate network. The following case study is based on excerpts from those three articles, with permission from Google and :login;.

We encourage you to read the original source material to learn more details:

- "BeyondCorp: A New Approach to Enterprise Security" (*https://research.google.com/pubs/pub43231.html*)
- "BeyondCorp: Design to Deployment at Google" (*https://research.google.com/pubs/pub44860.html*)
- "Beyond Corp: The Access Proxy" (*https://research.google.com/pubs/pub45728.html*)

By the early 2010s, Google was increasingly uncomfortable with the perimeter model of network defense. Creating high, impregnable "castle walls" was not going to protect us when tens of thousands of our employees performed much of their work while physically outside our offices, while on any given day we invited thousands of people inside. At the same time, as the critical role Google plays in the lives of billions of users continued to increase, so did the almost incalculable value we place on the user data entrusted to us.

In light of the scope and scale of our employee base and our corporate network, and the variety of ways in which our employees interact with corporate resources (as a mobile workforce using cloud services and a variety of client devices), it became obvious that the castle-wall metaphor was unsustainable. We needed a strategy much more

---

akin to a modern city than a medieval castle: a system that mediates access to applications, data, and services according to who you are, not which network you use.

With this security imperative in mind, Google revisited the state of the enterprise with a fresh set of eyes. We knew that we could do better than any of the conventional network security models deployed across the industry, so we took the radical step of redesigning our entire approach.

Starting from square one in re-envisioning internal network security, we invested over four years of design and iteration in creating a robust implementation of the zero trust model. While most enterprises assume that the internal network is a safe environment in which to expose corporate applications, we assume that an internal network is as fraught with danger as the public internet.

This new model dispenses with a privileged corporate network entirely. Instead, access depends solely on device and user credentials, regardless of a user's network location—be it an enterprise location, a home network, or a hotel or coffee shop. All access to enterprise resources is fully authenticated, fully authorized, and fully encrypted based upon device state and user credentials. We can enforce fine-grained access to different parts of enterprise resources. As a result, all Google employees can work successfully from any network, and without the need for a traditional VPN connection into the privileged network. The user experience between local and remote access to enterprise resources is effectively identical, apart from potential differences in latency.

When reading the following case study, keep in mind that we're well aware that Google is unique both in terms of its scale and in the amount of resources we were able to devote to this problem space. Because we weren't constrained by resources, we could act more or less purely motivated by ambitious goals that did away with the conventional network security paradigm.

Fast-forward from BeyondCorp's inception to 2017: hacking tools have advanced in sophistication and dropped massively in cost. Malicious efforts that might once have been worthwhile only when turned against Google-scale targets are now applicable to much smaller enterprises. While the risk profile of small- to medium-sized organizations has increased, so too have their options to protect themselves: the commercial network security industry has likewise matured. While Google had to build its security infrastructure from scratch, today there actually are enterprise network security offerings your organization can employ in moving away from the perimeter model. Regardless of individual components you're considering in this space, keep the core design principles and objectives that motivated Google in mind as you develop a strategy.

While technical and implementation details of BeyondCorp may have varying degrees of direct applicability to your enterprise or organization, many of the risk factors we designed to protect against are widely germane, and the fundamental design principles we employed should be directly relevant to all.

The Major Components of BeyondCorp

As shown in Figure 9-5, BeyondCorp consists of many cooperating components to ensure that only appropriately authenticated devices and users are authorized to access the requisite enterprise applications. The following sections describe individual components of BeyondCorp.

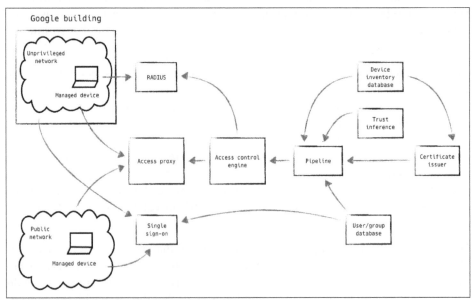

Figure 9-5. BeyondCorp components and access flow

Securely identifying the device

BeyondCorp securely identifies and tracks all managed devices using a master Device Inventory Database and device certificates.

Device inventory database. BeyondCorp uses the concept of a "managed device," which is a device that is procured and actively managed by the enterprise. Only managed devices can access corporate applications. A device tracking and procurement process revolving around our Device Inventory Database is one cornerstone of this model.

As a device progresses through its lifecycle, Google keeps track of changes made to the device. This information is monitored, analyzed, and made available to other parts of BeyondCorp. Because Google has multiple inventory databases, we use a meta-inventory database to amalgamate and normalize device information from these multiple sources, and to make the information available to downstream components of BeyondCorp. With this meta-inventory in place, we have knowledge of all devices that need to access our enterprise.

Device identity. All managed devices need to be uniquely identified in a way that references the record in the Device Inventory Database. One way to accomplish this unique identification is to use a device certificate that is specific to each device.

To receive a certificate, a device must be both present and correct in the Device Inventory Database. We store the certificate on a hardware or software Trusted Platform Module (TPM) or a qualified certificate store. A device qualification process validates the effectiveness of the certificate store, and only a device deemed sufficiently secure can be classed as a managed device. These checks are also enforced as certificates and are renewed periodically. Once installed, the certificate is used in all communications to enterprise services. While the certificate uniquely identifies the device, it does not single-handedly grant access privileges. Instead, it is used as a key to a set of information regarding the device.

Securely identifying the user

BeyondCorp also tracks and manages all users in a User Database and a Group Database. This database system tightly integrates with Google's HR processes that manage job categorization, usernames, and group memberships for all users.

An externalized, single sign-on (SSO) system is a centralized user authentication portal that validates primary and second-factor credentials for users requesting access to our enterprise resources. After validating against the User Database and Group Database, the SSO system generates short-lived tokens that can be used as part of the authorization process for specific resources.

Externalizing applications and workflows: The access proxy

All enterprise applications at Google are exposed to external and internal clients via an internet-facing access proxy that enforces encryption between the client and the application. The Access Proxy is configured for each application and provides common features such as global reachability, load balancing, access control checks, application health checks, and denial-of-service protection. This proxy delegates requests as appropriate to the backend application after the access control checks (described in the next section) complete. See "Leveraging and Extending the GFE" on page 194 for more details about AP features.

Implementing inventory-based access control

The level of access given to a single user and/or a single device can change over time. By interrogating multiple data sources, we are able to dynamically infer the level of trust to assign to a device or user. The Access Control Engine (described in more detail next) can then use this trust level as part of its decision process, as in the following examples:

- A device that has not been updated with a recent OS patch might be relegated to a reduced level of trust.
- A particular class of device, such as a specific model of phone or tablet, might be assigned a particular trust level.
- A user accessing applications from a new location might be assigned a different trust level.

We use both static rules and heuristics to ascertain these levels of trust.

An Access Control Engine within the Access Proxy provides service-level authorization to enterprise applications on a per-request basis. The authorization decision takes several factors into account:

- Information about the user, the groups to which the user belongs, the device certificate, and artifacts of the device, as reported by the Device Inventory Database
- The inferred level of trust in the user and the device
- If necessary, the Access Control Engine can also enforce location-based access control

For example, the following policies are possible with the Access Control Engine:

- Restrict access to Google's bug tracking system to fulltime engineers using an engineering device.
- Restrict access to a finance application to full- time and part-time employees in the finance operations group using managed non-engineering devices.

The Access Control Engine can also restrict parts of an application in different ways. For example, viewing an entry in our bug tracking system might require less strict access control than updating or searching the same bug tracking system.

Leveraging and Extending the GFE

A conventional approach might integrate each backend with the device trust inference service in order to evaluate applicable policies; however, this approach would significantly slow the rate at which we're able to launch and change products. Instead, Google implemented a centralized policy enforcement frontend Access Proxy (AP) to handle coarse-grained company policies.

BeyondCorp leverages the existing Google Front End (GFE) infrastructure as a logically centralized point of access policy enforcement. Funneling requests in this manner led us to naturally extend the GFE to provide other features, including self-service provisioning, authentication, authorization, and centralized logging. The resulting extended GFE is called the Access Proxy (AP). The following section details the features of the AP that are particularly pertinent to this case study. For details about its other features, see "Beyond Corp: The Access Proxy" (*https:// research.google.com/pubs/pub45728.html*).

The GFE provides some built-in benefits, such as load balancing for the backends and TLS management, that weren't designed specifically for BeyondCorp. The AP extends the GFE by introducing authentication and authorization policies.

User authentication

In order to properly authorize a request, the AP needs to identify the user and the device making the request. Authenticating the device poses a number of challenges in a multiplatform context, which we address in "Challenges with Multiplatform Authentication" on page 196.

The AP verifies user identities by integrating with Google's Identity Provider (IdP). Because it isn't scalable to require backend services to change their authentication mechanisms in order to use the AP mechanism, the AP needs to support a range of authentication options: OpenID Connect, OAuth, and some custom protocols.

The AP also needs to handle requests without user credentials, for example, a software management system attempting to download the latest security updates. In these cases, the AP can disable user authentication.

When the AP authenticates the user, it strips the credential before sending the request to the backend. Doing so is essential for two reasons:

- The backend can't replay the request (or the credential) through the Access Proxy.
- The proxy is transparent to the backends. As a result, the backends can implement their own authentication flows on top of the Access Proxy's flow, and won't observe any unexpected cookies or credentials.

Authorization

Two design choices drove our implementation of the authorization mechanism:

- A centralized access control list (ACL) engine queryable via remote procedure calls (RPCs)
- A domain-specific language to express the ACLs that is both readable and extensible

Providing ACL evaluation as a service enables us to guarantee consistency across multiple frontend gateways (e.g., the RADIUS network access control infrastructure, the AP, and SSH proxies). We chose to combine coarse-grained, centralized authorization at the AP with fine-grained authorization at the backend.

Mutual authentication between the proxy and the backend

Because the backend delegates access control to the frontend, it's imperative that the backend can trust that the traffic it receives has been authenticated and authorized by the frontend. This is especially important since the AP terminates the TLS handshake, and the backend receives an HTTP request over an encrypted channel.

Meeting this condition requires a mutual authentication scheme capable of establishing encrypted channels—for example, you might implement mutually authenticated TLS authentication and a corporate public key infrastructure. Our solution is an internally developed authentication and encryption framework called LOAS (Low Overhead Authentication System) that bidirectionally authenticates and encrypts all communication from the proxy to the backends.

One benefit of mutual authentication and encryption between the frontend and backend is that the backend can trust any additional metadata inserted by the AP (usually in the form of extra HTTP headers). While adding metadata and using a custom protocol between the reverse proxy and the backends isn't a novel approach (for example, see Apache JServe Protocol), the mutual authentication scheme between the AP ensures that the metadata is not spoofable.

As an added benefit, we can also incrementally deploy new features at the AP, which means that consenting backends can opt in by simply parsing the corresponding headers. We use this functionality to propagate the device trust level to the backends, which can then adjust the level of detail served in the response.

Challenges with Multiplatform Authentication

At minimum, performing proper device identification requires two components:

- Some form of device identifier
- An inventory database tracking the latest known state of any given device

Because BeyondCorp replaces trust in the network with an appropriate level of trust in the device, each device must have a consistent, non-cloneable identifier, while information about the software, users, and location of the device must be integrated in the inventory database.

Desktops and laptops

Desktops and laptops use an X.509 machine certificate and a corresponding private key stored in the system certificate store. Key storage, a standard feature of modern operating systems, ensures that command-line tools (and daemons) that communicate with servers via the AP can be consistently matched against the correct device identifier. Since TLS requires the client to present a cryptographic proof of private key possession, this implementation makes the identifier non-spoofable and non-cloneable, assuming it's stored in secure hardware such as a Trusted Platform Module (TPM).

Mobile devices

Instead of relying on certificates, we use a strong device identifier natively provided by the mobile operating systems. For iOS devices, we use the identifierForVendor, while Android devices use the device ID reported by the Enterprise Mobility Management application.

Migrating to BeyondCorp

Like virtually every other enterprise in the world, Google maintained a privileged network for its clients and applications for many years. This paradigm gave rise to significant infrastructure that is critical to the day-to-day workings of the company. While all components of the company will migrate to BeyondCorp, moving every network user and every application to the BeyondCorp environment in one fell swoop would be incredibly risky to business continuity. For that reason, Google has invested heavily in a phased migration that has successfully moved large groups of network users to BeyondCorp with zero effect on their productivity.

Deploying an unprivileged network

To equate local and remote access, BeyondCorp defines and deploys an unprivileged network that very closely resembles an external network, although within a private address space. The unprivileged network only connects to the internet, limited infrastructure services (e.g., DNS, DHCP, and NTP), and configuration management systems such as Puppet. All client devices are assigned to this network while physically located in a Google building. There is a strictly managed access control list (ACL) between this network and other parts of Google's network.

Workflow qualification

All the applications used at Google are required to work through the Access Proxy. The BeyondCorp initiative examined and qualified all applications, which accomplish tasks ranging from the simple (e.g., supporting HTTPS traffic) to the more difficult (e.g., SSO integration). Each application required an AP configuration and, in many cases, a specific stanza in the Access Control Engine. Each application went through the following phases:

1. Available directly from the privileged network and via a VPN connection externally.

2. Available directly from the privileged network and via the AP from external and unprivileged networks. In this case, we used split DNS. The internal name server pointed directly at the application, and the external name pointed at the AP.
3. Available via the AP from external, privileged, and unprivileged networks.

Cutting back on VPN usage

As more and more applications became available via the Access Proxy, we started actively discouraging users from using the VPN, employing the following strategy:

1. We restricted VPN access to users with a proven need.
2. We monitored use of the VPN and removed access rights from users who did not use VPN over a well-defined period.
3. We monitored the VPN usage for active VPN users. If all of their workflows were available through the AP, we strongly encouraged users to give up their VPN access rights.

Traffic analysis pipeline

It was very important that we moved users to the unprivileged network only when we were certain (or very close to certain) that all of their workflows were available from this network. To establish a relative degree of certainty, we built a traffic analysis pipeline. Our analysis proceeded as follows:

1. As input to this pipeline, we captured sampled netflow data from every switch in the company.
2. We analyzed this data against the canonical ACL between the unprivileged network and the rest of the company's network. This analysis allowed us to identify the total traffic that would have passed the ACL, plus an ordered list of traffic that would not have passed the ACL.
3. We could now attach the nonpassing traffic to specific workflows and/or specific users and/or specific devices.
4. We progressively worked through the list of nonpassing traffic to make it function in the BeyondCorp environment.

Unprivileged network simulation

To augment the traffic analysis pipeline, we also simulated unprivileged network behavior across the company via a traffic monitor that we installed on all user devices attached to Google's network. The traffic monitor examined all incoming and outgoing traffic on a per-device basis, validated this traffic against the canonical ACL between the unprivileged network and the rest of the company's network, and logged the traffic that did not pass the validations. The monitor had two modes:

Logging mode
> Captured the ineligible traffic, but still permitted said traffic to leave the device

Enforcement mode
> Captured and dropped the ineligible traffic

Migration strategy

With the traffic analysis pipeline and the unprivileged simulation in place, we defined and began implementing a phased migration strategy that entails the following:

1. Identifying potential sets of candidates by job function and/or workflow and/or location.
2. Operating the simulator in logging mode, identifying users and devices that have >99.9% eligible traffic for a contiguous 30-day period.
3. Activating simulator enforcement mode for users and devices that have >99.99% eligible traffic for that period. If necessary, users can revert the simulator to logging mode.
4. After operating the simulator in enforcement mode successfully for 30 days, recording this fact in the device inventory.
5. Along with inclusion in the candidate set, successful operation in the simulator's enforcement mode for 30 days provides a very strong signal that the device should be assigned to the unprivileged network.

Exemption handling

In addition to automating the migration of users and devices from our privileged to our new unprivileged network as much as possible, we also implemented a simple process for users to request temporary exemptions from this migration:

- We maintained a known list of workflows that were not yet qualified for Beyond-Corp.
- Users could search through these workflows, and with the correct approval levels, mark themselves and their devices as active users of a certain workflow.
- When the workflow was eventually qualified, its users were notified and were again eligible to be selected for migration.

Lessons Learned

The migration to BeyondCorp came with a set of challenges and kinks to be ironed out along the way. Hopefully the following lessons can save some time and headaches for other organizations seeking to implement a similar model.

Communication

Fundamental changes to the security infrastructure can potentially adversely affect the productivity of the entire company's workforce. It's important to communicate the impact, symptoms, and available remediation options to users, but it can be difficult to find the balance between over-communication and under-communication.

Under-communication results in the following problems:

- Surprised and confused users
- Inefficient remediation
- Untenable operational load on the IT support staff

Over-communication is also problematic:

- Change-resistant users tend to overestimate the impact of changes and attempt to seek unnecessary exemptions.
- Users can become inured to potentially impactful changes.
- As Google's corporate infrastructure is evolving in many unrelated ways, it's easy for users to conflate access issues with other ongoing efforts, which also slows remediation efforts and increases the operational load on support staff.

Engineers need support

Transitioning to a new network security paradigm doesn't happen overnight, and requires coordination and interaction among multiple teams. At large enterprise scale, it's impossible to delegate the entire transition to a single team. The migration will likely involve some backward-incompatible changes that need sufficient management support.

In our experience, the success of the transition largely depended on how easy it was for teams to successfully set up their service behind the Access Proxy. Making the lives of developers easier should be a primary goal, so keep the number of surprises to a minimum. Provide sane defaults, create walkthrough guides for the most common use cases, and invest in documentation. Provide sandboxes for the more advanced and complicated changes—for example, you can set up separate instances of the Access Proxy that the load balancer intentionally ignores but that developers can reach (e.g., temporarily overriding their DNS configuration). Sandboxes have proven extremely useful in numerous cases, like when we needed to make sure that clients would be able to handle TLS connections after major changes to the X.509 certificates or to the underlying TLS library.

Data quality and correlation

Poor data quality in asset management can cause devices to unintentionally lose access to corporate resources. Typos, transposed identifiers, and missing information are common. Such mistakes may happen when procurement teams receive asset shipments and add the assets to our systems, or may be due to errors in a manufacturer's workflow. Data quality problems also originate quite frequently during device repairs, when physical parts or components of a device are replaced or moved between devices. Such issues can corrupt device records in ways that are difficult to fix without manually inspecting the device.

The most effective solutions in this arena have been to find local workflow improvements and automated input validation that can catch or mitigate human error at input time. Double-entry accounting helps, but doesn't catch all cases. However, the need for highly accurate inventory data in order to make correct trust evaluations forces a renewed focus on inventory data quality. The accuracy of our data is at previously unseen levels, and this precision has had secondary security benefits. For example, the percentage of our fleet that is updated with the latest security patches has increased.

Sparse data sets

Upstream data sources don't necessarily share overlapping device identifiers. To enumerate a few potential scenarios:

- New devices might have asset tags but no hostnames.
- The hard drive serial might be associated with different motherboard serials at different stages in the device lifecycle.
- MAC addresses might collide.

A reasonably small set of heuristics can correlate the majority of deltas from a subset of data sources. However, in order to drive accuracy closer to 100%, you need an extremely complex set of heuristics to account for a seemingly endless number of edge cases. A tiny fraction of devices with mismatched data can potentially lock hundreds or even thousands of employees out of applications they need to be productive.

Conclusion

What began as an ambitious and long-term goal in late 2010 is in its final stages of completion, and the majority of Google employees now work completely within BeyondCorp. This process was an uphill battle at times, and its success entailed a large amount of time and resources.

Fortunately, an organization seeking to implement a zero trust network strategy today does have resources at hand to bootstrap this process. While this journey will by no means be trivial, there are a number of enterprise and commercial solutions available in this arena, and we hope that the rough blueprint outlined in this case study is helpful as you contemplate potential approaches. Keep the core motivations and design principles outlined here in mind while weighing your options and choosing the optimal security strategy for your needs.

Case Study: PagerDuty's Cloud Agnostic Network

Evan Gilman and Doug Barth

PagerDuty began building a zero trust network in 2013, and completed it in 2014. It has continued to evolve, and remains in production as of this writing. The authors would like to thank PagerDuty for its permission to use its name and describe some of the details behind its zero trust implementation. All opinions are those of the authors, and PagerDuty is not at fault for errors or inaccuracies contained herein.

PagerDuty is a platform that organizations use to power their incident response. Users are able to integrate their existing tools like monitoring, ticketing, and reporting systems using PagerDuty's API. Most users first configure their monitoring systems to route alerts through PagerDuty so PagerDuty can manage on-call rotations and escalations. Given the critical nature of the service being provided, a zero trust network was ideal to meet both the reliability and data privacy requirements of that system.

PagerDuty's zero trust network primarily deals with server-to-server interactions purely within a multiprovider public cloud environment. Cloud providers have varying network control plane capabilities. Some providers give none of the controls that are normally required for a traditional perimeter system like a stateful firewall, private addressing, network ACLs. In the most extreme case, hosts are placed onto the public internet and the host needs to secure itself. This disparity in provider capabilities makes running a provider-agnostic network exceptionally difficult using traditional perimeter concepts.

PagerDuty's system also makes heavy use of WAN communication in its normal operation. Business-critical systems are deployed across three separate regions with the goal of surviving the loss of an entire region without impacting normal business operations. Relying on the WAN for normal application operation places some heavy requirements on the system. The internet is generally a challenging network environment with the potential for unexpected high latency and packet loss. In addition, communications need to be encrypted and authenticated to ensure data privacy and integrity. By deploying a perimeterless zero trust network, failure isolation is achieved since each node in the cluster is responsible for just its own communication.

Configuration Management as an Automation Platform

The key asset used to construct PagerDuty's zero trust network is its configuration management tool, Chef. Chef was already being used to configure every virtual machine in the system, and so it is a readily available automation layer which could be leveraged to build a zero trust network. With configuration management, policy can be centrally managed in code while distributing the enforcement into the entire fleet.

This approach has a number of benefits:

- Network compute power scales as the number of instances increases. This scaling property removes the need to buy ever larger shared hardware as the network grows.
- Failures tend to be more isolated. Instead of having "the firewall," the system ends up having many smaller firewalls. A failure of a single firewall affects a much smaller set of traffic and oftentimes can be routed around.

Distributing policy throughout the network isn't without its downsides:

- Constant validation of expected policy state is required to ensure that all nodes are correctly enforcing the expected policy.
- Changes to policy are eventually consistent across the fleet. This can be a bit jarring if a system administrator expects to be able to make a change and see it take effect immediately.

While configuration management was an ideal place to quickly iterate on the zero trust ideas, it is not an ideal long-term solution. As these systems have become more mature, they have graduated out of Chef and into their own systems, which can be deployed and tuned for optimal performance.

Dynamically Calculated Local Firewalls

Without a consistent provider-supplied firewall solution, PagerDuty found it needed to ensure that each host was secured without relying on provider systems. To meet that need, Chef was taught how to generate IPtables configuration based on its existing knowledge of the system.

Servers in the system are categorized by their role, which captures the set of services and expected communication patterns that should exist for that role. Each server of a given role is identical in its configuration.

IPtables chains are constructed on each individual host that enumerates the IP addresses for servers of a particular role. These chains are then used to define the rules which allow expected access by role. If a flow does not match the whitelisted rules, its packets are dropped.

Here's an example of an IPtables configuration representing this arrangement:

```
Chain INPUT (policy ACCEPT 0 packets, 0 bytes)
target    prot in  out  source          destination
ACCEPT    all  lo  *    0.0.0.0/0       0.0.0.0/0
ACCEPT    all  *   *    0.0.0.0/0       0.0.0.0/0       state RELATED,ESTABLISHED
```

```
bastion  tcp  *  *  0.0.0.0/0         0.0.0.0/0    tcp dpt:22
lb       tcp  *  *  0.0.0.0/0         0.0.0.0/0    tcp dpt:80
lb       tcp  *  *  0.0.0.0/0         0.0.0.0/0    tcp dpt:443
LOG      all  *  *  0.0.0.0/0         0.0.0.0/0    limit: avg 10/min burst 5...
DROP     all  *  *  0.0.0.0/0         0.0.0.0/0

Chain bastion (1 references)
target   prot in out source           destination
ACCEPT   all  *  *  192.168.0.55     0.0.0.0/0
ACCEPT   all  *  *  192.168.5.4      0.0.0.0/0
ACCEPT   all  *  *  10.0.2.78        0.0.0.0/0
ACCEPT   all  *  *  172.16.0.132     0.0.0.0/0

Chain lb (2 references)
target   prot in out source           destination
ACCEPT   all  *  *  192.168.1.221    0.0.0.0/0
ACCEPT   all  *  *  192.688.1.222    0.0.0.0/0
```

Distributed Traffic Encryption

For network encryption and authentication, PagerDuty decided to implement an IPsec host-to-host mesh network. This network architecture has a number of benefits:

- All packets are encrypted and authenticated by every node in the system.
- Since encryption and authentication is distributed throughout the system, as the number of hosts grows, the capacity to provide this critical function grows as well.

Network encryption and authentication is normally viewed as an application-level concern, but requiring every application to provide these safety controls results in a less secure or less operable system. Application encryption can have issues with correctly implementing the encryption specification, lack the configuration controls to respond to security vulnerabilities, or introduce performance regressions into the system. For these reasons, PagerDuty decided to rely on the kernel's IPsec stack to provide this bit of critical infrastructure.

A system utilizing mutually authenticated TLS could provide similar benefits to an IPsec-based network. In order to provide the same guarantees, system administrators should separate the TLS infrastructure from the application.

Out-of-Process Encryption Is Increasingly Becoming the Standard

In many systems, encryption and authentication is considered an application concern, and applications usually provide this functionality using standard libraries. As the number of applications in a system has grown, systems are increasingly using out-of-process mechanisms for securing network communication.

By moving the encryption logic into a separate process, administrators gain a standard set of controls to use to respond to security vulnerabilities. In addition, having a separate process controlling the sensitive encryption process reduces the surface area for attacks that might want to expose secret data.

PagerDuty's network uses IPsec in transport mode. The phase 1 and phase 2 cipher suites use the strongest possible configuration available at the time. When choosing the cipher suites, RFC 6379 (*https://tools.ietf.org/html/rfc6379*) was referenced to ensure that the algorithms chosen were recommended to be used together.

IPsec communication is normally transmitted using ESP packets. Since some cloud provider's networks do not route ESP packets, all IPsec traffic is encapsulated in UDP packets.

PagerDuty's experience with operating an IPsec mesh network in production has been a bit mixed. The network has handled production throughput, and has grown with the fleet. During the initial rollout, communication failures did occur, often due to inconsistent state on either side of the IPsec relationship. Having metrics and logging to surface these issues was critical to operating the network. While having these failures was certainly frustrating, with a mesh network these failures were isolated to pairs of hosts, which often reduced the impact of the failure.

PagerDuty's initial rollout of the IPsec network utilized Chef and some simple scripts to configure pre-existing IPsec packages. As the network grew, the configuration of the system has moved out of Chef and into a dedicated service that can handle the sole responsibility of configuring this aspect of the system. Moving the logic into its own system was done to lessen the convergence time for deploying a change to the network. The Chef-based system required running an entire Chef convergence run to update all relevant hosts in the network—a heavyweight operation that handles more than just the network configuration.

Decentralized User Management

PagerDuty's user access control is deployed in a centralized fashion, much like the networking systems previously discussed. Instead of relying on a centralized LDAP system, local users and groups are programmatically constructed on each host in the network. This approach removes a dependency on the network, which helps the system continue to operate even during challenging periods.

While the enforcement of user access control is distributed into the network, the definitions of which users and groups should be created is centralized. This information could be captured in an LDAP server or some other database. In PagerDuty's case, it used Chef databags to define users and groups. Server roles are marked with the set of groups that should be created on that role. Chef uses this data to only create the users and groups on a particular server that need access to that infrastructure.

Rollout

PagerDuty's network, like most networks, is an ever-evolving system. The network transitioned from a traditional design to a zero trust network over time, while production traffic was flowing.

Changing a network architecture while critical production traffic is flowing can be difficult, so it was important that the rollout was planned to reduce risk. PagerDuty followed a slow rollout pattern:

1. New policies are defined.
2. Policies are deployed in a manner that does not affect the production system, but instead collects useful metrics or logs.
3. The metrics/logs are inspected over a long period of time to ensure that the behavior is desired.
4. The policy is slowly enabled across the fleet, growing from a small percentage to 100% coverage.

This simple procedure can be used to reduce the risk of most production changes. It is much better than the common approach of using a scheduled maintenance window.

The slow rollout pattern is used to deploy most changes in PagerDuty's systems. For the distributed firewall project, all hosts were initially configured to log packets which would be dropped at a later date. Firewall rules were created to classify traffic flows, which could be deployed without the risk of blocking any production traffic. With the rules deployed, the logged traffic was reduced; and once enough time had passed, the system was reconfigured to drop all non-whitelisted traffic.

The distributed traffic encryption followed the same rollout procedure. IPsec policies were first deployed into the fleet in a no-op configuration. These policies control whether a particular traffic flow should use IPsec for communication. IPsec supports three different states:

None
    IPsec will not be used.

Use
> IPsec will be optimistically used if a relationship can be negotiated.

Required
> IPsec must be used for traffic to be processed.

The initial set of policies were deployed in the *none* state. The end goal was to get the entire system to the *required* state by stepping through the *use* state. Based on testing of the failure modes of the *use* state, it was determined that intermediate stateful firewalls would block communication if the IPsec relationship were broken, as packets would fall back to a *none* policy. These packets would not be associated with an expected flow (remember that previously they were encrypted and wrapped in a UDP encapsulation packet) and so would be dropped.

Instead of configuring the entire network to a *use* state, smaller portions of the network were transitioned to a *use* state and then reconfigured to a *required* state. This phased approach minimized the amount of time the network was in the potentially risky *use* state while still allowing hosts to communicate as they reconfigured themselves. Chef calculated the minimum policy between a pair of hosts based on their preferred state.

Value of a Provider-Agnostic System

It goes without saying that building a provider-agnostic system requires significant engineering effort. For many system, this effort may not be justified. In PagerDuty's case, the business requirements determined that the effort was justified.

Having this provider-agnostic network in place provided a significant return on investment when PagerDuty decided to move off one of its cloud providers. Normally an effort like this would be a several month effort with many high-risk change windows.

In PagerDuty's case, this change was relatively straightforward. It took roughly six weeks from making the decision to having all production traffic moved over. The bulk of that time was spent researching new providers, testing the new provider's systems, and reworking the Chef automation. The actual changes were deployed to production in one week during normal business hours without any customer impact.

Summary

This chapter focused on the considerations that an organization that wants to move to a zero trust network needs to decide on. Where possible, it gave real-world recommendations to help readers through making these decisions.

It spent time discussing the importance of understanding the state of the system using system diagrams and capturing network flows from real production traffic.

Building all the zero trust control plane systems as standalone services can be a large up-front investment, so practical alternatives were explored.

The most important detail to remember is that zero trust is an architectural ideal, so this chapter discussed how to get started down the path by defining and capturing policy in a manner which can be later reused. It explored putting in place authentication proxies which can incorporate systems that aren't directly compatible with zero trust. It also explored whether organizations should start with client/server interactions or server/server interactions.

Finally, to help readers see how this type of endeavor played out in other organizations' systems, this chapter explored two concrete case studies. These case studies explore the particular approaches and trade-offs that were made to make zero trust a reality in existing production networks.

The next chapter focuses on how a hypothetical attacker might try to thwart a zero trust network.

CHAPTER 10

The Adversarial View

Most formal proposals in the technology industry include a section commonly known as "security considerations." In fact, the IETF mandates a security consideration section (*https://tools.ietf.org/html/rfc7322#section-4.8.5*) for all submitted RFCs.

This section is crucial for many reasons. First, it clearly communicates potential pitfalls, dangers, and caveats. This is extraordinarily important during the implementation and deployment phases, as it will help to ensure that the operator arrives at a design which retains the security properties that the system was originally designed for.

Second, it demonstrates that the authors have put good thought into the ways in which the system can be attacked. It is far too easy to design a seemingly secure system which harbors a major vulnerability just under the surface. And finally, it sets the stage for discussion on how to best approach and manage the security risks presented. As a result, including a security considerations section is generally considered best practice. Some might even view the work as deceptive without such a section, since it might indicate that the authors are trying to push a known-weak technology.

Even the strongest proposals will have *some* security considerations. For instance, the latest RFC for the TLS protocol has 12 pages worth. It is important to understand that a system is not inherently insecure simply because there are security considerations associated with it; rather, it should be a sign that the system as a whole is *more* secure.

In this chapter, we will discuss the potential pitfalls, dangers, and attack vectors associated with the zero trust model. If you were trying to penetrate a zero trust network, how might you do it?

Identity Theft

Practically all of the decisions and operations performed within a zero trust network are made on the basis of authenticated identity. In Chapter 6, we discussed the difference between informal and authoritative identity, such as the difference between your "human" identity and your government identity. Computer systems implement authoritative identity similar to the way governments do—and similar to the way your government identity can be stolen, so can your identity within a computer system.

If your identity is stolen or compromised, it might be possible for an attacker to masquerade their way through the zero trust authentication and authorization checks. This is, of course, extremely undesirable. Since identity in a computer system is typically tied to some sort of "secret" which is used to prove said identity, it is extraordinarily important to protect those secrets as well as we can.

These secrets can be protected in different ways, based on the type of component the identity belongs to. Careful consideration should go into choosing which methods to use for which components. We spoke about different ways to approach this problem in previous chapters.

Since a zero trust network authenticates both the device and the user/application, it is necessary for an attacker to steal at least two identities in order to gain access to resources within it, raising the bar when compared to traditional approaches in use today. These concerns can be additionally mitigated through the use of trust engine behavioral analysis.

While securing identity is a widespread industry concern, and is not specific to zero trust, its importance is large enough to justify calling it out as something which should be carefully handled, despite the fact that the zero trust model works to naturally mitigate this threat.

Distributed Denial of Service

A zero trust network is primarily concerned with authentication, authorization, and confidentiality, generally affected by tightly controlling access to all network resources. While the architecture strives to authenticate and authorize just about everything on the network, it does not provide good mitigation against denial-of-service (DoS) attacks on its own. Distributed DoS (DDoS) attacks that are volumetric in nature can be particularly troublesome.

Just about any system which can receive packets is vulnerable to volumetric DDoS, even those employing the zero trust architecture. Some implementations "darken" internet-facing endpoints through the use of pre-authentication protocols. We spoke a little about these in "Bootstrapping Trust: The First Packet" on page 139, the basic premise being to hide those endpoints behind a deny-all rule, adding narrow exceptions based only on signaling. While this method goes a long way in helping to keep the endpoint addresses obscured, it does not fundamentally mitigate DDoS attacks.

Zero trust networks, by nature, retain a great deal of information about what to expect on the network. This information can be used to calculate policy for more traditional traffic filtering defenses far upstream. For instance, perhaps only a few systems in the network actually communicate with the internet. In this case, we can use the policy to calculate coarse enforcement rules from the perspective of an upstream device, applying very broad enforcement with few exceptions. The advantages of this approach over the typical approach are two-fold:

- The configuration is fully automated.
- The traffic filtering mechanisms can remain stateless.

The second advantage is quite a large one, since it obviates the need for expensive hardware and complicated state replication schemes. In this way, these filtering devices act more like scrubbers than firewalls. Of course, this only makes sense if you operate a large network. If you have a few racks in a colocation facility, or are cloud native, you might prefer to leverage an online DDoS-prevention service.

The short of it is, DDoS is still a problem in the zero trust world, and while we might have a few new clever ways to address it, it will still require special attention.

Endpoint Enumeration

The zero trust model lends itself naturally to perimeterless networks, since a perimeter makes much less sense when the internal network is untrusted. The peer-to-peer nature of perimeterless networks make them generally easier to maintain than perimeter networks, which frequently include network gateways and tunnels like VPNs which pose scaling, performance, and availability challenges.

As a result of this architecture, it is possible for an adversary to build a system diagram by observing which systems talk to which endpoints. This is in contrast to architectures which leverage network gateways like VPNs, since an adversary observing VPN traffic can't see conversations with endpoints beyond the VPN gateway. It should be noted that this advantage is lost as soon as the traffic crosses the gateway—a classic property of the perimeter model.

It is here that we make a distinction between privacy and confidentiality. The zero trust model guarantees network confidentiality, but *not* privacy. That is, ongoing conversations can be observed and asserted to exist; however, the contents of the conversation are protected. Systems that provide network privacy attempt to obscure the fact that the conversation happened at all. Tor is a popular example of a system which provides network privacy. This is a wholly different problem space and is considered out of scope for the zero trust model.

If a limited form of privacy over public networks is desired, tunneling traffic through site-to-site tunnels is still an option in zero trust networks. This deployment will make it more difficult to see which individual hosts are communicating on either side of the tunnel. We should be clear that this additional privacy protection should not be considered critical in the network's security. In fact, in some ways it undermines the zero trust model itself, as hiding information in one part of the network and not another suggests that one is more trusted than the other.

Untrusted Computing Platform

We covered this in Chapter 5, but it's important to reiterate that zero trust networks require the underlying computing platform to be a trustworthy system. There's a distinction to be made here between the computing platform itself (think cloud hardware, virtual machine hypervisor) being trusted and the "device" being trusted. Oftentimes these two systems are conflated, but the attacks against each are subtly different due to their differing privilege levels.

Totally defending against untrustworthy computing platforms is practically impossible. Consider a system which used hardware that purposefully generated weak random numbers (which encryption systems depend on). Defending against that type of attacker would first involve detecting the problem, though this alone might be impossible if the attacker hides their capability most of the time.

Despite our inability to guard against a truly malicious computer platform, zero trust systems can still guard against simpler attacks against the platform. Encrypting persistent data and swapped-out memory pages will mitigate simpler attacks by malicious peers on the computing platform. It will also remove some small amount of trust in the platform's operators and therefore is recommended.

Social Engineering

Social engineering attacks, which trick trusted humans into taking action on a trusted device, are still very much a concern in zero trust networks. Whether they be phishing attacks, which craft written communication that is not obviously malicious, or via face-to-face communications like those that customer service departments have had to deal with, a zero trust network can only do so much to defend against attacks enabled by an unwitting participant.

For less sensitive resources, behavioral analysis of internal activity is the mechanism that is used to guard against this threat. That analysis is coupled with end user training that teaches users to think like an adversary and be suspicious of requests which are out of the ordinary.

For more sensitive resources, group authentication/authorization schemes like Shamir's Secret Sharing can help mitigate the effects of a single member of the group causing unintended actions to occur. This scheme can be very burdensome on a day-to-day basis, so the best plan is to save it for the truly critical assets.

Chapter 6 has more details on these mechanisms for defending against social engineering attacks.

Physical Coercion

Zero trust networks effectively mitigate many threats in the virtual world, but threats in the real world are another beast entirely. Valid users and devices can be effectively coerced to aid an attacker to gain access to a system that they shouldn't have access to. Border crossing can often be a place where government entities have substantial power over an individual who just wants to get to their destination. And someone with a blunt instrument can force even the most honest individuals to aid them (as demonstrated in Figure 10-1).

Figure 10-1. The reality of threats in a system (cartoon by XKCD: https://xkcd.com/538/)

The reality is that defending against these types of compromises is ill-advised. No security professional would ever tell someone in this situation to risk their physical well-being to protect the information that they have access to. Therefore, the best we can work toward as an industry is to keep only the least sensitive data and systems vulnerable to the compromise of a single individual. For higher-value targets, group authorization is an effective mitigation against these threats.

Subtler physical attacks against individuals (say someone is able to insert a USB device into an unguarded laptop) are best mitigated by a consistent process of cycling both devices and credentials. Scanning of unrotated devices can also help to mitigate these types of attacks.

If someone has physical access to your device, they can do a lot of damage. However, that statement should not be license to throw our hands up in the air and not at least try to mitigate these threats, particularly when it comes to securing data used for zero trust authentication/authorization. There are clear steps that can be taken to lessen the impact and duration of compromise even if someone has physical access to a device, and zero trust networks add those steps. You can read more about physical device security in Chapter 5.

Invalidation

Invalidation is a hard problem in computer science. In the context of a zero trust network, invalidation applies chiefly to long-running actions that were previously authorized but are no longer.

The definition of an action is largely dependent on your chosen authorization processes. For instance, if you authorize access on a request-by-request basis, an action would be considered as a single application-level request/operation. If, on the other hand, you authorize network flows (like a TCP session) instead of application requests, an action would be considered to be a single network session.

How quickly and effectively ongoing actions can be invalidated deeply affects security response. It is important to gauge how much risk you're willing to tolerate in this area as you design your zero trust network, since the answer has the potential to significantly affect how you might approach certain problems. For instance, if a new TCP session is the action being authorized, and some services maintain TCP sessions for multiple days on end, is it acceptable to say that an entity with revoked credentials might retain access for that long? Maybe not.

Luckily, we have some tools in our chest to address this problem. First, and perhaps most obvious, is to perform more granular authorizations on actions that are short-lived. Perhaps this means that the enforcement component authorizes application-level requests instead of new network sessions. While it is still possible to have long-running application requests, they are in practice less frequent than long-running network sessions.

Another approach, though somewhat naive, is to periodically reset network sessions, enforcing a maximum lifetime. When the application/client reconnects, it will be forced back through the authorization process.

The best approach though is to teach the enforcement component to track ongoing actions, and rather than reset them after a period of time, send another authorization request to the policy engine. If the policy engine decides that the action is now unauthorized, the enforcement component can forcibly reset it.

As you can see, these mechanisms still rely on a "pull" model, in which the enforcement component is forced to periodically reauthorize. As a result, sessions can only be invalidated as fast as the longest polling period configured in the enforcement component. While invalidation is best done as a push or event-based model, those approaches come with additional complexities and challenges which perhaps outweigh the benefits. Regardless, it can be seen that the problem is (at the very least) addressable.

Control Plane Security

We discussed many control plane services throughout this book, responsible for things like policy authorization and tracking inventory. Depending on needs, a zero trust control plane can comprise a nontrivial number of services, all of which play a crucial role in ensuring authorization security throughout the network. A natural question follows: how can you protect your zero trust control plane systems, and what happens if one is compromised?

Well, it's not good, that's for sure! It is possible to completely undermine the zero trust architecture if a control plane compromise is pervasive enough. As such, it is absolutely critical to ensure the security of these systems. This is not a weakness unique to the zero trust model—it exists even today in perimeter networks. If your perimeter firewall is compromised, what is the impact? Nevertheless, the concern is great enough to warrant a discussion.

Control plane security can begin through traditional means, providing very limited network connectivity and strict access control. Some control plane systems are more sensitive than others. For instance, compromising a data store housing historical access data is strictly less useful to an attacker than compromising the policy engine. In the former, an attacker may be able to artificially raise their level of trust by falsifying access patterns, where the latter leads to a complete compromise of zero trust authorization, allowing the attacker to authorize anything they please.

For the most sensitive systems (i.e., the policy engine), rigorous controls should be applied from the beginning. Requiring group authentication and authorization in order to make changes to these systems is a real option and should be heavily considered. Changes should be infrequent and should generate broadly seen messages or alerts. It should not be possible for a control plane change to go unnoticed.

Another good practice is to keep the control plane systems isolated from an administrative standpoint. Perhaps that means they live in a dedicated cloud provider account or are kept in a part of the datacenter that has more rigorous access control. Doing this allows access to be more carefully audited and minimizes the risk presented to control plane systems by their administrative facilities. Isolating these systems administratively does *not* mean that they are logically isolated from the rest of the network. Despite administrative isolation, it is important that control plane systems participate in the network just as any other service does. Attempts to isolate them can quickly lead back to a perimeterized design, which can be considered the worst-case scenario for zero trust control plane security.

As the network matures, zero trust enforcement can be slowly applied to the control plane systems themselves. Kind of like rewriting the C compiler in C, backing zero trust enforcement into the control plane ensures that tight security is applied homogeneously throughout the network and that there are no special cases. The propensity to introduce a chicken-and-egg problem should not deter you from this approach. Such problems are manageable and can usually be worked through if sufficient thought is put into them. The alternative (putting control plane systems in a perimeter network) would leave these systems the *least* protected of all, and is generally unacceptable in the context of a zero trust network.

Summary

This chapter attempts to approach the zero trust network from the opposite perspective of the administrators of the system. By putting ourselves into the mindset of a would-be attacker, we can evaluate the system as an adversary who has vast knowledge of how it is put together.

Some of the attacks against zero trust networks are well mitigated, while for others we are only able to detect the attack, at best. Even a zero trust network can be compromised by a determined adversary, as the inconvenience of defending against any theoretical attack is simply too high a price to pay in the day-to-day operation of such a network.

The reality is that every system is susceptible to an attacker with sufficient resources. When faced with the most advanced attacks, the best we can hope for is efficient and accurate detection. Starting from the assertion that a system has been compromised and working our way backward toward limiting the damage is sage advice that might allow us to sleep soundly.

While the zero trust model certainly introduces some new consideration points with regard to networked system security, it at the same time resolves many more. By applying the power of automation to tried-and-true security primitives and protocols, the authors are confident that the zero trust model will rise to replace the perimeter model as a more effective, scalable, and secure solution to the computer network security problem.

Index

Symbols
802.1X protocol, 17

A
active monitoring, 132-134
active response systems, 134
Address Allocation for Private Internets (RFC 1597), 6
Advanced Packaging Tool (APT), 123, 124
AES encryption, 141
AES key, 74
agents (see network agents)
API security, 130
application isolation, 131-132
application trust, 113-135
    active monitoring, 132-134
    active response systems, 134
    applications monitoring applications, 134
    build systems, 118-122
    distribution, 122-126
    human threats, 126-127, 135
    instance authorization, 127-129
    isolation, 131-132
    per-deployment credentials, 128-129
    runtime security, 130-134
    secure coding practices, 130-131
    source code, 115-118
    trusted application pipeline, 114
    upgrade-only policy, 127, 135
application whitelisting, 127
ASICs (application-specific integrated circuits), 164
asymmetric cryptography, 71
AtE (authenticate-then-encrypt) , 141

authentication, 28-30, 39, 99-108
    in application-layer endpoints, 176
    versus authorization, 44-45
    biometrics for, 105-105
    certificate-based, 26-27, 104
    versus encryption, 137-139
    groups, 108-110, 112
    human-driven, 32, 96-97, 126-127, 135
    with identity provider system, 183
    inventory management, 78-81
    load balancers and proxies, 184
    with local devices, 107
    location and, 89
    multifactor, 184
    using multiple channels, 100
    out-of-band checks, 106
    passwords, 102-103
    security tokens, 104
    session caching, 101
    SSO (single sign-on), 106-107
    strong, 175
    TOTP (time-based one-time password, 103
    TPM (trusted platform module), 73-77
    for trust, 99-100
    user, 16, 111
    X.509, 70-73
authentication/authorization components, 16-17
authoritative identity, 94, 111, 210
authorization
    application-centric, 183
    using device data, 88
authorization systems, 51-63
    architecture overview, 51-53

data scores, 60-62
data stores, 53, 63
enforcement, 52, 53-58, 62
low-latency, 54
policy engine, 52, 62
trust engine, 52, 58-60, 62
auto-scaling, 22
automated scanning, 133
automation systems, 15, 18

B
biometrics, 105-105
Bit9, 127
bookended filtering, 167-169
bootstrapping identity, 95-97
expectations, 97
government-issued identification, 95
human-driven authentication, 96-97
bootstrapping trust, 65-70
certificate provisioning and signing, 67-70
generating and securing identity, 66-67
in network traffic, 139-142
secure boot, 66
unique device certificate, 66
build artifacts, 121-123, 126
build system security, 118-122
artifact versions, 121-122
host security, 120
input/output security, 120
reproducible builds, 120
risks, 118-120
virtualized build environments, 121

C
caching, 101
CAPTCHAs, 110
case studies
Google BeyondCorp, 190-202
PagerDuty, 202-207
centralized filtering, 164
certificate authorities (CAs), 28-29, 70, 177
certificate chains, 70
certificate pinning, 177
certificate provisioning and signing, 67-70
certificate, unique device, 66
certificate-based authentication, 26-27, 66, 104
channel security, 100
CHILD_SA, 151
cipher suites, 148, 152, 156-159

authentication methods, 159
curve-based key agreements, 158
key exchange, 157-158
negotiation as weakness, 157
PFS (perfect forward secrecy), 158
client-to-server interactions, 189
cloud deployments, 18-19
Cloudflare DNS Root Zone Signing Ceremony, 109
code reviews, 118
code signing ceremonies, 126
code, trusting, 113
(see also application trust)
confidentiality/privacy distinction, 211
configuration management, 85-88
for inventory management, 85-87
secure source of truth, 87
configuration management (CM) systems, x, 78, 182-183
content addressable storage, 116-118
control plane, 3, 40
authenticating devices with, 70-77
automation and, 15
data compatibility across, 46
versus data plane, 36-38
protecting, 215-216
credential reuse, 108
credential rotation, 25, 27
credentials, 94
cryptographic keys, 26-26, 71-75, 158
cryptographic signatures, 124
cryptoprocessors, 67, 73
(see also TPMs)

D
data cleanliness, 46
data plane, 3, 40
automation and, 15
control plane versus, 36-38
data stores, 53, 60-62, 63
DDoS (Distributed Denial of Service) attacks, 210-211
device authentication, 16
device trust, 65-91, 113, 178
authenticating with the control plane, 70-77
authorization through device data, 88
bootstrapping, 65-70
local measurement, 83
reimaging, 178

remote measurement, 83-85
renewing, 81-85, 91
trust signals, 89-90
DHE protocol, 157
dial-in interfaces, 9
dialer-based attacks, 10-12
Diffie–Hellman key exchange, 151
DigiNotar, 67
directed acyclic graph (DAG) storage, 116-118
distributed source control, 116
distribution security, 122-126
    Advanced Packaging Tool (APT), 123
    build artifact promotion, 122-123
    integrity and authenticity, 123-124
    network trust, 125
DMZ (demilitarized zone), 2, 7, 8, 10
DNS Root Zone Signing Ceremony, 109
DREAD, 23
DSA authentication, 159

E

ECDHE protocol, 157
ECDSA authentication, 159
egress filtering, 167-168
email, evolution of, 6
encryption, 17
    AES, 141
    asymmetric versus symmetric, 161-162
    versus authentication, 137-139
    bulk, 161-162
    cryptographic keys, 26-26, 71-75
    cryptoprocessors, 67
    GnuPG, 141
    intra-datacenter, 18
    monitoring encrypted traffic, 35
    as priority, 175
    private key cryptography, 26-26, 29, 66,
        72-73, 76
    public key cryptography, 26-26, 71-72, 158
    separation of duties, 159-161
    with TPMs, 74-75
endorsement key (EK), 76
endpoint enumeration, 211
enforcement, 52, 53-54, 62
enumerating flows, 176
exclusion zone, 2
    (see also DMZ (demilitarized zone))
Extensible Authentication Protocol (EAP), 151

F

filtering, 147, 163-171
    bookended, 167-169
    egress/ingress, 167-168
    host filtering, 164-167
    intermediary, 169-170
    perimeter, 169-170
firewall exceptions, 12
firewalls, 52, 163, 164-167
    hardware, 9
    on-host, 164-166
    perimeter (see perimeter security)
flow database, 176
forward proxy mode, 188
fuzzing, 131, 132
fwknop, 140-142

G

general number field sieve, 158
geolocation, 111
Git, 116-117
GnuPG encryption, 141
golden images, 65
Google
    BeyondCorp case study, 190-202
    BeyondCorp paper, x, 52
Google Front End (GFE) infrastructure, 194
government-issued identification, 95
group authentication, 112

H

hardware security modules (HSMs), 67
hardware-backed measurement, 83
hashing, 123-124, 125
Heartbleed, 80
historical data stores, 62, 89
HMAC (hashed message authentication code),
    141
host filtering, 164-167
human-driven authentication, 32, 96-97,
    126-127, 135

I

identity
    authoritative, 94, 111, 210
    bootstrapping (see bootstrapping identity)
    generating and securing, 66-67
    informal, 94, 210

storing, 97-98, 111
identity provider system, 184
identity recovery system attacks, 95
identity theft, 210
implementing zero trust model, 173-208
    building a system diagram, 178-180
    case studies
        Google BeyondCorp, 190-202
        PagerDuty cloud agnostic network,
            202-207
    choosing scope, 173-178
    client-side versus server-side migrations,
        189
    configuration management (CM) systems,
        182-183
    initial controller-less architecture, 182-186
    load balancer and proxy authentication, 184
    network flows in, 180
    policy distribution, 185-186
    policy, defining and installing, 186-187
    priorities list for, 174-178
    relationship-oriented policy, 185
    zero trust proxy deployment, 187-189
informal identity, 94
ingress filtering, 167
injection attacks, 130
insider threats, 24
intermediary filtering, 169-170
intermediary keys, 74
internal network attack launches, 11
Internet Assigned Numbers Authority (IANA),
    4
Internet Key Exchange (IKE), 150-154
    cipher suites, 152
    for device authentication, 154
    IKE_SA_INIT and IKE_AUTH, 151
Internet Threat Model, 24
Internet, early, 5
invalidation, 214-215
inventory data stores, 61
inventory management, 78-81, 85-87
    and configuration management systems
        (CMSs), 78
    data sources, 78
    expectations for, 79
    secure introduction, 80-81
IP address evolution, 4-9
IP Address Network Translator (RFC 1631), 7
IPsec, 145-154, 171

and IKE (Internet Key Exchange), 150-154
application support issues, 149
cipher suite selection, 152
device support issues, 148
for device authentication, 154
network support issues, 147-148
security associations (SA), 152
tunnel mode versus transport mode, 153

L

least privilege, 30-33, 39
load balancers, 52, 184
local authentication, 107
location-related data, 89
low-latency authorization systems, 54

M

machine learning, 59
man-in-the-middle attacks, 108
management information base (MIB), 47
managing trust (see trust management)
Merkle tree, 116
message authenticity, 162
Microsoft server isolation, 150
Modern Chef, 81
multifactor authentication, 184
multiplatform authentication challenges, 196
mutually authenticated TLS, 155
    (see also TLS (Transport Layer Security))

N

NAC (Network Access Control), 17
NAT (network address translation), 7-8, 10
network address translation (NAT), 7-8
network agents, 41-49
    creating, 43, 48
    data fields in, 43
    data volatility, 42
    defining, 42
    exposing, 45-46
    overview, 41-43
    roles of, 43-45, 49
    scoring of, 59
    standardization of, 46-48
network communication patterns, 90
network filtering (see filtering)
network flows, 180-182
    (see also network traffic)

network models, 142-150
    layers in, 142-145
    OSI, 143-145
    TCP/IP, 145
    zero trust controls in, 145-150
network policy, 33, 36, 39, 43-45
network traffic, 137-171
    encryption versus authentication, 137-139
    enumeration of flows, 176
    filtering, 163-171
    first packet problem, 139-142, 171
    IPsec, 145-154, 171
    security applications for, 145-150
    TLS (Transport Layer Security), 155-163,
        171

O

OIDs (object identifiers), 47-48
opportunistic attackers, 24
OSI network model, 143-145
out-of-band checks, 106
outbound network security, 11

P

Packages file, 124
PagerDuty, case study, 202-207
passphrases, 74
passwords, 102-103
PASTA, 23
patient zero, 10
payload, 142
PCRs (platform configuration registers), 75-76
PDU (protocol data unit), 24
perimeter filters, 169-170
perimeter security model, 4-9
    example attack, 12-15
    shortcomings of, 12-15, 20
    versus zero trust model, 16-18, 19
perimeterless networks, 211
PFS (perfect forward secrecy), 158
phoning home, 10
physical coercion, 213-214
PKI (see public key infrastructure (PKI))
policy distribution, 185
policy engine, 52, 54-58, 62
    defining policy, 58
    isolation from enforcement layer, 54
    policy rules storage, 55

traditional versus zero trust network policy,
    56-57
Postel, Jon, 4
pre-authentication, 81, 139-139, 210
privacy/confidentiality distinction, 211
Private Enterprise Number, 48
private IP address space, 6
private key cryptography, 26-26, 29, 66, 72-73,
    76
privilege, elevated/reduced, 31
    (see also least privilege)
Project Calico, 169
proxies, 52
public key cryptography, 26-26, 71-72, 158
public key infrastructure (PKI), 28-30, 39, 178
    binding keys to entities, 29
    importance of, 29
    private versus public, 29-30
    privately held systems, 177

Q

quotes, 76

R

RADIUS protocol, 55
RAT (remote access tool), 12
Red October project, 109
registration authority (RA), 28, 70
reimaging, 82
relationship-oriented network policy, 185
Release file, 124-124, 125
remote access tool (RAT), 12
remote attestation, 76-77, 83
Remote Authentication Dial-In User Service
    (RADIUS), 55
remote measurement, 83-85
replay attacks, 107
repository security, 116
reproducible builds, 120
resource managers, 69-70
response wrapping, 128
reverse proxy mode, 188
RFC 1597, 6
RFC 1631, 7
RFC 3439, 145
RFC 3552, 24
RFC 6238, 103
RFC 6379, 152
RFC-style prioritized lists, 174-175

risk determination, 32
rotation, 25, 82-83
RSA authentication, 159
RSA protocol, 158
RSA token, 35
runtime security, 130-134
    active monitoring, 132-134
    isolation, 131-132
    secure coding practices, 130-131

S

scanning, automated, 133
script kiddies, 24
SDN (software-defined network), 170
sealed data, 76
searchable inventory, 87
secrets, 26-28, 128-129
secure boot, 66
secure coding practices, 130-131
secure introduction, 80-81
secure zone, 8
    (see also DMZ (demilitarized zone))
security considerations, 209-216
    control plane security, 215-216
    DDoS (Distributed Denial of Service)
        attacks, 210-211
    endpoint enumeration, 211
    identity theft, 210
    invalidation, 214-215
    physical coercion, 213-214
    social engineering attacks, 212
    untrusted computing platforms, 212
security policies
    defining, 33-36, 186
    rolling out, 187-187
security policies, defining, 39
security tokens, 104, 185
server-to-server interactions, 189
session caching, 101
Shamir's Secret Sharing, 108, 213
shared kernel environments, 132
Shor's algorithm, 158
signing, 123-124, 125
SMS messaging, 103
SNMP (Simple Network Management Proto-
    col), 47-48
social engineering attacks, 212
software-backed measurement, 83
source code, 115-118

authenticity and audits, 116-118
    code reviews, 118
    repository security, 116
SPA (Single Packet Authorization) implementa-
    tion, 139-142
SPI (Security Parameter Index), 152
SSL configuration, 26
    (see also TLS configuration)
SSO (single sign-on), 106-107
state-level actors, 24, 25
storage root key (SRK), 74
STRIDE, 23
strong authentication, 175
Suite B Cryptographic Suite, 152
supply chain security, 114
system diagram, building, 178

T

targeted attackers, 24
TCP/IP network model, 145
threat evolution, 9-12
threat models, 23-25, 39
    attacker-based, 24
    common models, 23-24
    defining, 23
    Internet Threat Model, 24
TLS (Transport Layer Security), 26, 126,
    145-146, 149, 155-163, 171
    authentication considerations, 163
    bulk encryption, 161
    cipher suites, 156-159
    infrastructure concerns with, 146
    key exchange, 157
    message authenticity, 162
    separation of duty, 159-161
    TLS handshake, 155
TOTP (time-based one-time password), 103
TPMs (trusted platform modules), 73-77
    encryption with, 74-75
    PCRs (platform configuration registers),
        75-76
    quotes, 76
    remote attestation, 76-77
traditional network security architecture, 2
    (see also perimeter security model)
traffic (see network flows, network traffic)
traffic sources, 111
training data, 59

Transport Layer Security (TLS) (see TLS (Transport Layer Security))
Trike, 23
trust, 16
    application trust (see application trust)
    bootstrapping (see bootstrapping trust)
    device trust (see device trust)
    user trust (see user trust)
trust anchor, 22
trust chain, 22
trust delegation, 21-22
trust engine, 52, 58-60, 62
    machine learning techniques, 59
    scored entities, 59-60
trust levels, 15
trust management, 21-40
    authentication, 28-30, 39
    control plane versus data plane, 36-38, 40
    defining trust policies, 33-36
    least privilege, 30-33, 39
    strong authentication, 25-28
    threat models, 23-25
    variable trust, 33-36, 39
trust score, 17, 34-36, 42, 44
trust signals, 89
    historical access, 89
    location, 89
    network communication patterns, 90
    time since image, 89
trusted insiders, 24
Trusted Network Connect (TNC), 17
trusted platform modules (TPMs), 67
trusted third parties, 128

U

U2F (Universal 2nd Factor), 104, 185
UAF standard, 107
UDP packets, 139
untrusted computing platforms, 212
untrusted zone, 8
upgrade-only policy, 127, 135
UPnP, 170
user authentication, 111
user directories, 97-98
user trust, 93-112
    access patterns, 110

    awareness and speaking up, 110
    bootstrapping identity, 95-97
    government-issued identification, 95
    group authentication, 108-110
    how to authenticate, 101-108
    human-driven authentication, 96-97
    identity authority, 93-95
    physical safety and, 102, 213-214
    storing identity, 97-98
    user directories, 97-98
    when to authenticate, 99-101
user/application authentication, 16

V

variable trust, 39
VAST, 23
Vault, 128
version control systems (VCS), 116
virtualization, 132
virtualized build environments, 121
VPNs (virtual private networks), 3, 17, 17
vulnerability scanning, 84

W

webs of trust (WoTs), 28
workloads, 169

X

X.509 certificates, 104, 151
X.509 security, 29
X.509 standard, 26, 70-73, 75

Z

zero trust model/networks
    architecture example, 3
    compared to other threat models, 24-25
    defined, ix
    disadvantages of, 2
    lack of standards for, 56-57
    overview, 1-3
    versus perimeter security model, 16-18, 19
    realizing (see implementing zero trust model)
zero trust proxies, 187-189
ztmn4losf

About the Authors

Evan Gilman is an engineer with a background in computer networks. With roots in academia, and currently working in the public internet, he has been building and operating systems in hostile environments his entire career. An open source contributor, speaker, and author, Evan is passionate about designing systems that strike a balance with the networks they run on.

Doug Barth is a software engineer who loves to learn and share his knowledge with others. He has worked on systems of various sizes at companies like Orbitz and PagerDuty. He has built and spoken about monitoring systems, mesh networks, and failure injection practices.

Betsy Beyer, who contributed the Google BeyondCorp case study, is a technical writer for Google Site Reliability Engineering in NYC and a coauthor of *Site Reliability Engineering: How Google Runs Production Systems* (O'Reilly). She has previously written documentation for Google Datacenters and Hardware Operations teams. Before moving to New York, Betsy was a lecturer on technical writing at Stanford University. She holds degrees from Stanford and Tulane.

Colophon

The animal on the cover of *Zero Trust Networks* is a squat lobster, a type of crustacean found in the *Galatheoidea* and *Chirostyloidea* superfamilies; there are over 1,000 species, most of which spend their lives on the sea floor. Despite their name, squat lobsters are more closely related to hermit crabs than lobsters.

The squat lobster does not have a shell on its back, and protects itself by squeezing into crevices or under rocks. Its claws remain out, ready to fend off predators, defend its territory, and scavenge for food floating by or buried in the sand. A squat lobster's arms can grow to be many times longer than its body. These crustaceans do appear similar to lobsters, with a segmented thorax and large claws, but are generally flatter and smaller.

The meat of squat lobsters is known as langostino (derived from the Spanish word for lobster, *langosta*). It is often used in seafood dishes as a less expensive alternative to lobster.

Many of the animals on O'Reilly covers are endangered; all of them are important to the world. To learn more about how you can help, go to *animals.oreilly.com*.

The cover image is from *Pictorial Museum of Animated Nature*. The cover fonts are URW Typewriter and Guardian Sans. The text font is Adobe Minion Pro; the heading font is Adobe Myriad Condensed; and the code font is Dalton Maag's Ubuntu Mono.

Learn from experts.
Find the answers you need.

Sign up for a **10-day free trial** to get **unlimited access** to all of the content on Safari, including Learning Paths, interactive tutorials, and curated playlists that draw from thousands of ebooks and training videos on a wide range of topics, including data, design, DevOps, management, business—and much more.

Start your free trial at:
oreilly.com/safari

(No credit card required.)

Lightning Source UK Ltd.
Milton Keynes UK
UKHW032314121218
333862UK00001B/1/P